Günter Ladwig

Efficient Optimization and Processing of
Queries over Text-rich Graph-structured Data

Efficient Optimization and Processing of Queries over Text-rich Graph-structured Data

by
Günter Ladwig

Dissertation, Karlsruher Institut für Technologie (KIT)
Fakultät für Wirtschaftswissenschaften
Tag der mündlichen Prüfung: 19.02.2013
Referenten: Prof. Dr. Rudi Studer, Prof. Dr. Heiner Stuckenschmidt

Impressum

Karlsruher Institut für Technologie (KIT)
KIT Scientific Publishing
Straße am Forum 2
D-76131 Karlsruhe
www.ksp.kit.edu

KIT – Universität des Landes Baden-Württemberg und
nationales Forschungszentrum in der Helmholtz-Gemeinschaft

KIT Scientific Publishing 2013
Print on Demand

ISBN 978-3-7315-0015-5

Efficient Optimization and Processing of Queries over Text-rich Graph-structured Data

Zur Erlangung des akademischen Grades eines

**Doktors der Ingenieurwissenschaften
(Dr.-Ing.)**

von der Fakultät für Wirtschaftswissenschaften
des Karlsruher Instituts für Technologie (KIT)
genehmigte Dissertation von

Dipl.-Inform. Günter Ladwig

Tag der mündlichen Prüfung: 19.02.2013
Referent: Prof. Dr. Rudi Studer
Korreferent: Prof. Dr. Heiner Stuckenschmidt

This thesis is dedicated to the memory of my mother,
Barbara Ladwig (1945 - 1991)

Abstract

Many databases today are text-rich in that they not only capture structured, but also unstructured data. Hybrid data can take many forms, from databases that store text documents and structured data extracted from these documents to large parts of the Web that no longer consist of textual documents only, but often include large amounts of structured data. The combination of structured and unstructured data, also known as the integration of databases (DB) and information retrieval (IR), has been an important topic for some time and has also attracted commercial interest. In research, this problem has gained much attention, particularly the topic of *querying* text-rich structured data that we call *hybrid data*.

There are a multitude of query languages that have been proposed to access unstructured and structured data or a combination of both, i.e. hybrid data. In the same way that we distinguish data, we can also largely categorize these query languages into three classes: unstructured, structured, and hybrid queries. The efficient evaluation of all three types of queries is an important concern and is becoming even more so with the growing amount of data that has to be processed and queried. The central challenges associated with query processing, regardless of query type, is that the *search space for finding valid query answers is very large*. On a high level, the challenge is then to minimize the search space in order to reduce the effort for producing query results and thereby increasing overall query performance. In terms of query processing, this can be achieved by either decrease the amount of data to be processed or processing the data more efficiently. This thesis aims to tackle the challenge in both ways and examines processing techniques for all three types of queries.

Concerning unstructured keyword queries, we propose a solution that employs much more *compact index structures* for neighborhood lookups, thereby reducing the search space for query answers. Using these indexes, keyword search result exploration is reduced to the traditional database problem of top-k join processing, enabling results to be computed efficiently. In particular, this computation can be performed on data streams successively loaded from disk (i.e. does not require the entire input to be loaded at once into memory). To support this, we propose a *top-k procedure* based on the rank join operator, which not only computes the *k*-best results, but also selects query plans in a top-*k* fashion during the process. In experiments using large real-world datasets, the solution reduced storage requirements and also outperformed the state-of-the-art in terms of performance and scalability.

Concerning structured queries over RDF data graphs, the topic of *Linked Data query processing* has recently gained attention. Linked Data query processing incurs new challenges associated with the large amount of data sources, the limited access patterns that can be used to access the sources, and the lack of up-to-date knowledge about the sources. We propose a novel query processing strategy that combines knowledge available about previously indexed data sources with knowledge gained at run-time through online discovery of new sources to perform *run-time adaptation of query plans*. Data sources are ranked according to their importance in order to report results as early as possible. This ranking is adapted at run-time to incorporate new knowledge and thereby increases query performance. We propose the *symmetric index hash join* (SIHJ), a novel operator that deals with the unpredictable nature of accessing data distributed over a large number of sources by employing stream-based processing techniques while still supporting the use of data stored in local indexes when available. Compared to previously proposed operators, SIHJ guarantees completeness with regard to the retrieved data sources and improves performance significantly.

We observe that the problems of source selection and data processing have been treated as separate in previous work. To this end, we propose a *multi-objective optimization* framework for *joint optimization of several query optimization objectives*, cost and output cardinality in particular. We propose a *dynamic programming (DP) solution* for the multi-objective optimization of this integrated process of source selection and query processing. It produces a set of Pareto-optimal query plans, which represent different trade-offs between optimization objectives. The challenge of using DP here is that after retrieval, sources can be re-used in different parts of the query, i.e. the source scan operators can be shared. Depending on the reusability of these operators, the cost of subplans may vary such that the cost function is no longer monotonic with regard to the combination of subplans. We provide a tight-bound solution, which takes this effect into account. In experiments on real world Linked Data, *Pareto-optimal plans* computed by our approach show benefits over suboptimal plans generated by existing solutions.

Concerning hybrid queries, different types of languages have been proposed. However, we note there exists no standard hybrid query language for the more general graph-structured RDF data. We propose a full-text extension to SPARQL that extends Basic Graph Patterns (BGP) to *Hybrid Graph Patterns* (HGP) and thereby captures proprietary extensions employed by various RDF stores. We discuss the various types of hybrid search queries that can be supported with this model. Moreover, while there are many proposals for processing hybrid queries and ranking hybrid results, the problem of *building indexes* for supporting efficiently hybrid search is largely unexplored. We have identified two main directions of works. First, there are *database extensions*, which add keyword search support to databases by using a separate inverted index for textual data. The other direction is to build *native indexes* capturing both structured and textual data. We systematically study the differences among the various choices for native indexes and database extensions. We propose a *general hybrid search index schema HybIdx* that can be used to specify access patterns needed by the various query types. We perform a comprehensive experiment using several benchmark datasets and queries to systematically study HybIdx in several scenarios, from the text-centric retrieval of documents in Wikipedia and TREC collections annotated with structured data to structure-centric retrieval of data in IMDB and YAGO up to "pure" hybrid data formed by combining Wikipedia and DBpedia. Compared to native approaches, HybIdx provides superior performance for relational and document queries (outperforms the second best approach by up to three orders of magnitude) and yields results close to the ones achieved by the best "focused" solution for entity queries. As opposed to these solutions, it is more complete regarding the types of hybrid search queries that can be supported.

While hybrid graph patterns make it easier for users to specify structured queries, knowledge of the structure in the data is still required. This structure information is useful, making up the difference between structured and keyword queries. However, users might be able to capture only some but not all the structure information of a query. Addressing this, we propose to add to BGPs not only the use of keywords but also the capability to relax its structure, using *Flexible Hybrid Graph Patterns* (fHGP). The flexibility introduced by fHGP results in ambiguity. We show how an *fHGP can be translated into a set of unambiguous HGPs*. Then, based on the introduced semantics of HGP, these HGP-interpretations of an fHGP can be processed using the proposed index scheme HybIdx. Instead of producing all results, top-k processing based on the *pull/bound rank join* (PBRJ) template for instance, can be used to restrict attention to the best results and to terminate early. Hence, processing fHGP interpretations can be cast as a multi-query processing problem. The main technical contribution is the *Multi-Query PBRJ*. Compared to PBRJ, this extension processes several interpretations simultaneously to share their intermediate results. We introduce novel optimizations that are only possible with the Multi-Query PBRJ. With this, we show that run-time join order optimization is actually orthogonal to the top-k mechanisms, and propose the use of probing sequence selectors to achieve that. We propose score bounds specific to the interpretations that are tighter than the PBRJ bound obtained for the whole query (all interpretations). They enable more aggressive pulling and bounding, hence earlier reporting of top-k results. Experiments show that sharing results of queries processed simultaneously is several (3-5) times faster than processing the queries one-by-one (without sharing). Further, the join order optimization and more aggressive interpretation-specific pulling/bounding leads to consistent improvements.

Acknowledgements

This thesis would not have been possible without the support and guidance of many people. First, I would like to thank my advisor Prof. Dr. Rudi Studer who provided the opportunity and the support I needed for my research. I would also like to thank Dr. Duc Thanh Tran, my frequent co-author and advisor that supported and motivated me during my work on this thesis.

Many thanks also go out to my current and former colleagues at AIFB who provided an incredibly friendly and supportive atmosphere that I very much enjoyed working in. In particular, I would like to thank Daniel M. Herzig, Dr. Andreas Harth, Dr. Philipp Sorg, and Andreas Wagner, who all contributed in one way or the other to my work and research. Prof. Dr. Philipp Cimiano first employed me as a student assistant during his time at AIFB, thereby introducing me to research work in the first place, for which I am also thankful.

Most of all, I am indebted to my family and friends for their support and encouragement, without which this thesis would not have been possible. I would like to thank Sarah for tolerating the many evenings and weekends spent in front of the computer and her loving support. I would not be where I am today without my parents Barbara and Helmut, whom I love very much. I dedicate this thesis to the memory of my mother who left us much too early.

Günter Ladwig

Contents

Chapter 1

Introduction

In this first chapter, this thesis motivates the topic of processing queries over hybrid data. Section 1.1 introduces the concept of hybrid data as being composed of unstructured data (i.e. textual documents) and structured data (i.e. data adhering to a schema). Many databases today are text-rich in that they not only capture structured, but also unstructured data. Hybrid data can take many forms, from databases that store text documents and structured data extracted from these documents to large parts of the Web that no longer consist of textual documents only, but often include large amounts of structured data. The combination of structured and unstructured data, also known as integration of databases (DB) and information retrieval (IR) integration, has been an important topic for some time and has also attracted commercial interest. Section 1.2 presents different types of queries that can be used to access hybrid data, namely unstructured (keyword), structured, and hybrid queries. Section 1.3 then motivates the main topic of this thesis with the challenge of processing queries over hybrid data and the two main ways to deal with this challenge, namely (1) reducing the amount of data that has to be processed for obtaining query answers and (2) processing the data more efficiently. In Section 1.4 we present several research hypotheses that target the efficient processing of unstructured, structured, and hybrid queries.

In Section 1.5 we present the main contributions presented in the thesis, namely techniques for processing different types of queries over hybrid data, and relate them to the stated challenges. Finally, Section 1.6 presents the organization of this thesis.

1.1 Hybrid Data

Traditionally, data has been categorized as being either *unstructured* or *structured*. The former designates data that does not adhere to a pre-defined data model (or schema) and commonly refers to (collections of) textual documents. The latter refers to data that conforms to a data model that may specify data types, constraints, and even semantics. The relational model is a popular model for structured data, however much structured data is also stored as RDF, XML, or in a variety of other data models.

However, the distinction between unstructured and structured data is not as clear-cut as the previous definitions would suggest and has not been for some time now. On the one hand, structural information is often added to unstructured data. For example, fields such as *author* and *title* may be used in document collections. On the other hand, databases today often store large amounts of textual data in addition to (or as part of) structured data. Data mining and text analysis systems are also able to extract structured information from unstructured text, thereby establishing a direct correspondence between the two categories of data. Another example is the Web, which today not only contains textual documents, but also a large amount of structured data. This includes metadata associated with Web pages, but also semi-structured and highly structured information made publicly available as Linked Data[1]. Largely contributing to this trend are community efforts such as the Linked Open Data project. It has promoted the publishing and linking of data across sources, resulting in a large amount of freely available Linked Open Data (LOD) on the Web, which is now in the order of billions of RDF triples linked via millions of mappings. While most information today is still stored in unstructured formats, the amount of structured data has been increasing rapidly. These developments give rise to *hybrid data*, i.e. data that consists of unstructured as well as structured information.

A prominent example of hybrid data is the combination of Wikipedia, a repository of unstructured information (i.e. Wiki pages), and DBpedia, which contains structured RDF data extracted from Wikipedia pages. Fig. 1.1 shows the Wikipedia page of the city Berlin and RDF data in DBpedia extracted from that page. The structured data can unambiguously satisfy complex information needs using a query language such as SPARQL. Retrieving complex information from unstructured text is a more complicated process involving natural language processing and dealing with ambiguities. However, the unstructured text still carries information that is not part of the structured data, which may be the case due to various reasons: the automated extraction process may not be sophisticated enough or too expensive, there is no pre-defined schema to represent a given piece of information, or a particular statement in natural language may be not

---

[1]http://linkeddata.org, retrieved 2013-01-18

Berlin

From Wikipedia, the free encyclopedia

Berlin is the capital city of Germany and one of the 16 states of Germany. With a population of 3.5 million people, Berlin is Germany's largest city and is the second most populous city proper and the ninth most populous urban area in the European Union. Located in northeastern Germany on the River Spree, it is the center of the Berlin-Brandenburg Metropolitan Region, which has about 4½ million residents from over 180 nations. Due to its location in the European Plain, Berlin is influenced by a temperate seasonal climate. Around one third of the city's area is composed of forests, parks, gardens, rivers and lakes.

```
<rdf:RDF>
  <rdf:Description rdf:about="http://dbpedia.org/resource/Berlin">
    <rdf:type rdf:resource="http://schema.org/City" />
    <rdf:type rdf:resource="http://schema.org/Place" />
    <rdf:type rdf:resource="http://dbpedia.org/ontology/PopulatedPlace" />
    <dbp:populationTotal rdf:datatype="&xsd;integer">
      3499879
    </dbp:populationTotal>
    <dbp:populationAsOf rdf:datatype="&xsd;date">
      2011-11-30
    </dbp:populationAsOf>
    <dbp:elevation rdf:datatype="&xsd;double">
      34.0
    </dbp:elevation>
    <dbp:country rdf:resource="http://dbpedia.org/resource/Germany" />
    <dbp:areaCode xml:lang="en">030</dbpedia-owl:areaCode>
    <dbp:leader rdf:resource="http://dbpedia.org/resource/Klaus_Wowereit" />
    <owl:sameAs rdf:resource="http://sws.geonames.org/2950159/" />
```

Figure 1.1: Wikipedia page[2] about Berlin (unstructured), and structured data (excerpt) extracted from it in DBpedia (RDF/XML format).

be representable at all in the chosen structured data model. The combination of both structured and unstructured data therefore promises to deliver more value than either part on its own.

Dealing with unstructured and structured data in an integrated fashion is a problem that has attracted large investments from enterprises. For example, the web search engine by Google not only provides search for unstructured Web pages, but today also searches over structured data (called Knowledge Graph[3]) to provide better and more specific results to its users. In research, the area targeting this problem also known as DB & IR integration [Wei07], has gained much attention, particularly the topic of *querying* text-rich structured data that we call hybrid data. Due to the rapid increase of text-rich RDF data (e.g. Linked

---

[2]http://en.wikipedia.org/wiki/Berlin, retrieved 2013-04-08
[3]http://www.google.com/insidesearch/features/search/knowledge.html, retrieved 2013-01-18

Data in RDF or RDF embedded in Web pages called RDFa[4]), is also relevant for the Web setting.

1.2 Querying Hybrid Data

There are a multitude of query languages that have been proposed to access unstructured and structured data or a combination of both, i.e. hybrid data. In the same way that we distinguish data, we can also largely categorize these query languages into three classes: unstructured, structured, and hybrid queries.

On the one end of the spectrum between unstructured and structured, there are unstructured *keyword queries*, a paradigm that has been popular for a long time. Keyword queries can be used to access unstructured data and there is large body of work on information retrieval [BYRN99] that is concerned with the efficient and effective retrieval of textual documents or entities. This work also includes search over Web documents, which has been commercialized in Web search engines such as Google[5] or Bing[6]. Recently, keyword queries have also been employed to query structured data [YQC10]. This topic has gained research interest in the last decade and promises to be a lightweight and intuitive query paradigm for accessing structured and hybrid data stored in databases. In contrast to the traditional information retrieval processing of keyword queries, the results are usually complex structures, e.g. trees or graphs, instead of single elements (entities or documents). The efficient processing of such queries is therefore an important research topic.

On the other end of the spectrum are *structured query languages*, such as SQL (relational databases), XQuery (XML databases), and SPARQL (RDF stores). These query languages allow users to formulate highly complex queries involving joins, unions, and other expressive constructs. The efficient evaluation of these types of queries has been an important topic in database and Semantic Web research for a long time. In recent years, with the proliferation of the Web of Data and the increasing amount of data that is accessible as Linked Data, the evaluation of structured queries over remote Linked Data sources has gained attention and has become the subject of dedicated research. The processing of structured queries in this setting includes the identification of relevant sources,

---

[4]http://www.w3.org/TR/xhtml-rdfa-primer/, retrieved 2013-01-18
[5]http://www.google.com, retrieved 2013-01-18
[6]http://www.bing.com, retrieved 2013-01-18

often at run-time, and the efficient online processing of data retrieved from a multitude of remote sources.

Both, unstructured and structured queries, have been shown to be effective paradigms for accessing hybrid data. The lack of structure in keyword queries make them easy to formulate and use, which is one of the main reasons for their popularity. However, that same lack of structure also limits their expressivity, especially when employed by expert users. Structured queries, such as SPARQL queries, on the other hand support expressive constructs that make use of the structure in the data to formulate queries that can satisfy complex information needs. However, these languages require detailed knowledge of the syntax and the data schema, such as the names of attributes and relations between data elements. This makes formulating these types of queries a complex task, often only accomplished by expert users.

For both paradigms there are also approaches that extend the capabilities of each paradigm with features of the other. Keyword query approaches have been extended with limited structural constraints [DH07]. Structured query languages have been extended with full-text search capabilities, usually through the use of special query predicates[7,8]. These trends suggest that there exists a middle point between these approaches that combines features of both, i.e. *hybrid queries*. These types of queries aim to support querying unstructured and structured data in an integrated fashion. There are various proposals for such query languages that combine features of unstructured and structured queries.

1.3 Query Processing

The general architecture of query processing engines is similar for all types of queries. Given a particular query, the first task is selecting the subset of data that is necessary for answering the query and then determining how the selected data should be processed such that valid answers are produced. This process is usually also guided by some given optimization criteria, such as cost or result quality, if applicable. The decisions made in this step are captured as logical and physical operations in a query plan. Hence, this step is also called *query*

---

[7]Full-Text Search in MSSQL: http://msdn.microsoft.com/en-us/library/ms142571.aspx, rtrvd. 2013-01-18

[8]SPARQL Full Text Search: http://www.w3.org/2009/sparql/wiki/Feature:FullText, retrieved 2013-01-18

planning or query optimization. The next step[9] is then the *execution* of the query plan, i.e. loading and retrieving data and then processing it according to the operations specified in the query plan.

The efficient evaluation of all three types of queries is an important concern and is becoming even more so with the growing amount of data that has be processed and queried. The central challenges associated with query processing, regardless of query type, is that the *search space for finding valid query answers is very large*. For example, consider keyword queries over a large data graph: a valid answer to a keyword query might be constituted as a subgraph that connects relevant nodes in the data graph for each of the keywords in the query. Given that each keyword might be associated with hundreds or thousands of nodes and that there are often millions of connections in such graphs, obtaining all (or the best) answers is a non-trivial task as large amounts of data have to loaded and a large number of candidate answers have to be generated and checked for validity.

On a high level, the challenge is then to reduce the search space in order to reduce effort for producing query results and thereby increasing overall query performance. In terms of query processing, there are two main ways to reduce the search space:

- We may *reduce the amount of data to be processed*, i.e. instead of processing all data in the system, we focus only on the part of the data that is absolutely necessary for obtaining query answers. For example, in the keyword query setting, special data structures might be used, such that only a relevant part of the whole data graph has to be loaded and processed, thereby reducing the required effort.

- We may *process data more efficiently* by employing intelligent algorithms that require less resources to obtain query answers. For example, the query planner can generate query plans that minimize the number of unnecessary intermediate results or we may terminate processing early after all relevant query answers have been found.

These challenges have been a research subject in a large body of previous and ongoing research in different contexts. They are also the main topics of this thesis, where they are examined in the context of processing queries over hybrid data.

---

[9]There are also systems that do not have such a clear distinction between the planning/optimization and execution of query plans (e.g. adaptive systems that change query plans during execution), but this is not relevant for the purpose of this discussion.

1.4 Hypotheses

In this work, we examine a number of hypothesis that are concerned with improving the performance of queries over hybrid data as stated in the previous section.

Unstructured Queries. While evaluating keyword queries over structured data is a relatively recent research area, Steiner trees or graphs that connect elements in the data graph have been established as the general model for keyword query answers [DYW$^+$07, LOF$^+$08]. In the current state of the art, the computation of such graph structures is optimized by materializing the neighborhoods of data elements [LOF$^+$08]. In particular, every maximal neighborhood of nodes and edges is indexed, i.e. when it is not completely covered by another neighborhood. This leads to the first hypothesis:

Hypothesis 1. *Given a set of data elements and their neighborhoods in a data graph, determining coverage at the level of paths, instead of graphs, allows for more fine-grained pruning and thereby reduces the size of the materialized index.*

In Chapter 3 we extend the 2-hop cover concept to compute and materialize the neighborhood and prune at the level of paths. We show that this leads to reduced storage requirements and improves query performance.

Structured Queries. In this thesis we examine structured SPARQL queries in the setting of Linked Data query processing, where queries are evaluated over a multitude of Linked Data sources that are retrieved at run-time. In previous work, two main strategies for discovering sources have been proposed. The *bottom-up strategy* takes advantage of links in Linked Data sources to discover new sources and thereby iteratively expanding the search space at run-time for query answers. The *top-down strategy* maintains a source index that is used to discover sources in an offline process at compile-time. This leads to the following hypothesis:

Hypothesis 2. *The combination of compile-time knowledge about sources with knowledge gained at run-time can be used to perform run-time refinements and thereby improve early result reporting, i.e. first query results are reported earlier.*

In Chapter 4 we describe the mixed query evaluation strategy and show in experiments that it outperforms previous approaches in terms of early result reporting.

Also in the Linked Data query processing setting, previous approaches perform source selection and query optimization in separate and independent steps. First, sources are selected according to some criteria (e.g. to maximize the output cardinality), then query optimization algorithms are applied, e.g. to minimize the execution cost. This is problematic because these criteria are not always complementary. For instance, there is an inherent trade-off between output cardinality and cost: to produce more results, we have to retrieve more sources, which in turn increases processing cost. We therefore propose to extend the scope of query optimization to support the joint optimization of several objectives, i.e. to perform *multi-objective query optimization*. Applying the classic dynamic programming (DP) algorithm for multi-objective query optimization poses two main challenges: 1) query plans for different combinations of sources would be treated as not comparable, limiting the number of plans that can be pruned at each step of the DP algorithm, and 2) the re-use of sources in different parts (i.e. by sharing operators) of the query means that the cost of subplans may vary such that the cost function is no longer monotonic with regard to the combination of subplans. This leads to the following hypothesis:

Hypothesis 3. *By introducing tight bounds that maintain the monotonicity with regard to the combination of subplans, the optimal substructure of the multi-objective query optimization problem is preserved when employing operator sharing, such that the classic dynamic programming algorithm for query optimization can be applied. Further, relaxing the comparability constraint enables the optimizer to prune suboptimal plans more aggressively. The generated query plans then represent the trade-off between the optimization objectives.*

In Chapter 5 we describe the relaxation of the comparability constraint and prove that the maximal benefit bound restores the monotonicity and thereby maintains the optimal substructure of the query optimization problem.

Hybrid Queries. Different languages for hybrid queries have been proposed, such as content-and-structure queries for XML document retrieval [AYLP04], and a combination of paths and keywords for XML data retrieval [AYLP04]. Also, there are a number of proprietary extensions of SPARQL that allow keywords to be used as RDF terms at any position of a basic graph pattern (BGP), which we designate as hybrid graph patterns (HGP). This query model can be used to formulate a wide range of query types, i.e. entity, attribute, relation and document queries. Concerning the implementation we can distinguish between two main directions. On the one hand there are database extensions, which add keyword search support to databases by using a separate inverted index for textual data [WTLF11]. The other direction is to build native indexes capturing both structured and textual data [DH07, WLP+09, BMV11]. While the former approaches support all previously mentioned types of queries, storing the textual data in a separate index requires more joins, leading to worse performance than native approaches. However, the proposed native approaches do not support all types of queries, being focused on a specific type of queries, e.g. entity queries [DH07]. This leads to the following hypothesis:

Hypothesis 4. *Hybrid queries combine structural constraints with keyword matching and can largely be categorized by the types of required access patterns as entity, attribute or relation queries. Hybrid indexes that combine RDF terms and keyword terms in their index keys and cover all possible access patterns improve query performance by reducing the number of joins necessary for answering hybrid queries.*

In Chapter 6 we present HybIdx as an instance of a general hybrid indexing scheme that efficiently supports all types of queries.

Further, we propose to add to BGPs not only the use of keywords but also the capability to relax its structure, using flexible hybrid graph patterns. This allows users to add structural constraints where they have the knowledge to do so and to use keywords otherwise. However, this relaxation also introduces ambiguity. A flexible hybrid graph pattern is therefore evaluated by first translating it into a set of unambiguous hybrid graph pattern interpretations and then forming the union of their results. Instead of producing all results, top-k processing based on the pull/bound rank join (PBRJ) template for instance, can be used to restrict attention to the best results and to terminate early. Adapting this to the multi-query case leads to the following hypothesis:

Hypothesis 5. *The execution of multiple queries (interpretations) can be made more efficient by introducing interpretation-specific score bounds that are tighter than previous bounds and applying run-time join order optimization in addition to sharing intermediate results between the different interpretations.*

In Chapter 7 we introduce the Multi-Query-PBRJ template for executing a set of interpretations that extends the PBRJ template to execute multiple queries simultaneously and provide new bounding schemes and pulling strategies that use tighter bounds. Further, we show that run-time join order optimization is actually orthogonal to the top-k mechanisms, and propose the use of probing sequence selectors to achieve that.

1.5 Contribution of this Thesis

In general, this thesis is concerned with the performance aspects of processing queries over hybrid data (in the form of text-rich data graphs). To this end, the thesis makes the following contributions:

- Several approaches for processing **keyword queries** over structured data have been previously proposed that can largely be categorized as schema-based and schema-agnostic approaches. In our contribution we focus on the latter category of approaches where keyword queries are evaluated directly over the data graph to obtain answers in the form of *Steiner graphs*. For supporting keyword search on structured data, current solutions require large indexes to be built that redundantly store subgraphs called neighborhoods. Further, for exploring keyword search results, large graphs have to be loaded into memory. In [LT11a], we propose a solution that employs much more *compact index structures* for neighborhood lookups, thereby reducing the search space for query answers. Using these indexes, keyword search result exploration is reduced to the traditional database problem of top-k join processing, enabling results to be computed efficiently. In particular, this computation can be performed on data streams successively loaded from disk (i.e. does not require the entire input to be loaded at once into memory). For supporting this, we propose a *top-k procedure* based on the rank join operator, which not only computes the k-best results, but also selects query plans in a top-k fashion during the process. In experiments using large real-world datasets, the solution reduced storage requirements and also outperformed the state-of-the-art in terms of performance and scalability.

- Concerning **structured queries** over RDF data graphs, the topic of *Linked Data query processing* has recently gained attention. These approaches make use of the Linked Data principles that mandate how structured RDF data should be published on the Web. In contrast to more traditional databases and RDF stores, queries are evaluated by retrieving data sources via live HTTP lookups during query processing and also discovering new data sources by following links contained in the data sources. Linked Data query processing however also incurs new challenges associated with the large amount of data sources, the limited access patterns that can be used to access the sources, and the lack of up to date knowledge about the sources. In [LT10], we propose a solution that tackles these challenges in various ways. We propose a novel query processing strategy that combines knowledge available about previously indexed data sources with knowledge gained at run-time through online discovery of new sources to perform *run-time adaptation of query plans*. Data sources are ranked according to their importance in order to report results as early as possible. This ranking is adapted at run-time to incorporate new knowledge and thereby increases query performance. In [LT11b], we propose the *symmetric index hash join* (SIHJ), a novel operator that deals with the unpredictable nature of accessing data distributed over a large number of sources by employing stream-based processing techniques while still supporting the use of data stored in local indexes when available. Compared to previously proposed operators, SIHJ guarantees completeness with regard to the retrieved data sources and improves performance significantly. This work was recognized with the Best Linked Open Data Paper Award at the 8th Extended Semantic Web Conference in 2011.

The results of this work were also contributed to establish a benchmark suite for federated query processing. FedBench [SGH+11] aims to support benchmarking various configurations of federated query processing over Linked Data, such as SPARQL endpoint federation and the Linked Data query processing setting studied in our work [LT10, LT11b]. The benchmark consists of several real-world datasets and several query sets for the various scenarios.

Further, existing works focus on the ranking and pruning of sources [LT10, HHK+10], or on the efficient processing of data while it is retrieved from sources [HBF09, LT11b], i.e. joins and traversal algorithms for retrieving and processing data from sources. However, there exists no *systematic approach for query plan optimization*, especially the kind that considers both the problems of source selection and data processing in a holistic way. We also observe that due to long execution times resulting from the large number of sources and their high processing cost, result completeness is often no longer affordable. Instead of assuming completeness and optimizing exclusively for cost, other criteria such as relevance, quality and cardinality of results, and trustworthiness of sources may be considered. This is problematic because these criteria are not always complementary. For instance, there is an inherent trade-off between output cardinality and cost: to produce more results, we have to retrieve more sources, which in turn increases processing cost. Taking this trade-off into account, we propose a *multi-objective optimization* framework in [LT12b]. In particular, we propose an optimization framework for Linked Data query processing, which incorporates both standard query operators and source selection. That is, we propose to extend the scope of query optimization from "how to process to data" to "which data to process". Further, this framework supports the *joint optimization of several objectives*, cost and output cardinality in particular. We propose a *dynamic programming (DP) solution* for the multi-objective optimization of this integrated process of source selection and query processing. It produces a set of Pareto-optimal query plans, which represent different trade-offs between optimization objectives. The challenge of using DP here is that after retrieval, sources can be re-used in different parts of the query, i.e. the source scan operators can be shared. Depending on the reusability of these operators, the cost of subplans may vary such that the cost function is no longer monotonic with regard to the combination of subplans. We provide a tight-bound solution, which takes this effect into account. In experiments on real world Linked Data, *Pareto-optimal plans* computed by our approach show benefits over suboptimal plans generated by existing solutions.

- Dealing with structured and unstructured data in an integrated fashion is a problem that is actively studied in the area of DB & IR integration [Wei07]. This research recognizes that exploiting the full richness of structure information in hybrid data requires expressiveness that goes beyond mere keywords. For this, different types of languages for formulating **hybrid queries** have been proposed, including content-and-structure queries for XML document retrievals, XQuery Full-Text, and a combination of paths and keywords called FleXPath for XML data retrieval. However, we note there exists no standard hybrid query language for the more general graph-structured RDF data. Moreover, while there are many proposals for processing hybrid queries and ranking hybrid results [TSW05, DH07, KSI+08, PIW10, AYLP04], the problem of *building indexes* for supporting efficiently hybrid search is largely unexplored. We have identified two main directions of works. On the one hand there are *database extensions*, which add keyword search support to databases by using a separate inverted index for textual data [HD05]. The other direction is to build *native indexes* capturing both structured and textual data [DH07, WLP+09, BMV11]. However, there is no work that systematically studies the differences among the various choices for native indexes and database extensions. To this end, we make the following contributions in [LT12a]. We propose a full-text extension to the standard RDF query language SPARQL, extending SPARQL Basic Graph Patterns (BGP) to *Hybrid Graph Patterns* (HGP). We discuss the various types of hybrid search queries that can be supported with this model. We propose a *general hybrid search index schema* that can be used to specify access patterns needed by these various query types and we present *HybIdx* as one instance of this scheme. Further, we perform a comprehensive experiment using several benchmark datasets and queries to systematically study existing solutions and HybIdx in several scenarios, from the text-centric retrieval of documents in Wikipedia and TREC collections annotated with structured data to structure-centric retrieval of data in IMDB and YAGO up to "pure" hybrid data formed by combining Wikipedia and DBpedia. The main conclusions of this experimental study are: native solutions are faster than database extensions by up to an order of magnitude; native solutions that focus on one type of queries, i.e. entity queries, are fastest because of smaller index size. Compared to these, HybIdx provides superior performance for relational and document queries (outperforms the second best approach by up to three orders of magnitude) and yields results close to the ones achieved by the best "focused" solution for entity queries [DH07]. As opposed to these solutions, it is more complete regarding the types of hybrid search queries that can be supported.

While hybrid graph patterns make it easier for users to specify structured queries, knowledge of the structure in the data is still required. Users have to express their information needs in technical terms, i.e. in terms of triple patterns. For example, they need to know when and how to specify joins between two patterns (by using variables that have the same name). This structure information is useful, making up the difference between structured and keyword queries. However, users might be able to capture only some but not all the structure information of a query. Addressing this, we propose in [LT12c] to add to BGPs not only the use of keywords but also the capability to relax its structure, using *Flexible Hybrid Graph Patterns* (fHGP). The flexibility introduced by fHGP results in ambiguity. we show how an *fHGP can be translated into a set of unambiguous HGPs*. Then, based on the introduced semantics of HGP, these HGP-interpretations of an fHGP can be processed using the proposed index scheme HybIdx. Instead of producing all results, top-k processing [IAE04, ISA$^+$04, IAE$^+$06] based on the pull/bound rank join (PBRJ) template for instance, can be used to restrict attention to the best results and to terminate early. Finally, results of all its interpretations can be combined to produce results for an fHGP. Hence, processing fHGP interpretations can be cast as a multi-query processing problem. We show that processing interpretations one-by-one is however inefficient, as results for several interpretations often overlap, meaning this multi-query processing can be optimized by sharing intermediate results. The main technical contribution in [LT12c] is the *Multi-Query PBRJ*. Compared to PBRJ, this extension processes several interpretations simultaneously to share their intermediate results. We introduce novel optimizations that are only possible with the Multi-Query PBRJ. With this, we show that run-time join order optimization is actually orthogonal to the top-k mechanisms, and propose the use of probing sequence selectors to achieve that. We propose score bounds specific to the interpretations that are tighter than the PBRJ bound obtained for the whole query (all interpretations). They enable more aggressive pulling and bounding, hence earlier reporting of top-k results. We implement our approach and top-k baselines for processing HGP-interpretations of an fHGP. Experiments show that sharing results of queries processed simultaneously is several (3-5) times faster than processing the queries one-by-one (without sharing). Further, the join order optimization and the more aggressive interpretation-specific pulling/bounding lead to consistent improvements.

The relation of the contributions to the aforementioned challenges of (1) reducing the amount of necessary data and (2) the efficient processing of the data is shown in Fig. 1.2.

1.6 Organization of this Thesis

Chapter 2 presents a formal model for hybrid data based on RDF and introduces the query types that are subject of this thesis, namely unstructured, structured and hybrid queries. For each query type, a formal model is presented with a short summary of challenges associated with each type of query. Chapters 3 - 7 are the main part of this thesis. In these chapters, the contributions of this thesis towards the efficient processing of unstructured, structured, and hybrid queries are discussed:

- Chapter 3 presents index structures and join algorithms for efficient processing of unstructured keyword queries.

- Chapters 4 & 5 discuss structured Linked Data queries and presents the contributions towards stream-based query processing and multi-objective query optimization, respectively.

- Chapter 6 presents indexes for hybrid search and Chapter 7 discusses the efficient processing of flexible hybrid queries.

All proposed approaches in these main parts of the thesis were experimentally evaluated, the results of which are presented in the respective chapter. The thesis concludes with a summary in Chapter 8. The appendix contains the queries used in the evaluations presented in the main part of the thesis.

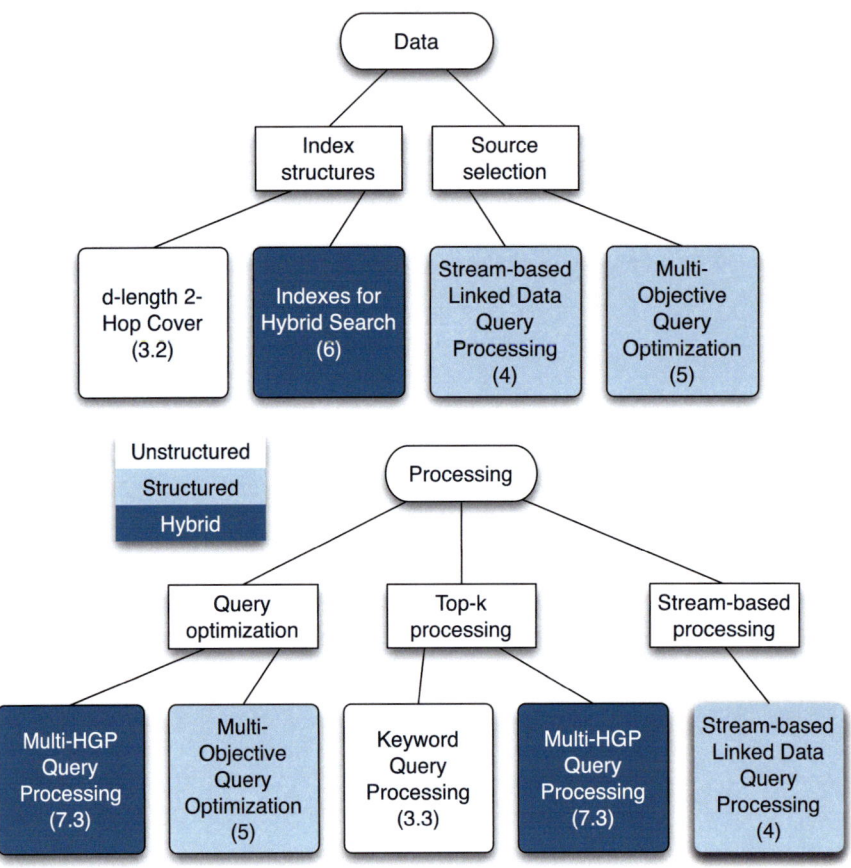

Figure 1.2: Categorization of the contributions presented in this thesis (corresponding chapter or section is indicated in parentheses). The background color indicates the type of query the contribution is associated with.

Chapter 2

Basics

The second chapter of this thesis presents the data and query model that is used in later chapters and introduces the challenges associated with processing unstructured, structured, and hybrid queries. Section 2.1 discusses the data model that is used to represent hybrid data, namely the RDF data model. We will show how this data model can be used to represent a large class of data models for unstructured and structured data, from document collections to relational data. Sections 2.2 - 2.4 then give formal definitions of unstructured, structured, and hybrid queries, respectively. We also discuss the challenges associated with processing queries of each type. This chapter concludes with a short introduction of query compilation and execution in Section 2.5.

2.1 Data Model

We use the Resource Description Framework[1] (RDF) as the basic model for hybrid data, omitting the special RDF semantics of blank nodes for the sake of generality: Namely, it can be considered as a general model for graph-structured data encoded as triples of the form $\langle subject, predicate, object \rangle$. These triples are composed of unique identifiers (URI references) and literals (e.g., strings or other data values) as follows:

Definition 2.1 (RDF Triple, RDF Term, RDF Graph). *Given a set of URI references $\mathcal{U}$ and a set of literals $\mathcal{L}$, elements in $\mathcal{U} \cup \mathcal{L}$ are called* RDF terms, $\langle s, p, o \rangle \in \mathcal{U} \times \mathcal{U} \times (\mathcal{U} \cup \mathcal{L})$ *is an* RDF triple, *and a set of RDF triples is an* RDF *graph. The elements in an RDF triple $\langle s, p, o \rangle$ are called* subject, predicate, *and* object, *respectively.*

---

[1] http://www.w3.org/RDF/, retrieved 2013-01-18

Note that an RDF graph is a labeled, directed multi-graph, where subjects and objects are nodes and the predicate is the label of an edge between them. We further distinguish predicates in the RDF graph as *relations* or *attributes*:

Definition 2.2 (Relation, Attribute). *Let $\langle s, p, o \rangle$ be an RDF triple in RDF graph G. We call p a relation if o is an URI reference, or attribute if o is a literal. The object of an attribute triple is also called* attribute value. *We denote the set of all attributes values in G as N_A. URI references that are subjects or objects are called* entities. *The set of all entities in G is N_E. Attributes and relation predicates are disjoint, i.e. a predicate may not be used as a relation and an attributes in the same RDF graph G.*

Given this general model, real-world entities s can be represented as URIs and via $\langle s, p, o \rangle$ triples, associated with attribute values (o as literals) or relations to other entities (o as entities). Clearly, this model can be used to capture structured data of different kinds as well as text-rich data, i.e. hybrid data. For instance, (structured) document entities can be represented as URIs and long textual descriptions might be associated with several types of entities as attribute values. In fact, some RDF resources are already text-rich as they are associated with long names and descriptions that can be decomposed into several words. Also, data stored in relational databases (RDBMS) can be mapped to an RDF representation, e.g. by using the R2RML mapping language[2].

Definition 2.3 (Keyword Term). *The function text $: \mathcal{U} \cup \mathcal{L} \to \mathcal{K}$ maps a URI or a literal to a bag of words (also called* keyword terms, *with shorthand term) $K \in \mathcal{K}$, where $\mathcal{K}$ is the set of all bags of keyword terms $K = \{k_1, \ldots, k_i, \ldots, k_n\}, k_i \in \mathcal{W}$, and $\mathcal{W}$ is the vocabulary of all keyword terms. As a shorthand we also define keyword terms over sets of RDF terms, text$(T) := \bigcup_{t \in T} text(t)$, where $T \subseteq \mathcal{U} \cup \mathcal{L}$.*

We do not specify a concrete implementation of the *text* function. A straightforward implementation would be to extract terms directly if the argument is a literal (using standard IR tokenization techniques) and to extract terms from the URI or associated labels (e.g. *rdfs:label*) if the argument is an URI reference.

We model hybrid data as data graphs associated with a textual representation, as captured by the *text* function:

Definition 2.4 (Hybrid Data). *Hybrid data is a tuple $G = (G^R, text)$, where G^R is an RDF graph and text a function mapping RDF terms in G^R to bags of keyword terms.*

---

[2]http://www.w3.org/TR/r2rml/, retrieved 2013-01-18

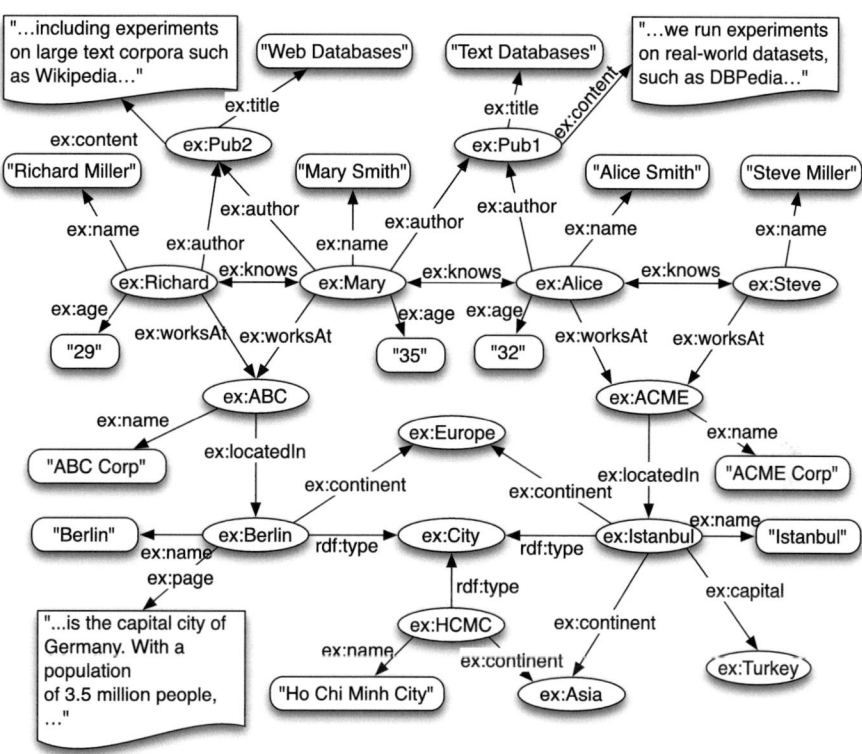

Figure 2.1: Example hybrid data containing information about locations, publications, people and their relationships. This data will be used in examples throughout this thesis.

Throughout the thesis we use the following notation conventions: variables are single letters prefixed with a question mark (e.g. $?s$), literals are enclosed in quotation marks (e.g. *"Berlin"*), keyword terms are lower-case words (without quotation marks) (e.g. *berlin*), and URIs are identified by the use of namespace abbreviations (e.g. *ex:Berlin*).

Example 2.1. *An example RDF graph formed by RDF triples is shown in Fig. 2.1. For presentation, URI references are shortened using the abbreviation* ex: *for URI namespaces where* ex: *stands for* http://example.org/. *Literal nodes are marked with enclosing question marks, e.g. "Berlin" or "Istanbul". The literal representing the attribute value for* ex:page *contains a large number* *of words. Applying the text function to that literal yields the terms {capital, city, germany, ...}. Similarly, for the URI ex:Berlin, we have the term {berlin}.*

2.2 Unstructured Queries

Especially for lay users, *keyword search* has been regarded as an effective mechanism because it helps to circumvent the complexity of structured query languages, and hide the underlying data representation. Without knowledge of the query syntax and data schema, users can obtain possibly complex structured results, including tuples from relational databases, XML data, data graphs, and RDF resources [HWYY07, TWRC09]. As opposed to document retrieval, results in this structured data setting may encompass several resources that are connected over possibly very long paths (e.g. joined database tuples, XML trees, RDF resources connected over paths of relations).

There are two directions of research that aim at supporting this. On the one hand, there are *schema-based approaches* implemented on top of off-the-shelf databases [HGP03, LYMC06, LLWZ07, QYC09]. These approaches find candidate networks, which represent valid join sequences that are employed as queries to retrieve the final results. The main advantage here is that the power and optimization capabilities of the underlying database engine can be fully utilized. On the other hand, there are *schema-agnostic approaches* [KPC+05, HWYY07, LOF+08], which operate directly on the data. Since they do not rely on a schema, the applicability of these approaches is not limited to structured data. For instance, semi-structured RDF data [TWRC09] as well as the combination of structured, semi-structured and unstructured data [LOF+08] have been supported.

In this work, we focus on the latter type, also called *native approaches*. Given a keyword query $Q = \{k_1, \ldots, k_n\}$, these approaches first find matching elements in the data graph. Next, structures connecting these so-called *keyword elements* are explored. These structures constitute the query results, which are called Steiner trees [DYW+07], or *Steiner graphs* [TWRC09, LOF+08].

2.2.1 Query Model

Before formally defining keyword queries and their answers, we define the length of paths in a graph and the distance between two nodes. These concepts are later used in the formal definition of keyword query answers, namely Steiner graphs.

Definition 2.5 (Paths). *Let G be an RDF graph. The* length *of a path denotes the number of edges in the path. We use* distance *between u,w to denote the length of the shortest path between u and w. Two graph elements (nodes or edges) are* connected *if they appear together in a path (no matter the directions of edges in that path).*

Definition 2.6 (Keyword Query). *A* keyword query *is a set of keyword terms $Q = \{k_1, \ldots, k_n\}$, where each $k_i \in \mathcal{W}$.*

Query keywords match entities' attribute value nodes, or labels of attribute or relation edges. Thus, keyword matches can always be associated with some entities. We call these matching entities *keyword elements*:

Definition 2.7 (Keyword Element). *Given a keyword query $Q = \{k_1, \ldots, k_n\}$ consisting of keywords, a node $n_k \in N_E$ is a* keyword element *for $k \in Q$ iff there is a triple $\langle n_k, p, a \rangle$ in G and k is relevant for $text(p)$ or $text(a)$. The set of all keyword elements for k is denoted as N_k.*

For processing a keyword query, we first find keyword elements in the data graph. Then, we search for substructures that connect the keyword elements. The most commonly used substructures are Steiner trees [KPC+05], i.e. minimal rooted trees in the data graph, which contains at least one keyword element for every keyword in the query. Instead of rooted trees, general graphs have also been used [TWRC09, LOF+08]. This notion of Steiner graph is also employed in this work:

Definition 2.8 (Keyword Query Answer). *An* answer *to a keyword query $Q = \{k_1, \ldots, k_n\}$, also called* Steiner graph, *is a subgraph of G denoted as $G_S = (N_S, E_S)$, which satisfies the following conditions:*

- *For every $k \in Q$ there is at least one keyword element $n_k \in N_S$. The set of keyword elements containing one n_k for every $k \in Q$ is $N_K \subseteq N_S$.*

- *For every possible pair $n_i, n_j \in N_K$ and $n_i \neq n_j$, there is a path $n_i \leadsto n_j$ such that every $n_i \in N_K$ is connected to every other $n_j \in N_K$.*

We call such a graph a d-length Steiner graph when direct paths, *i.e. paths that connect exactly two keyword elements n_i, n_j such that there is no other keyword element n_k in the path between n_i and n_j, have length d or less (we use $n_i \leadsto^d n_j$ to denote these paths).*

21

This captures the standard semantics of keyword query answers [KPC$^+$05, TWRC09]. Limited by its internal index structure, EASE [LOF$^+$08] departs from this and employs an alternative semantics: while it also searches for Steiner graphs, it implicitly assumes one "center keyword element" that is connected to all other keyword elements over a maximum distance d. While this leads to a more restricted search space, results corresponding to the standard semantics may be missed. In this work, we support the standard semantics. That is, we do not assume the existence of a center keyword element. The d-length restriction only implies that for every keyword element n_i in the Steiner graph, there is *at least one* other keyword element connected to it via a path of length d or less (i.e., the directly connected one), while all other keyword elements may be (indirectly) connected to it via longer paths.

The computation of top-k Steiner graphs typically requires a monotonic function for ranking. Widely used in keyword search is the score of a node calculated using a probabilistic IR model. Scores which measure nodes' prestige have also been incorporated – PageRank for instance [HHP06]. Besides, keyword search solutions generally rest on the assumption that more compact Steiner graphs more likely match the user needs, i.e. the length of paths connecting two keyword elements has a negative effect on the rank. The solution proposed here is orthogonal to the ranking function being used. For ease of exposition, we use path length as the only metric:

Definition 2.9. *Let G_S be a Steiner graph and P be the set of direct paths that connect its keyword elements, the* rank *of G_S is determined by $Score(G_S) = \sum_{p \in P} Score(p)$, where $Score(p) = \frac{1}{length(p)}$.*

Example 2.2. *Let $Q = \{miller, corp\}$ be an example keyword query that consists of two keywords, to be evaluated on the example graph in Fig. 2.1. First, keyword elements are retrieved for each of the keywords. Keyword miller appears in the ex:name attribute of ex:Richard and ex:Steve, which are therefore keyword elements for miller (see Def. 2.7). Keyword elements for corp are ex:ACME and ex:ABC. Next, structures connecting these elements are explored, which are the results for the keyword query. Fig. 2.2 shows two such results, each of which connects keyword elements for both keywords. The results are therefore valid according to Def. 2.8.*

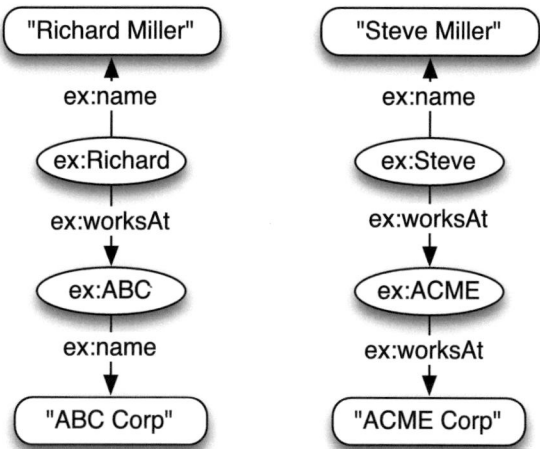

Figure 2.2: Two example results for keyword query $Q = \{miller, corp\}$.

2.2.2 Challenges

Since the search space for evaluating keyword queries may be large, two main directions have been investigated for optimization. One is based on materializing paths [HWYY07]. The fastest solution proposed recently, called EASE, is based on materializing even more complex structures in the form of graphs, which capture entire neighborhoods of data elements [LOF+08]. This can improve online performance because instead of searching, pre-computed structures retrieved from the index can be used. The other direction is to improve the efficiency of the exploration algorithm [KPC+05, DYW+07]. The main drawbacks of current state-of-the-art is that materialized indexes [LOF+08], which redundantly store neighborhood information may become too large. Further, existing search strategies for efficient result exploration assume the entire data to be available in memory, a requirement that is too limited when the amount of data is large.

The index structures and algorithms proposed so far are very specific to the keyword search problem. In this work, we aim to reduce this problem to more standard database ones to leverage the vast body of existing work. In particular, we propose the concept of *native keyword search databases*, which solve the keyword search problem using two standard database operations, *data access* and *join*. Instead of loading the data entirely at once and exploring results in memory, keyword search is supported through a series of fine-granular data access (path lookups) and join operations (path and graph joins). For supporting these operations, we build upon existing work on index structures and top-k join processing.

2.3 Structured Queries

SPARQL[3] is the established query language for RDF data. Specialized RDF databases, called triple stores, provide structured querying capabilities to local users, but also via remote access, in which case they are referred to as *SPARQL endpoints*.

However, in recent years, the amount of RDF data published as *Linked Data* on the Web has been increasing rapidly. Datasets made publicly available on the Web as Linked Data cover different domains, including life sciences (e.g. DrugBank, UniProt, PubMed), geographic locations (e.g. World Factbook, Geo Names), media and entertainment (MusicBrainz, Last.FM, BBC Programmes). There are also cross-domain encyclopedic datasets such as Freebase and DBpedia (the structured data counterpart of Wikipedia). Besides enterprises, such as media companies like BBC and Last.FM, several governments (e.g. US, UK) recently started to make data of public interest available to citizens, including CO2, Mortality, Energy and Postcodes.

SPARQL endpoints providing structured querying capabilities are available for some of these datasets such that federated query processing over Linked Data is possible. However, the need for managing these endpoints represents technical and economic entry barriers. Not all data providers can and want to serve their data through endpoints. Instead, they mostly follow the *Linked Data principles* [BHBL09], which dictate how to publish and access Linked Data and how to establish links between them. According to these principles, structured data about an entity can be made available as Linked Data essentially by publishing an "entity Web page", called *Linked Data source*, that has an URI. Dereferencing this URI via HTTP should return structured data about that entity. This data may contain other URIs representing links to related entities (related Linked Data sources). Thus, as an alternative to managing structured data through federated endpoints, Linked Data represents a simple mechanism for publishing, accessing and linking structured data on the Web just like Web pages.

As a result of this Linked Data movement, a large number of structured data sources, including the ones mentioned above, has been made accessible

---

[3]http://www.w3.org/TR/rdf-sparql-query/, retrieved 2013-01-18

through HTTP lookups, while only a few of them can actually be retrieved via SPARQL endpoints. Given an information need represented as a structured query, federation over SPARQL endpoints is only a partial solution. It can be used to retrieve some parts of the results, while harnessing all structured data available as Linked Data requires (1) *offline* crawling and importing it into an endpoint (2) or processing these queries *online* – using HTTP URI lookup as the only one access pattern. In this regard, the problem of *Linked Data query processing* [HBF09, HHK⁺10, LT10, LT11b, Har11] has recently gained attention. Given a structured query, the goal is to efficiently compute and retrieve results from Linked Data sources at run-time via URI lookups.

In this work, we focus on the efficient execution of SPARQL queries over RDF data that is published as Linked Data. We now formalize Linked Data and the structured query model (SPARQL basic graph patterns) for our purposes and then present challenges associated with Linked Data query processing.

2.3.1 Linked Data

Linked Data on the Web today is basically RDF data managed according to the Linked Data principles [BHBL09]:

1. Use URIs to name things.

2. Use HTTP URIs so that people can look up those names.

3. When someone looks up an URI, provide useful information, using the standards (RDF, SPARQL).

4. Include links to other URIs, so that they can discover more things.

An HTTP URI reference is also called a Linked Data source, whose constituent triples contain other HTTP URI references that lead to other sources:

Definition 2.10 (Linked Data Source / Graph). *A Linked Data source, identified by an HTTP URI d, is a set of RDF triples* $\langle s, p, o \rangle$, *denoted as* T^d. *There is a* link *between two Linked Data sources* d_i, d_j *if* d_j *appears as the subject or object in at least one triple of* d_i, *i.e.* $\exists t \in T^{d_i}, t = \langle d_j, p, o \rangle \lor t = \langle s, p, d_j \rangle$ *or vice versa,* $\exists t \in T^{d_j}, t = \langle d_i, p, o \rangle \lor t = \langle s, p, d_i \rangle$. *With D as the set of all Linked Data sources, the* Linked Data *graph is constituted as* $T^D = \{t | t \in T^{d_i}, d_i \in D\}$.

Src. 1: http://example.org/Mary

```
ex : Mary
    ex : name  'Mary  Smith '  ;
    ex : knows  ex : Richard  ;
    ex : knows  ex : Alice  ;
    ex : worksAt  ex : ABC  .
```

Src. 2: http://example.org/Alice

```
ex : Alice
    ex : name  'Alice  Smith '  ;
    ex : knows  ex : Mary  ;
    ex : knows  ex : Steve  ;
    ex : worksAt  ex : ACME  .
```

Src. 3: http://example.org/ABC

```
ex : ABC
    ex : name  'ABC  Corp '  ;
    ex : locatedIn  ex : Berlin  .
```

Src. 4: http://example.org/ACME

```
ex : ACME
    ex : name  'ACME  Corp '  ;
    ex : locatedIn  ex : Istanbul  .
```

Src. 5: http://example.org/Richard

```
ex : Richard
    ex : name  'Richard  Miller '  ;
    ex : knows  ex : Mary  ;
    ex : worksAt  ex : ABC  .
```

Figure 2.3: Example Linked Data sources containing data from Fig. 2.1.

Example 2.3. *Fig. 2.3 shows the content (derived from Fig. 2.1) of five example Linked Data sources: ex:Mary, ex:Richard, ex:Alice, ex:ABC, and ex:ACME. In this case, the Linked Data sources contain only triples where the source URI appears as the subject, which is a common property of published Linked Data. Note that the sources follow the Linked Data principles and include links to other Linked Data sources (e.g. ex:Mary links to ex:Alice via predicate ex:knows).*

2.3.2 Query Model

The standard for querying RDF data is SPARQL, of which *basic graph patterns* (BGP) are an important fragment that captures a wide range of information needs:

Definition 2.11 (Basic Graph Pattern)**.** *Let $\mathcal{V}$ be the set of all variables. A triple pattern (TP) $\langle s, p, o \rangle \in (\mathcal{V} \cup \mathcal{U}) \times (\mathcal{V} \cup \mathcal{U}) \times (\mathcal{V} \cup \mathcal{U} \cup \mathcal{L})$ is a triple where the subject, predicate, and object can either be a variable or a constant (an RDF*

term). A basic graph pattern (BGP) is a set of triple patterns, $Q = \{t_1, \ldots, t_n\}$.
Two TPs that share a variable form a join *pattern.*

Analogously to the triples in an RDF graph, the triple patterns in a basic
graph pattern also form a graph. In principle, this graph does not have to be
connected (when referring to connectedness we treat the graph as undirected).
In practice, however, BGP queries we find in logs (e.g. queries against DBpedia
[MLAN11] or queries in the USEWOD2012[4] query logs) are always connected.
Accordingly, we focus on connected BGPs only.

Computing answers to a BGP query over the Linked Data graph amounts to
the task of *graph pattern matching*:

Definition 2.12 (BGP Result). *Let G be an RDF graph, Q be an BGP query, and*
$\mathcal{V}$ *be the set of all variables. Let μ' be the function that maps elements in Q to*
elements in G:

$$\mu' : \mathcal{V} \cup \mathcal{U} \cup \mathcal{L} \to \mathcal{U} \cup \mathcal{L} \begin{cases} v \mapsto \mu(v) & \text{if } v \in \mathcal{V} \\ t \mapsto t & \text{if } t \in \mathcal{U} \cup \mathcal{L} \end{cases}$$

where the mapping $\mu : \mathcal{V} \to \mathcal{U} \cup \mathcal{L}$ is employed to map variables in Q to RDF
terms in G. A mapping μ is a result to Q if it satisfies $\langle \mu'(s), \mu'(p), \mu'(o) \rangle \in G$,
$\forall \langle s, p, o \rangle \in Q$. *We denote the set of all result bindings for query Q over graph*
G as $\Omega_G(Q)$ (we omit G if clear from context), i.e. $\mu \in \Omega_G(Q)$. The set of all
bindings for a single triple pattern $t \in Q$ is $\Omega_G(t)$.

Intuitively, a result to a BGP query Q is a mapping μ of all variables in the
BGP to elements of the RDF graph G such that the substitution of all variables
with their mapped terms in μ forms a subgraph of G.

Figure 2.4: Example BGP query that asks for the names of companies people
known by *ex:Mary* work at.

---

[4]http://data.semanticweb.org/usewod/2012/, retrieved 2013-01-18

Example 2.4. *Fig. 2.4 shows an example BGP query over the Linked Data sources shown in Fig. 2.3. A BGP query is answered by retrieving bindings for each triple pattern in the query and then joining them to obtain final results. For example, bindings for the triple pattern $t_1 = \langle ex{:}Mary, ex{:}knows, ?x \rangle$ can be retrieved from from source ex:Mary, i.e. $?x \to ex{:}Alice$ and $?x \to ex{:}Richard$. Then, bindings for the second pattern $t_2 = \langle ?x, ex{:}worksAt, ?y \rangle$ can be retrieved from sources ex:Mary, ex:Richard, ex:Alice as they all contain triples matching the pattern. However, only the bindings from ex:Richard and ex:Alice will join with the bindings for the first pattern to obtain the intermediate results for $?x$ and $?y$:*

$$?x \to ex{:}Alice, ?y \to ex{:}ACME$$
$$?x \to ex{:}Richard, ?y \to ex{:}ABC$$

The last pattern is evaluated in the same manner, obtaining final results for $?x, ?y$ and $?z$:

$$?x \to ex{:}Alice, ?y \to ex{:}ACME, ?z \to \text{``ACME Corp''}$$
$$?x \to ex{:}Richard, ?y \to ex{:}ABC, ?z \to \text{``ABC Corp''}$$

2.3.3 Challenges

A BGP query is evaluated by first obtaining *triple bindings* for each of the triple patterns $q \in Q$ and then performing a series of joins to combine the bindings. This is done for every two patterns that share a variable (called the join variable), forming a join pattern. In the Linked Data context, there might be no endpoints providing structured querying capabilities to directly retrieve bindings for triple or join patterns. Instead, using URI lookups only, entire sources have to be retrieved and their data matching triple patterns have to be extracted and joined to produce results. The main challenges we identified for this setting are as follows:

- **(C1) Limited Access Patterns.** Via HTTP lookups, Linked Data sources can only be retrieved as a whole. Thus, processing sources that have only little or no contributions to the final result incurs a large and unnecessary overhead.

- **(C2) Heterogeneous Access Patterns.** Some Linked Data is available in SPARQL endpoints or might be managed locally using RDF stores. Exploiting the richer querying capabilities and faster performance provided by these endpoints requires dealing with different access patterns, i.e. URI lookups and SPARQL queries.

- **(C3) Large Number of Sources.** According to the Linked Data principles [BHBL09], each URI can be dereferenced and the document returned represents a virtual "data source". This dramatically increases the number of Linked Data sources that need to be considered.

- **(C4) Dynamics of Sources.** Linked Data sources are added and removed and sources' content changes rapidly over time. Due to this dynamics, it is not safe to assume that information about all sources can be obtained. In particular, sources might be a priori unknown and can only be discovered at run-time.

2.4 Hybrid Queries

Different types of *hybrid query languages* have been proposed, including content-and-structure queries (e.g. based on XQuery) for XML document retrievals [TSW05], and a combination of paths and keywords called FleX-Path [AYLP04] for XML data retrieval. Also, there are proprietary full-text extensions[5] to SPARQL used by RDF store vendors. SPARQL is a standard for querying RDF using BGPs. data, comprise the triple The full-text extensions allow keywords to be used as RDF terms at any position of the triple patterns so that users do not need to know URIs but can specify a query using their own words. An example query is for instance

$$\langle ?x, type, city\rangle, \langle ?x, continent, europe\rangle, \langle ?x, capital, ?y\rangle$$

which contains only variables and keywords (e.g. *type* is a keyword, which is not the same as the URI *rdf:type*). In this work we introduce the notion of a *Hybrid Graph Pattern* (HGP) as an extension to SPARQL BGP to capture the semantics of these proprietary extensions[6].

While HGPs make it easier for users to specify structured queries, knowledge of the structure in the data is still required. Users have to express their information

---

[5]http://www.w3.org/2009/sparql/wiki/Feature:FullText, retrieved 2013-01-18

[6]Most RDF stores use a "magic" predicate to specify keywords. The pattern $\langle ?x, type, city\rangle$ would be executed as $\langle ?x, ?p, ?o\rangle, \langle ?p, text:contains, type\rangle, \langle ?o, text:contains, city\rangle$, where *text:contains* signifies that the keyword should appear in the RDF term bound to the subject variable.

needs in technical terms, i.e. in terms of triple patterns. For example, they need to know when and how to specify joins between two patterns (by using variables that have the same name). This structure information is useful, making up the difference between structured and keyword queries. However, users might be able to capture only some but not all the structure information of a query. Addressing this, we propose to add to BGPs not only the use of keywords but also the capability to relax its structure, using *Flexible Hybrid Graph Patterns* (fHGP). Basically, they are "incomplete" HGPs where not all positions have been specified. For example, the fHGP

type:city, *continent:europe*, *capital*

can be seen as three incomplete triple patterns of an HGP, where the first two contain only two specified elements and the last only one element. This way, fHGPs enable the use of structure knowledge when available, but also just keywords otherwise (using patterns with one element, e.g. *capital*).

2.4.1 Hybrid Query: HGP

The core feature of SPARQL is the Basic Graph Pattern (BGP), which is composed of triple patterns $\langle s, p, o \rangle$, where each s, p, and o are either variables or constants. As constants, RDF terms are specified in BGP queries such that matching results are corresponding RDF terms in the data. For instance, we specify the pattern $\langle ?s, ex{:}name, \text{"Ho Chi Minh City"} \rangle$, where $?s$ is a variable, to obtain the corresponding triple $\langle ex{:}HCMC, ex{:}name, \text{"Ho Chi Minh City"} \rangle$. Given hybrid data where RDF terms, and especially literals, contain a large number of words, it is desirable to query data not only with entire RDF terms, e.g. *"Ho Chi Minh City"*, but some containing words, i.e. keyword terms, such as *Ho* or *Chi*, to obtain results with RDF terms that contain these words.

With the introduced *text* function that represents the textual data embedded in structured data and the resulting model of hybrid data, we can now query for RDF triples and subgraphs as well as the textual data contained in them. We extend the notion of BGP such that not only RDF terms but also keyword terms can be used as constants. This yields a kind of hybrid queries called *Hybrid Graph Pattern* (HGP):

Definition 2.13 (Hybrid Graph Pattern). *Let $\mathcal{V}$ be the set of all variables. A hybrid triple pattern (HTP) $\langle s, p, o \rangle \in (\mathcal{V} \cup \mathcal{U} \cup \mathcal{K}) \times (\mathcal{V} \cup \mathcal{U} \cup \mathcal{K}) \times (\mathcal{V} \cup \mathcal{U} \cup \mathcal{L} \cup \mathcal{K})$ is a triple where the subject, predicate and object can either be a* variable *in*

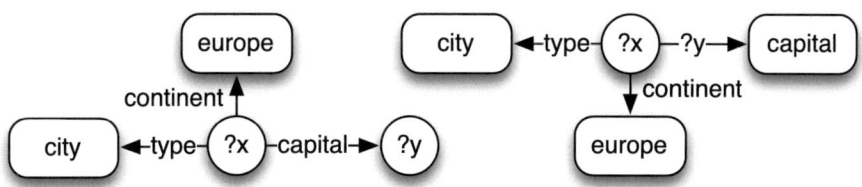

Figure 2.5: Two example hybrid graph patterns that aim at the same information need: "cities in Europe that are capitals". In the left query, the capital status of a city is expressed by a *capital* keyword at the predicate position, whereas in the other query, it is expressed by the *capital* keyword at the object position, i.e. *capital* should appear in the literal value.

$\mathcal{V}$ *or a constant. The latter is either an* RDF term *in* $\mathcal{U} \cup \mathcal{L}$ *or a* bag of keyword terms *in* $\mathcal{K}$. *Two HTPs* t_i *and* t_j *that share a common variable* v, *establish the* join condition (v^i, v^j), *where* v *is called the* join variable, *and* v^i *and* v^j *denotes the variable* v *in* t_i *and* v *in* t_j, *respectively. A* hybrid graph pattern *(HGP) is a set of HTPs,* $Q = \{t_1, \ldots, t_n\}$.

In principle, HGPs do not have to be connected. However, we assume that HGPs formulated by users will always be connected (in the same way as BGPs) and thus restrict our attention to *connected HGPs* that contain a path between any two nodes.

Example 2.5. *Fig. 2.5 shows two example HGPs, which are composed of variables and keyword terms only. Further, HGPs can also contain a keyword term and an RDF term, e.g.* $\langle ?x, name, "Istanbul" \rangle$, *and also allow keywords at subject position:* $\langle istanbul, capital, ?o \rangle$.

Processing HGPs. The usual SPARQL semantics can be used for evaluating HGPs without keywords terms (i.e. those which are BGPs). Extending this semantics to incorporate keyword terms, a result to an HGP query can be defined as follows:

Definition 2.14 (HGP Result). *Let* $G = (G^R, text)$ *be a hybrid data graph, Q be an HGP query, and* $\mathcal{V}$ *be the set of all variables and* $\mathcal{K}$ *the set of all bags of* *keyword terms. Let μ' be the function that maps elements in Q to elements G^R:*

$$\mu' : \mathcal{V} \cup \mathcal{U} \cup \mathcal{L} \cup \mathcal{K} \rightarrow \mathcal{U} \cup \mathcal{L} \begin{cases} (1)\ v \mapsto \mu(v) & \textit{if } v \in \mathcal{V} \\ (2)\ K \mapsto t & \textit{if } K \in \mathcal{K} \\ (3)\ t \mapsto t & \textit{if } t \in \mathcal{U} \cup \mathcal{L} \end{cases}$$

where the mapping $\mu : \mathcal{V} \rightarrow \mathcal{U} \cup \mathcal{L}$ is employed to map variables in Q to RDF terms in G^R. A mapping μ is a result to Q if it satisfies $\langle \mu'(s), \mu'(p), \mu'(o) \rangle \in G^R$, $\forall \langle s, p, o \rangle \in Q$. We denote the set of all result bindings for HGP Q over G^R as $\Omega_{G^R}(Q)$ (we omit G^R if clear from context), i.e. $\mu \in \Omega_{G^R}(Q)$. The set of all bindings for a single hybrid triple pattern $t \in Q$ is $\Omega_{G^R}(t)$.

In other words, computing results amounts to the task of *graph pattern matching*, where the query graph pattern is matched against the data graph and the results are matches to variables in the query. The matching of (1) variables v and (3) RDF terms t in the query to RDF terms in the data is analogous to BGP matching (see Definition 2.12). The HGP extension to BGP matching is (2), the mapping of bags of keyword terms in the query, K, to the textual representation of RDF terms in the data, t. For this we propose the semantics commonly used in Information Retrieval (IR) tasks, the one based on *IR-style relevance*: an RDF term t is considered a match to K if $text(t)$ is relevant for K, otherwise t is not a match. Usually, $text(t)$ will be relevant if it contains one or more of the keyword terms in K, however other forms of relevancy are also possible (e.g. synonyms or related terms).

HGP Query Types. BGP has shown to be a powerful querying paradigm that supports various types of common searches. As examples, the search for *entities* (e.g. documents or other types such as people and companies) can be expressed as star-shaped BGP queries, whose triple patterns share the same variable at their subject position. This "center node" variable stands for the entities to be retrieved. Moreover, relational queries that are more complex, involving several *entities and their relations*, can be expressed as general BGPs, i.e. those composing of triple patterns that have different variables at their subject position (as well as variables in other positions). To this expressiveness of BGP, HGP adds the capability to use of keywords at any position, thus does not require users to know specific RDF terms.

2.4.2 Flexible Hybrid Query: fHGP

While HGPs enable querying RDF terms using keywords, they still require users to express information needs in more technical terms, i.e. as triple patterns.

To use them effectively, users are supposed to have technical knowledge such as how to join triple patterns (by specifying join variables that are shared by triple patterns). Keyword queries on the other hand, which do not capture triple structure but simply bags of terms, are intuitive. However, they do not allow users to exploit the structure in the data, given their knowledge thereof. For instance, users may want to specify that *Istanbul* is not any keyword but the *name* of the city they looking for. We propose the following combination, which exploits the richness in structure provided by HGPs and the intuitiveness of keyword-based querying:

Definition 2.15 (fHGP). *A flexible hybrid triple pattern (fHTP) is a sequence $f = (e_1, \ldots, e_n)$ with no more than three elements, i.e. $|f| \leq 3$, where each $e_i \in f$ is either a constant (RDF term or bag of keywords) or a variable. A* flexible hybrid graph pattern *(fHGP) is a set of fHTP $Q = \{f_1, \ldots, f_n\}$.*

Example 2.6. *An example fHGP that can be used to express the information needs captured by the two queries in Fig. 2.5 is $Q = \{(type, city), (continent, europe), (capital)\}$. Using a more intuitive syntax, we can also write Q as $\{type:city, continent:europe, capital\}$.*

2.4.3 Challenges

Concerning hybrid queries, we focus on two ways to improve performance: first, the construction of native indexes that allow for the efficient retrieval of hybrid patterns and, second, dealing with the ambiguity introduced by flexible hybrid graph patterns by employing efficient top-k processing techniques.

Indexes for Hybrid Search. While there are proposals for processing hybrid queries and ranking hybrid results [TSW05, DH07, KSI⁺08, PIW10, AYLP04], the problem of *building indexes* for supporting efficient hybrid search is largely unexplored. We have identified two main directions of works. On the one hand there are *database extensions*, which add keyword search support to databases by using a separate inverted index for textual data [WTLF11]. The other direction is to build *native indexes* capturing both structured and textual data [DH07, WLP⁺09, BMV11]. However, there is no work that systematically studies the differences among the various choices for native index design and in particular, differences between native indexes and database extensions.

In this thesis, we first discuss the various types of hybrid search queries that can be supported with the previously introduced hybrid graph pattern model and then propose a general hybrid search index scheme that can be used to specify access patterns needed to support these various query types. We propose HybIdx as one instance of this scheme and experimentally compare it to existing solutions.

Processing Flexible Hybrid Graph Patterns. While fHGPs do relax the syntax of HGPs to reduce the burden of structured query formulation, it also introduces ambiguities. First, an fHTP with a single element may denote the subject, the predicate, or the object of an HTP, i.e. several HTPs can be seen as candidate interpretations for an fHTP. Further, a set of fHTPs, i.e. and fHGP, may capture only few or no join conditions at all. Thus, combining results obtained for them is another challenging problem. Solving this requires searching through the space of all possible join conditions to connect HTP-interpretations of several fHTPs, and to form connected graphs as HGP-interpretations of an fHGP.

Second, we note that the HGP proposed here is in spirit similar to the proprietary SPARQL full-text extensions provided by RDF store vendors such as Virtuoso and OWLIM. The full-text support is implemented by vendors using a separate inverted index that is employed to retrieve all RDF terms matching a given keyword. In principle, they can be used to compute a solution to an fHGP simply by retrieving solutions to all of its HGP-interpretations. However, this is not feasible in practice, as the number of HGP-interpretations obtained for a HGP is large.

In this thesis, we provide a mechanism to compute all HTP-interpretations of an fHTP and HGP-interpretations of an fHGP, respectively. Then, for computing results to a set of HGP-interpretations, we make use of inverted indexes as implemented by RDF stores vendors. However, instead of computing all results, we apply top-k join processing techniques. Extending top-k techniques geared towards single queries, we provide novel solutions to the problem of simultaneously processing multiple HGP queries.

2.5 Query Compilation and Execution

In this section, we will shortly introduce the main concepts of modern query processing systems. These will be used when presenting contributions throughout the rest of this thesis. Most database systems offer a declarative query interface, i.e. the query specifies which data the user is interested in, but not how the data should be retrieved or computed. Rather, this decision is left to the database system, which chooses among multiple alternative ways to answer the given query that may have different run-time characteristics [Neu05]. Fig. 2.6 shows

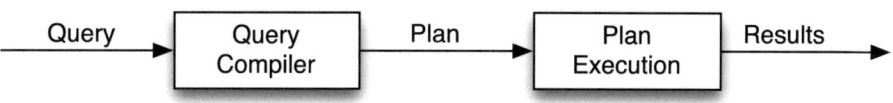

Figure 2.6: Architecture of query processing systems

the general architecture that most implementations adopt as a consequence. The input query is first processed by the *query compiler* that analyzes the query and tries to find the best way to answer it, resulting in a *query plan*. This plan is passed to the *query executor* that actually executes the query according to the query plan to finally obtain the *results*. In the following, we will shortly describe both of these steps while focusing on those parts that are most relevant for the content of this thesis.

2.5.1 Overview

The task of the query compiler is to create a query plan that specifies how the query should be evaluated by the query execution engine [EN00]. The main problem here is the task of *query optimization*, i.e. finding the best way to execute a given query according to pre-defined optimization criteria, such as cost. Because the problem of query optimization is of such importance, the terms *query optimizer* and query compiler are often used interchangeably.

In the following we will describe the process of query compilation with the help of an example structured SPARQL query. Note that the concepts described here can be directly transferred to other types of queries, such as the unstructured and hybrid queries described earlier, or even SQL queries in relational database systems. Fig. 2.7 shows the example BGP query from Fig. 2.4 in SPARQL syntax.

First, the query is *parsed* and transformed into an abstract syntax tree, which is then subject to semantic analysis. If no syntactic or semantic errors in the query are detected, the output of these steps is an internal *logical representation* of the original query. Fig. 2.8 shows the logical representation of the query as an abstract syntax tree. In the next step, the logical representation is transformed into a *physical query plan*. Where the logical representation describes the semantics of the query and its results, the physical plan specifies the steps that need to be taken to compute the results of the query. This transformation is usually

```
SELECT ?x ?z WHERE {
    ex:Mary ex:knows ?x .
    ?x ex:worksAt ?y .
    ?y ex:name ?z .
}
```

Figure 2.7: Example BGP query from Fig. 2.4 in SPARQL.

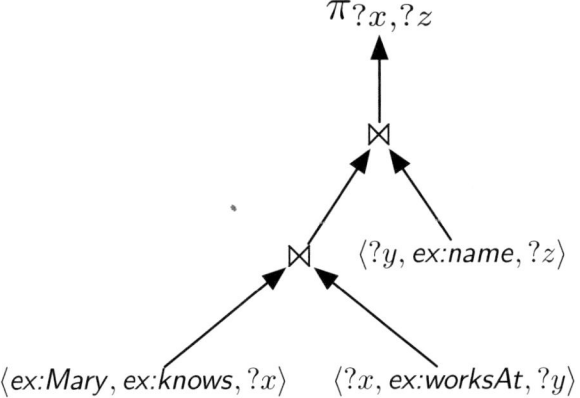

Figure 2.8: Logical representation of the example query.

cost-based, i.e. the query optimizer constructs a plan that will execute the query with minimal costs [Neu05].

After a physical query plan has been constructed it is then passed to the query execution engine, where the query results are obtained by performing the operations specified in the query plan.

2.5.2 Generating Physical Query Plans

Physical query plans are usually represented as trees of *query operators*. A query operator specifies a single operation that is required to execute the query. Operators are arranged in a tree, where results flow from the leaves of the tree to its root. Operators may have zero or more input operators that appear as children in the tree. For example, a join operator may have two input operators whose output are the operands of the join. Fig. 2.9 shows one such physical plan for the example query. In contrast to the logical representation, the physical plan specifies exactly which operators should be executed. In order to obtain

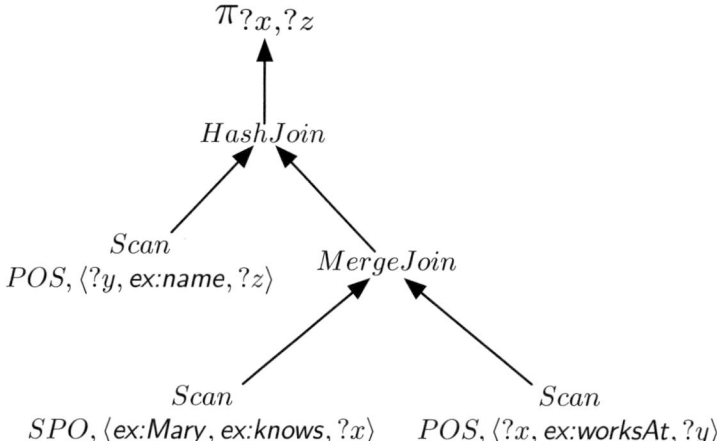

Figure 2.9: Physical query plan for the example query. Nodes in plan repre-
        sent the operators to be executed, e.g. in contrast to the logical
        representation, the concrete join algorithms are specified.

such a physical plan from a logical representation the query optimizer performs
certain choices and transformations, of which we will discuss the choice of
operators and the transformation of join ordering. Typically, many other types of
transformations are also applied that aim to reduce the cost of query processing,
e.g. filter push-down [SML10].

Query Operators. There are typically several ways to accomplish the logical
operations in a query. For example, in SPARQL, triple patterns are the basic
mechanism used to specify which data should be processed (roughly comparable
to a relation in SQL). In most cases, there are multiple ways to load all triples
matching a particular triple pattern. For example, the engine can perform either
a scan of all triples in the database or use an index scan to retrieve a smaller
subset. In Fig. 2.9 only index scans are used to access the underlying data. For
example, the triple pattern $\langle ex{:}Mary, ex{:}knows, ?x \rangle$ is retrieved from the POS
index that stores the triple values in a suitable order [NW08]. Apart from the
choice of access plans, query engines often support multiple implementations
of the same logical operations that may differ only in their costs. For example,
when inputs are sorted on the join variable, a merge join may be more efficient
than a hash join.

Join Ordering. Join ordering is a special case of plan rewriting where the
order of operators in the operator tree is changed. For example, Fig. 2.10 shows

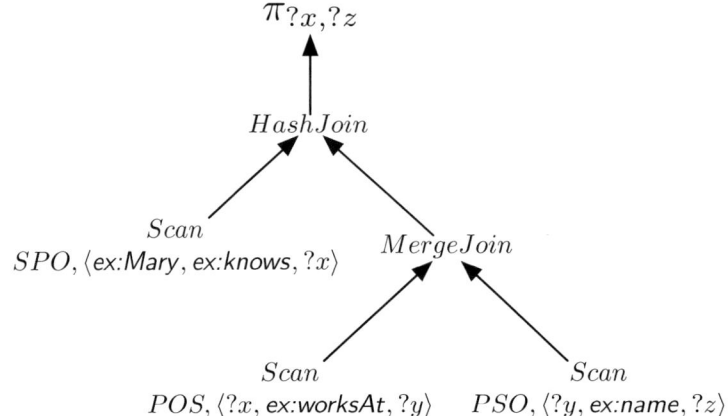

Figure 2.10: Alternate physical query plan with a different join order.

an alternate physical plan for the same query. Compared to the first physical plan, the order in which the data obtained from the scan operators are processed is different. The plan in Fig. 2.9 executes the join $\langle ex{:}Mary, ex{:}knows, ?x \rangle \bowtie \langle ?x, ex{:}worksAt, ?y \rangle$ first, whereas the plan in Fig. 2.10 executes the join $\langle ?x, ex{:}worksAt, ?y \rangle \bowtie \langle ?y, ex{:}name, ?z \rangle$ first. Note that both plans are equivalent in the final results they produce, a constraint that is enforced by the plan generator. The plans only differ in their intermediate results, which may result in one plan having lower costs than the other.

2.5.3 Optimization Algorithm

Based on the described transformations (and others), the plan generator can generate all possible physical plans that conform with the logical representation. In order to choose the best plan, query optimizers employ a *cost model* that is used to estimate the costs of executing a given physical plan. To this end, the query engine usually maintains statistics about the data that allow for the estimation of the input and output cardinalities of the operators in the plan. For example, the cost model for a join operator may take the size of its inputs and the estimated selectivity of the join as arguments and return the cardinality of its output and the estimated cost of obtaining that output.

In practice, generating all possible physical plans is not feasible due to the large plan space created by the multitude of choices for individual operators and their order. To this end, more advanced algorithms are employed that are able to prune partial plans that can never lead to an optimal plan as early as possible. One such algorithm is the dynamic programming algorithm for query optimization [SAC⁺79]. Here, the plan is constructed in a bottom-up fashion starting with the access plans at the leaves of the operator tree. Due to the optimal substructure of the query optimization problem, the algorithm can prune suboptimal partial plans at each step while preserving the overall optimality of final plans.

2.5.4 Query Execution

After a suitable physical plan with minimal cost has been created by the query optimizer, the plan is then executed by the query engine. A storage layer manages disk access on top of which the database system maintains data structures, such as B+-trees, that are used to provide efficient access to the data. These data structures offer a high-level interface that hides the actual storage implementation. This interface is used by implementation of the various operators that represent the basic building blocks of query plans [Neu05]. The actual execution is achieved by executing the individual operators in the order specified by the query plan. To this end, the database system also manages temporary buffers such that the output of one operator can be used as the input of another operator. Alternatively, some engines also offer pipelined execution, where operators process input and provide output in an incremental fashion, thereby providing results before query execution is finished.

2.5.5 Adaptive Query Processing

While most commercial database systems employ the compile-then-execute architecture described in the previous sections, there has been considerably interest in systems that perform *adaptive query processing*. In contrast to traditional systems, where the query plan is created once at compile-time and then never changed, adaptive systems may change the plan at run-time. Changing the query plan at run-time is beneficial when there is either not enough knowledge at compile-time to create an optimal query plan (e.g. in streaming databases) or the estimates made at compile-time turn out to have been incorrect. However, adapting the query plan is also associated with challenges that need to be overcome. These include the detection of when to change the query plan and the problem of how to change the plan. For example, some join operators accumulate state during query execution that then has to be migrated to the new query plan in order to preserve correctness. The survey by Deshpande et al. [DIR07] gives an overview of adaptive query processing and its advantages and challenges.

Chapter 3

Processing Unstructured Queries

3.1 Introduction

Especially for lay users, *keyword search* has been regarded as an effective mechanism because it helps to circumvent the complexity of structured query languages, and hide the underlying data representation. Without knowledge of the query syntax and data schema, users can obtain possibly complex structured results, including tuples from relational databases, XML data, data graphs, and RDF resources [HWYY07, TWRC09]. As opposed to document retrieval, results in this structured data setting may encompass several resources that are connected over possibly very long paths (e.g. joined database tuples, XML trees, RDF resources connected over paths of relations).

In this chapter, we present our contributions towards the efficient execution of keyword queries over hybrid data. As already introduced in Chapter 2.2, we propose the concept of *native keyword search databases*, which solves the keyword search problem using two standard database operations, *data access* and *join*. Existing database work on join processing covers different aspects, from join implementation, to join order optimization to top-*k* join on input streams. Breaking down the keyword search problem into these two operations allows us to leverage this vast body of research. In this work, we built upon existing work to propose index structures and algorithms for native keyword search databases.

The main contributions can be summarized as follows:

- We propose a new *processing strategy* for dealing with the keyword search problem that is based on the standard database operations data access and join.

- For efficient data access, we extend the *2-hop cover* concept [STW04, CY09] to pre-compute and materialize the neighborhoods of data elements.

Existing work indexes every maximal neighborhood, i.e. when it is not completely covered by one another [LOF$^+$08]. In this work, we determine coverage at the level of paths, instead of graphs. Indexing only maximal paths reduces the space requirements.

- For efficient and scalable Steiner graph search, we propose an extension of the hash rank join [IAE02] called *push rank join* to terminate early after the top-k results have been found. Instead of reading the entire graph into memory, this procedure operates on input streams.

- The main difference between join processing in keyword search and a standard database is that different query plans may lead to different, but also valid results. Instead of focusing on one single optimal plan, a large number of query plans have to be considered to generate all top-k answers. The *push-based top-k rank join procedure* proposed in this chapter not only computes the best results according to one plan, but also selects plans in a top-k fashion during the process.

- We evaluated our approach by comparing it to state-of-the-art native keyword search approaches [LOF$^+$08, KPC$^+$05], using several large real-world datasets. Our solution reduced storage requirement (up to 86%) and improved scalability (by several factors) and performance (over 50% on average).

In this chapter, we use the definitions of keyword queries and their results as Steiner graphs first given in Section 2.2. For ease of reading, we repeat the important definitions here:

Definition 2.6 (Keyword Query). *A keyword query is a set of keyword terms $Q = \{k_1, \ldots, k_n\}$, where each $k_i \in \mathcal{W}$.*

Definition 2.7 (Keyword Element). *Given a keyword query $Q = \{k_1, \ldots, k_n\}$ consisting of keywords, a node $n_k \in N_E$ is a keyword element for $k \in Q$ iff there is a triple $\langle n_k, p, a \rangle$ in G and k is relevant for text(p) or text(a). The set of all keyword elements for k is denoted as N_k.*

Definition 2.8 (Keyword Query Answer). *An answer to a keyword query $Q = \{k_1, \ldots, k_n\}$, also called Steiner graph, is a subgraph of G denoted as $G_S = (N_S, E_S)$, which satisfies the following conditions:*

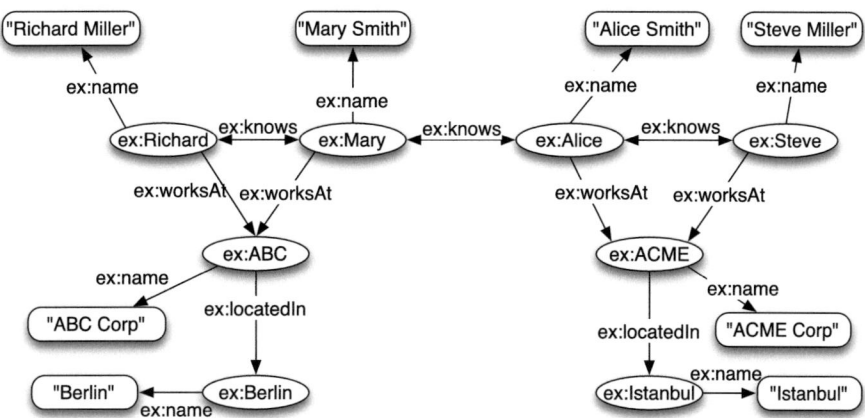

Figure 3.1: Excerpt of the example hybrid data from Fig. 2.1 used throughout this chapter.

- *For every $k \in Q$ there is at least one keyword element $n_k \in N_S$. The set of keyword elements containing one n_k for every $k \in Q$ is $N_K \subseteq N_S$.*

- *For every possible pair $n_i, n_j \in N_K$ and $n_i \neq n_j$, there is a path $n_i \leadsto n_j$ such that every $n_i \in N_K$ is connected to every other $n_j \in N_K$.*

We call such a graph a d-length Steiner graph when direct paths, i.e. paths that connect exactly two keyword elements n_i, n_j such that there is no other keyword element n_k in the path between n_i and n_j, have length d or less (we use $n_i \leadsto^d n_j$ to denote these paths).

Fig. 3.1 shows an excerpt of the hybrid data example in 2.1 that is used in the examples throughout this chapter.

3.2 d-length 2-Hop Cover

A 2-hop cover is a compact representation of connections in a graph that has been previously used to answer reachability and distance queries [STW04, CY09]. In this work, we propose to leverage this concept for retrieving paths between two keyword elements. Our data graph is directed. However, while it is essential to find paths during the computation of Steiner graphs, the direction of the edges that establish these paths are irrelevant (and only have to be preserved for outputting the actual results). For the efficient retrieval of paths, we propose the d-length 2-hop cover, which in contrast to the 2-hop cover employed in existing work, only considers paths up to length d. First, we define the neighborhood of a node u that captures paths from u to nodes in its vicinity:

Definition 3.1 (Neighborhood). *A neighborhood label (or short: neighborhood) $NB_u \subseteq G$ of a node $u \in N$ (also called the center node of NB_u) is the union set of nodes and edges that are connected to u via some paths. The set of paths between u and a node $w \in NB_u$ is denoted as $P(u,w)$, and its $Score(P(u,w))$ is defined as $max\{Score(p)|p \in P(u,w)\}$. The combined information is represented as a path entry (u,s,w) (or short: (u,w)), where u is the center node of NB_u, $w \in NB_u$ and $s = Score(P(u,w))$. A d-neighborhood of node u is the set of nodes and edges connected to u via paths of length d or less.*

A d-length 2-hop cover of a graph G is a graph labeling of G that assigns all nodes in G a 2-hop label, such that all paths in G are covered.

Definition 3.2 (d-length 2-hop Cover). *A labeling of a graph $G = (N,E)$, which consists of a set of neighborhood labels is a d-length 2-hop cover, if the following two conditions hold for any two nodes $u,v \in N_E$: 1) if there is a path of length d or less between u and v then $NB_u \cap NB_v \neq \emptyset$; 2) all paths of length d or less between the center nodes u and v are of the form $\langle u,\ldots,w,\ldots,v \rangle$, where $w \in NB_u \cap NB_v$ (w is called a hop node).*

This cover is used to find all paths of length d or less between two nodes by forming the intersection of their neighborhoods, i.e. the set of paths between u and v is ($+\!\!+$ denotes the concatenation of two paths):

$$P(u,v) = \{p_{uw} +\!\!+ p_{wv} | w \in NB_u \cap NB_v,$$
$$p_{uw} \in P(u,w), p_{wv} \in P(w,v), Length(p_{uw}p_{wv}) \leq d\}$$

Example 3.1. *Let a 2-hop cover of the graph in Fig. 3.1 contain the 1-neighborhoods of ex:Berlin and ex:Mary as their respective labels NB_B and NB_M. Then, we can find all paths between the two nodes by forming the intersection of NB_B and NB_M, which would contain the path through node ex:ABC.*

3.2.1 Construction

The problem of constructing a 2-hop cover of minimal size has been reduced to the minimum set cover problem that is NP-hard [CHKZ03]. Consequently, approximative algorithms are necessary for dealing with large graphs [STW04, CY09]. The basic idea is as follows: in a greedy manner, one neighborhood is selected at every iteration to prune redundant paths in other neighborhoods. The goal is to reduce redundancy as much as possible, while preserving the 2-hop cover property.

We adopt existing algorithms in two directions. (1) Firstly we define a trivial d-length 2-hop cover for the keyword search setting, which is used as a basis for later pruning. (2) Then, the *d-length* restriction is taken into account during the pruning of paths.

Basically, we observe that a trivial d-length 2-hop cover is simply the set of *d-neighborhoods*:

Theorem 3.1. *The set of d-neighborhoods constructed for every node $u \in N$ in $G(N,E)$ is a valid d-length 2-hop cover.*

Proof Sketch.   By definition, a d-neighborhood of a node u contains all nodes in $G(N,E)$ reachable from u via a path of length d or less. Thus, for all $u,v \in N$, $u \in NB_u$ and $v \in NB_v$, if $u \leftrightsquigarrow^d v$ then $u \in NB_v$ and $v \in NB_u$. Hence, $NB_u \cap NB_v$ must be not empty (this ensures condition 1). Further, we know the set $NB_u \cap NB_v$ contains hop nodes for all paths of length $2 \times d$ or less, which include all paths of length d or less (this ensures condition 2).   □

Then, the following intuition is employed for pruning redundant paths captured by this trivial d-length 2-hop cover: Given two nodes $u,v \in N$ that are connected via the set of paths $P_{uv} = \langle u,\ldots,w,\ldots,v \rangle$ of length d or less, NB_u contains some "partial paths" $P_{wv} = \langle w,\ldots,v \rangle$ that are also in NB_v, and vice versa NB_v contains the parts $P_{uw} = \langle u,\ldots,w \rangle$ that are also in NB_u. Then, these parts are redundant in the sense that after removing P_{wv} from NB_u and P_{uw} from NB_v, all the paths in P_{uv} are still preserved and can be computed via hop nodes in $NB_u \cap NB_v$.

The approximate algorithm for this consists of $|N-1|$ iterations. At each step, a neighborhood NB_i is selected (based on "pruning power" simply measured in terms of node counts), marked as complete, and used for pruning other neighborhoods not completed yet. Neighborhood pruning is discussed in the example below.

The goal of the pruning step is to reduce the size of the previous result as much as possible, while still retaining the d-length 2-hop cover property. The basic operation prunes a neighborhood NB_1 of node n_1 using another neighborhood NB_2 of node n_2 by removing all paths from NB_1 that are already covered in NB_2.

Algorithm 3.1 shows the pruning algorithm. It takes two neighborhoods as arguments: the neighborhood to be pruned NB_j and the neighborhood NB_i that is used for pruning. The algorithm first checks if the center node of $n_i \in NB_i$ is in NB_j. If this is not the case NB_i cannot be used to prune NB_j. Otherwise, we create a queue (for a breadth-first search) and use n_i as the start node.

The main loop of the algorithm works as follows: first node n is dequeued from Q. Next, we retrieve outgoing edges of n in both neighborhoods and store them in E_i, E_j, respectively. Here, outgoing edges are not related to the actual direction of the edges. During breadth-first-search, we treat the graph as undirected, traversing in both directions. The element n is either the center node n_i or a node that lies on a path between n_i and a leaf node. Outgoing edges of n in this sense traverse towards the leaf node (no matter the direction), i.e. lie on the paths between n and the leaf node. We form the intersection E of E_i, E_j, which then contains redundant edges that occur in both neighborhoods. They are added to the set of pruneable edges E_P. Finally, we enqueue all target nodes of the edges in E to proceed with the search.

When the search completes, E_P contains all pruneable edges, which are then removed from NB_j.

Algorithm 3.1: Prune neighborhood

Input: NB_j, NB_i and center nodes n_j, n_i
Data: node queue Q, set of edges E_P to prune
Output: pruned neighborhood NB'_j

1   **if** $n_i \notin NB_j$ **then**
2 | return

3   initialize Q and enqueue n_i
4   **while** $Q \neq \emptyset$ **do**
5 | $n = Q$.dequeue()
6 | E_i = all outgoing edges of n in NB_i
7 | E_j = all outgoing edges of n in NB_j
8 | $E = E_i \cap E_j$
9 | add all edges in E to E_P
10 | enqueue all target nodes of edges in E in Q

11   remove all edges in E_P from NB_j

Theorem 3.2. *Given a graph $G_E = (N_E, E_R)$ and a set of d-neighborhoods for all nodes in N_E, the set of pruned neighborhoods constructed using Algorithm 3.1 is a d-length 2-hop cover.*

Proof Sketch. At each step of the construction algorithm we choose a d-neighborhood NB_i to prune all other neighborhoods. We prove that the d-length 2-hop cover property still holds for the pruned d-neighborhoods. We show that for every two nodes $n_j, n_k \in N_E$ that are connected via a set of paths P of length d or less, pruning NB_j and NB_k using NB_i "preserves" P.

Let P_1 be the set of all paths in NB_j between n_j, n_k through n_i, i.e. $P_1 = \{\langle n_j \ldots n_i \ldots n_k \rangle \in NB_j\}$. For each $p_1 \in P_1$ the pruning algorithm removes from NB_j only outgoing edges on the part $\langle n_i \ldots n_k \rangle$ of p_1, where $\langle n_i \ldots n_k \rangle$ is both in NB_j and NB_i. Alg. 3.1 breadth-first-searches starting from n_i in NB_j, removes only edges from NB_j that are both in NB_j and NB_i, and traverses from n_i towards n_k. Analogously, $P_2 = \{\langle n_k \ldots n_i \ldots n_j \rangle \in NB_k\}$ is the set of all paths in NB_k between n_k, n_j through n_i. When pruning this neighborhood, the algorithm removes only outgoing edges on the part $\langle n_i \ldots n_j \rangle$ of $p_2 \in P_2$ from NB_k, where $\langle n_i \ldots n_j \rangle$ is both in NB_k and NB_i. Further, note that n_i is both in NB_j and NB_k. Thus, the parts $\langle n_i \ldots n_k \rangle$ removed from NB_j must be in NB_k and likewise, $\langle n_i \ldots n_j \rangle$ is in NB_j.

Thus, the algorithm removes from NB_j only those parts that are captured both by NB_i and NB_k, and likewise, removes from NB_k only those parts that are both in NB_i and NB_j. As a result, all parts P of length d or less between n_j and n_k can be reconstructed from parts that are either in P_1 or P_2. $\square$

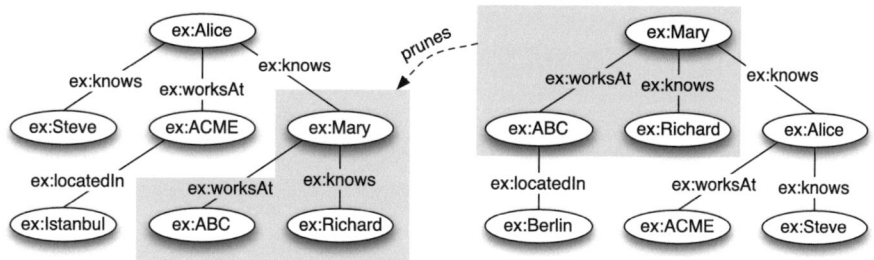

Figure 3.2: Pruning NB_A using NB_M (the figures shows only excerpts of the neighborhoods).

Example 3.2. *Fig. 3.2 shows the two not yet pruned neighborhoods NB_A and NB_M of ex:Alice and ex:Mary, respectively. Here, we prune NB_A using NB_M by starting a simultaneous breadth-first search towards the leaf nodes from ex:Mary. All edges in NB_A that also occur in NB_M are marked and later removed from NB_A. The part pruned this way is highlighted in Fig. 3.2.*

Note that the procedure here operates at the level of paths while existing work on keyword search applies pruning at the level of neighborhoods, i.e. a neighborhood is discarded only when it is completely covered by another [LOF+08].

3.2.2 Storage

We store neighborhoods as well as the actual paths. We define the path and path entry indexes, which are used during the computation of Steiner graphs.

Definition 3.3 (Path Entry Index). *The path entry index I_{PE} maps nodes $u \in N$ to a list of path entries (u, s, w), sorted by $s = Score(P(u, w))$, where $w \in NB_u$.*

Definition 3.4 (Path Index). *The path index I_P maps a path entry (u, w) to a list of paths $P(u, w)$, sorted by $Score(p)$ for $p \in P(u, w)$.*

Node	Entries
ex:Mary	$(ex{:}Mary, 2.0, ex{:}Mary)$
	$(ex{:}Mary, 1.0, ex{:}Richard)$ $(ex{:}Mary, 1.0, ex{:}Alice)$ $(ex{:}Mary, 1.0, ex{:}ABC)$
	$(ex{:}Mary, 0.5, ex{:}Berlin)$ $(ex{:}Mary, 0.5, ex{:}Steve)$ $(ex{:}Mary, 0.5, ex{:}ACME)$

Table 3.1: Example path entry index for node *ex:Mary*.

Example 3.3. *Tab. 3.1 shows an index entry for node ex:Mary from the running example. It contains path entries from ex:Mary to all hop nodes in the neighborhood with their associated scores. Recall that this is simply the maximal score of paths from ex:Mary to a hop node. Tab. 3.2 shows an excerpt of the path index for nodes in the neighborhood of ex:Mary. For example, the key $(ex{:}Mary, ex{:}ACME)$ can be used to retrieve all paths (and their scores) from ex:Mary to ex:ACME. In this case there are two such paths.*

Center,Hop	Paths
ex:Mary, ex:Richard	1.0 $\langle$ex:Richard, ex:knows, ex:Mary$\rangle$ 1.0 $\langle$ex:Mary, ex:knows, ex:Richard$\rangle$
ex:Mary, ex:Berlin	0.5 $\langle$ex:Mary, ex:worksAt, ex:ABC$\rangle\langle$ex:ABC, ex:locatedIn, ex:Berlin$\rangle$
ex:Mary, ex:ACME	0.5 $\langle$ex:Mary, ex:knows, ex:Alice$\rangle\langle$ex:Alice, ex:worksAt, ex:ACME$\rangle$ 0.5 $\langle$ex:Alice, ex:knows, ex:Mary$\rangle\langle$ex:Alice, ex:worksAt, ex:ACME$\rangle$

Table 3.2: Example path index for nodes in the neighborhood of *ex:Mary*.

3.3 Keyword Query Processing

In this section we present the process of answering keyword queries using a d-length 2-hop cover.

3.3.1 Basic Join Operations

Given a keyword query Q and its keyword elements N_K, the goal is to find Steiner graphs. The basic idea is to use the pruned neighborhoods of the d-length 2-hop cover to find paths between every pair of keyword elements and iteratively join them until they all are connected. For this, we (1) firstly perform *data access* operations to retrieve the neighborhoods for every keyword, called *keyword neighborhoods*, (2) then perform *neighborhood join* to merge two keyword neighborhoods to obtain a *keyword graph* and then successively (3) apply *graph joins* to combine a keyword neighborhood with a keyword graph.

Definition 3.5 (Keyword Neighborhood). *Given a keyword k and its keyword elements N_k, the keyword neighborhood NB_k of k is the union set of path entries retrieved from the index I_{PE}. It captures the neighborhoods of all keyword elements in N_k, i.e. $NB_k = \bigcup_{n \in N_k} I_{PE}(n)$.*

Definition 3.6 (Neighborhood Join). *Given two keyword neighborhoods NB_{k_1}, NB_{k_2}, the neighborhood join $\bowtie_{NB}$ combines two path entries (n_{k_1}, w) in NB_{k_1} and (n_{k_2}, w) in NB_{k_2} that match on w:*

$$NB_{k_1} \bowtie_{NB} NB_{k_2} = \{(n_{k_1}, w) \mathbin{+\!\!+} (n_{k_2}, w) |$$
$$(n_{k_1}, w) \in NB_{k_1}, (n_{k_2}, w) \in NB_{k_2},$$
$$distance((n_{k_1}, w) \mathbin{+\!\!+} (n_{k_2}, w)) \leq d\}$$

The result $(n_{k_1}, w) \mathbin{+\!\!+} (n_{k_2}, w)$ establishes a path between n_{k_1} and n_{k_2} with w being the hop node. A join of 2 or more path entries such as $(n_{k_1}, w) \mathbin{+\!\!+} (n_{k_2}, w)$

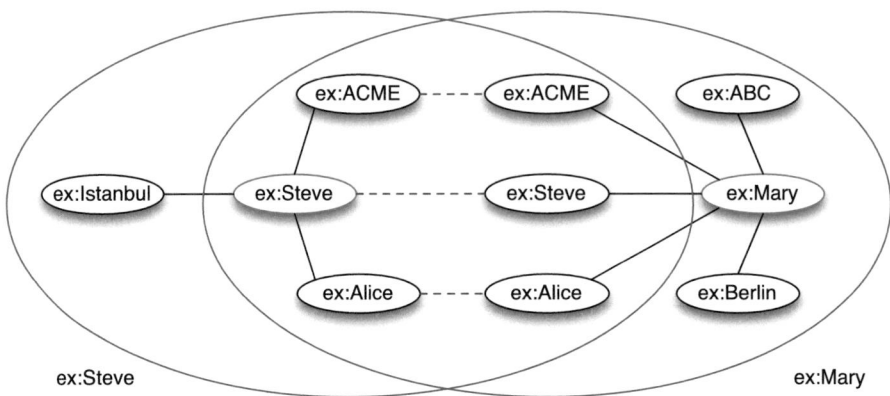

Figure 3.3: Joining the 2-neighborhoods for *ex:Steve* and *ex:Mary*.

form a keyword graph $G_K = (N_K, PE_K)$ with N_K subdivided into the two disjoint sets of center nodes N_K^C and hop nodes N_K^H. For every path entry $(n, w) \in PE_K$, we have $n \in N_K^C$ and $w \in N_K^H$.

Based on this $\bowtie_{NB}$ operation, we provide Theorem 3.3 for computing results of 2-keyword queries.

Theorem 3.3. *Given a 2-keyword query $Q = \{k_1, k_2\}$ and the retrieved keyword neighborhoods NB_{k_1}, NB_{k_2}, the keyword graphs resulting from $NB_{k_1} \bowtie_{NB} NB_{k_2}$ are d-length Steiner graphs for Q.*

Proof Sketch. In this 2-keywords setting, the set of all *d*-length Steiner graphs for $Q = \{k_1, k_2\}$ is exactly the set of all paths of length *d* or less between the pairs of nodes $n_1 \in N_{k_1}, n_2 \in N_{k_2}$. By definition of the *d*-length 2-hop cover, the intersection $NB_{n_1} \cap NB_{n_2}$ contains the hop nodes for all paths of length *d* or less between n_1 and n_2. The neighborhood join $NB_{k_1} \bowtie NB_{k_2}$ leverages this, joining all paths in NB_{k_1} with paths in NB_{k_2} on the hop node $w \in NB_{n_1} \cap NB_{n_2}$. The result comprises all paths connecting the pairs of nodes $n_1 \in N_{k_1}, n_2 \in N_{k_2}$ that are of length *d* or less, i.e. all *d*-length Steiner graphs for Q. $\square$

Example 3.4. *Fig. 3.3 illustrates the neighborhood join between the neighborhoods of ex:Steve and ex:Mary. The overlap is illustrated with dashed lines and includes the nodes ex:ACME, ex:Steve, and ex:Alice. Note that the edges between nodes in this graph stand for paths instead of single edges, e.g. in the data graph ex:Mary and ex:Berlin are only connected indirectly (via ex:ABC). Fig. 3.4 shows a keyword graph in the result of the neighborhood join.*

Figure 3.4: A keyword graph in the join result of *ex:Steve* and *ex:Mary*.

A keyword graph resulting from the neighborhood join contains only path entries in NB_{k_1} and NB_{k_2}, which connect the two keyword elements n_{k_1} and n_{k_2}. Thus, only hop nodes in these paths remain, while other nodes in the neighborhood of n_{k_1} and n_{k_2} have been eliminated during the process. For the subsequent graph join $\bowtie_G$, which takes a keyword graph G_K and a keyword neighborhood NB_k as inputs, these hop nodes still have to be considered because they might help in connecting G_K with NB_k. In order to include these candidates during the execution of $\bowtie_G$, a keyword graph is expanded with path entries discarded previously to obtain a keyword graph neighborhood:

Definition 3.7 (Keyword Graph Neighborhood). *Given a keyword graph* $G_K = (N_K^C \uplus N_K^H, PE_K)$, *the* keyword graph neighborhood NB_{G_K} *is a set of graph entries constructed from* G_K *and a path entry* (n, w), *i.e.* $NB_{G_K} = \{G_K + (n, w) | (n, w) \in I_{PE}(n), n \in N_K^C\}$, *where every* $G_K + (n, w)$ *forms a graph entry denoted as* G_K^+.

As a result of this expansion, each graph entry G_K^+ contains a "free" path entry (n, w), whose hop node w is yet not connected. Similar to $\bowtie_{NB}$, this hop node is used as the join attribute of the $\bowtie_G$ operation:

Definition 3.8 (Graph Join). *Given a keyword neighborhood* NB_{k_i} *and a keyword graph neighborhood* NB_{G_K}, *the result of a* graph join $\bowtie_G$ *is the combination of path entries* $(n_{k_i}, w) \in NB_{k_i}$ *and graph entries* $G_K^+(N_K, PE_K) \in NB_{G_K}$ *defined as* $NB_{k_i} \bowtie_G NB_{G_K} = \{G_K^+(N_K, PE_K) + (n_{k_i}, w) | \exists (n_{k_j}, w)((n_{k_j}, w) \in PE_K)\}$.

The result of this operation is also a keyword graph, which however, connects more than two keyword elements via a number of path entries. For each entry, we use the path index to retrieve all paths between its center and hop nodes and join them along the edges of the keyword graph to construct the final Steiner graphs.

Example 3.5. *Fig. 3.5 show two entries in the keyword graph neighborhood of the join result. Here, the keyword graph from Fig. 3.4 was expanded with additional hop nodes, ex:ABC and ex:ACME that are used in further joins.*

Fig. 3.6 shows final results of the join derived from the keyword graph. Note that here the directionless edges in the keyword graph have been replaced with concrete paths from the data graph, obtained from the path entry index.

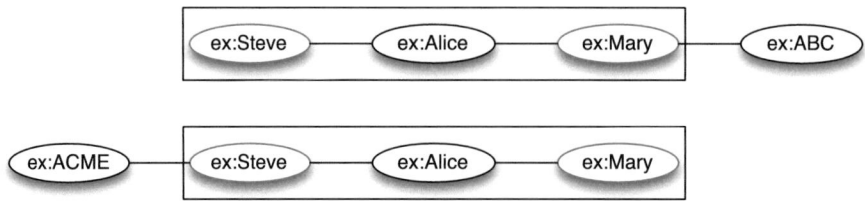

Figure 3.5: Two entries in a keyword graph neighborhood.

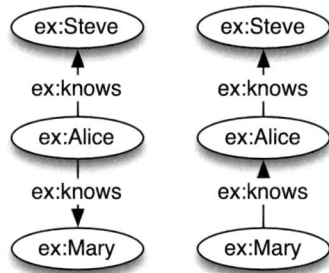

Figure 3.6: Steiner graphs for keyword graph.

3.3.2 Integrated Query Plan

A query Q can be processed according to a *query plan*. It is a sequence of join operators $(\bowtie_{NB}^1, \bowtie_G^2, \ldots, \bowtie_G^{|K|-1})$, starting with the operator $\bowtie_{NB}$ joining two keyword neighborhoods (called base inputs), followed by $\bowtie_G$ operators that combine a base input with a graph. Since the base inputs represent elements retrieved for the keywords, a plan also represents a particular order of query keywords.

The principle difference to standard database join processing is that in keyword search, connections between two keywords are not known in advance. This is why typically connections have to be explored at run-time by traversing edges of the data graphs that are loaded into memory. For this, efficient techniques for searching results in the data graph [KPC+05, DYW+07], or pruning joined neighborhoods [LOF+08] have been proposed.

For "searching" keyword search results via join processing, we observe there is no single optimal plan but different plans might produce different results, or even no results at all, as illustrated by Example 3.6.

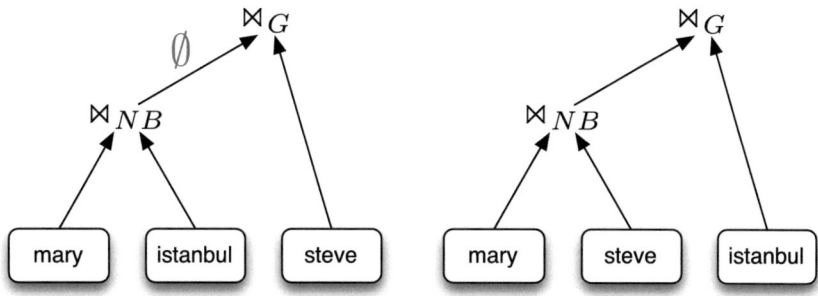

Figure 3.7: Two query plans for query $Q = \{istanbul, steve, mary\}$.

Example 3.6. *Consider query* $Q = \{istanbul, steve, mary\}$. *For* $d = 2$, *keywords* steve *and* istanbul *are connected and* mary *is connected to* steve, *but not to* istanbul. *Fig. 3.7 shows two query plans for query Q. The first join on the keyword neighborhoods of* mary *and* istanbul *produces empty results as there are no paths of length d or less. However, results can be produced when the keyword neighborhoods of* steve *and* istanbul *or* steve *and* mary *are joined first.*

Now, we provide Theorem 3.4 to compute keyword search results for queries with more than 2 keywords, using an *integrated query plan*:

Theorem 3.4. *Let G be the data graph, Q be an n-keyword query, and P(Q) represents all permutations of keywords in the set Q where each* $p \in P(Q)$ *stands for a query plan, keyword graphs resulting from executing all* $p \in P(Q)$ *capture all Steiner graphs for Q that can be obtained from G.*

Proof Sketch. Let $N_K = \{N_{k_1}, \ldots, N_{k_i}\}$ be the set of keyword elements obtained for Q. We must generate (1) all graphs from G, which (2) contain an element $n_{k_i} \in N_K$ for every $k_i \in Q$, (3) all these keyword elements are pairwise connected, and (4) direct paths between two keyword elements are of length d or less. The integrated plan contains different orders of joins. Every join is either $\bowtie_{NB}$ or $\bowtie_G$. As both operations rest on the same concept of d-length 2-hop cover (i.e. join two path entries on a hop node), the resulting paths are of length d or less (4). Every plan joins every keyword element with one another, ensuring they all are pairwise (directly or indirectly) connected (3). Also, since every plan contains all keywords, (2) is trivially satisfied. Taken (2+3+4) together, we can conclude that every plan (i.e. order of join) results in Steiner graphs of one particular structure. Since the integrated plan contains all possible orders,

Steiner graphs of all possible structures that may exist in the data graph are taken into account (1). □

As illustrated in Example 3.7, the integrated query plan consists of operators at levels $l = 0, \ldots, |Q|$. Level 0 represents data access operators, employing $|Q|$ base inputs. Level 1 to $|Q|-1$ contain join operators. Only $\bowtie_{NB}$ operators are needed at level 1. Subsequent levels consist exclusively of $\bowtie_G$ operators, which always combine a graph with a base input such that there is a correspondence between level and the number of inputs, i.e. every join operator at level l consumes exactly $l+1$ base inputs. That is, operators at level $|Q|-1$ have inputs for all query keywords in Q. In fact, every operator at this level can be seen as representing one particular plan (i.e. particular order of keywords). Level $|Q|$ has a single union operator that combines results from different plans.

The total number of join operators can be computed by taking all permutations of the set of base inputs Q as the total number of join order plans and multiply this by $|Q|-1$, which is the number of join operators for every plan. More precisely, the permutations of the set Q represent only the upper bound. The number of join operators at level 1 is in fact $N(1) = C(|Q|, 2) = |Q|(|Q|-1)/2$, which denotes all 2-combinations of the set $|Q|$. At this level, where only $\bowtie_{NB}$ operators are applied, the order of the base inputs is not relevant (and thus it suffices to consider all 2-combinations instead of permutations). The order of the subsequent $\bowtie_G$ operations is however relevant and distinguishes one plan from another. At each subsequent level $l > 1$, l-permutations of the set $|Q|$ have to be considered. These different orders however, share overlapping parts. To eliminate this redundancy and minimize the number of join operators, we employ join operators whose outputs can be connected to more than one subsequent operators at the next level. Based on this, we construct a join operator at level $l > 1$ by combining inputs of a possibly "shared" operator of the previous level with a base input not processed yet. Since the number of base inputs not processed by an operator at level $l-1$ is $|Q|-l$, the number of join operators at level l is $N(l) = N(l-1)(|Q|-l)$ (indicating all combinations of inputs from previous join operators and base inputs not processed yet). Thus, the total number of join operators is:

$$N(K) = N(1) + \sum_{l=2}^{|K|-1} (|K|-l)N(l-1)$$

Complexity. Given the number of join operators, the upper bound on complexity of keyword query processing can be established as follows. In worst case, the result of a join is the cross product of its inputs. Here, input size is given by the

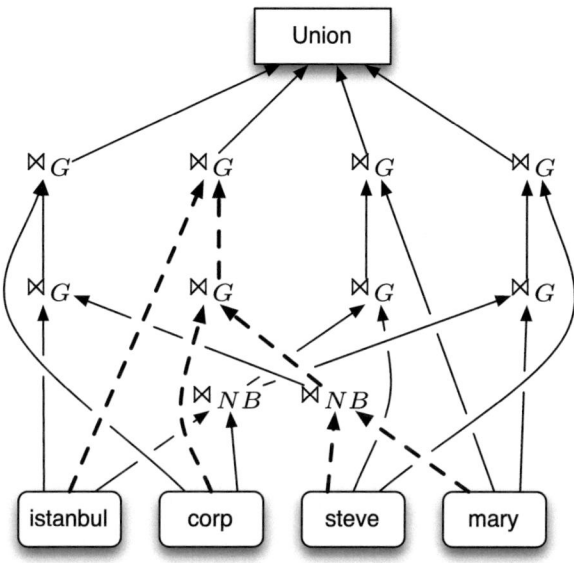

Figure 3.8: Excerpt of an integrated query plan. The subplan for join order *steve* $\bowtie_{NB}$ *mary* $\bowtie_G$ *corp* $\bowtie_G$ *istanbul* is highlighted with dashed lines.

number of path entries in each keyword neighborhood, which can be calculated as $|N_k| \cdot b^d$ for each $k \in Q$, where b is the average branching factor of the pruned d-neighborhood: b^d gives the number of paths in the neighborhood while $|N_k|$ denotes the total number of neighborhoods that can be obtained for a keyword k. The upper bound can then be calculated as $N(Q) \cdot \max\{|N_k| \cdot b^d | k \in Q\}^2$. Note that due to pruning at the level of paths, the branching factor of the neighborhoods is smaller than the one of the original graph.

Example 3.7. *Fig. 3.8 shows an excerpt of the integrated query plan for a query of size 4. One subplan for the join order* $\langle$*steve* $\bowtie_{NB}$ *mary* $\bowtie_G$ *corp* $\bowtie_G$ *malta*$\rangle$ *is emphasized. The figure also shows that intermediate results such as the one produced by st eve* $\bowtie_{NB}$ *mary is used for this as well as for another plan.*

3.3.3 Top-k Keyword-Join Processing

Different top-k query processing techniques have been proposed to reach early termination after obtaining the top-k results [IBS08]. Of particular interest in this context is the top-k join, which produces ranked join results without consuming all inputs [IAE02].

A top-k join operator, also called *rank join*, takes two inputs that are sorted by the scores of their elements and iteratively processes them as data streams (i.e. no random access) to produce k top results. Crucial in top-k processing is the *threshold T*, an upper bound maintained for every join operator to capture the maximum score that can be achieved using as yet unprocessed input tuples. A join result can be reported if its score is higher than T. For a join between the inputs 1 and 2, $T = \max(Agg(s_1^{max}, \bar{s}_2), Agg(\bar{s}_1, s_2^{max}))$ where $Agg(\cdot)$ returns the score for the joined result, s_i^{max} denotes the best score of all tuples of input i, and $\bar{s}_i$ denotes the score of the tuple lastly seen from i. The last seen score and threshold decrease as new tuples are processed (because they arrive at a decreasing order of scores).

This concept of rank join is utilized for top-k query processing in a pull-based architecture: each operator in the query plan has a *next* method that is called to produce the next result (i.e. a reportable result whose score exceeds T); a tree-shaped query plan is employed where the root operator calls the next method of lower level operators, which in turn call next on the base inputs. Processing inputs this way is guaranteed to preserve the top-k property, i.e. the resulting k results have best scores. This follows directly from the notion of threshold, as results reported by the next methods have scores greater than T, and thus are guaranteed to have scores greater than all other result candidates that can be produced using remaining tuples.

Top-k Processing. We adopt this top-k query processing to our setting, as early termination can avoid the processing of a possibly large amount of join operators in the integrated query plan. Further, implementing $\bowtie_G$ and $\bowtie_{NB}$ as *rank join* naturally enables us to treat data as input streams. Instead of loading large graphs into memory [LOF$^+$08] at once, we use rank join to incrementally access and process streams of path entries. We note that the only difference to the standard query plan is that in the integrated query plan, the root is a union operator. We apply the notion of threshold to obtain a *rank union* operator in order to preserve the top-k property. The threshold of a union operator $\cup$ is defined as $T(\cup) = max\{T_\bowtie | \bowtie \in \cup_\bowtie\}$, where $T_\bowtie$ is the threshold of a rank join operator $\bowtie$, and $\cup_\bowtie$ is the set of all rank join operators that feed into $\cup$. A result for $\cup$ can be reported when its score is higher or equal to $T(\cup)$. Processing the integrated query plan with the rank version of our operators (i.e. operators with thresholds for result output) using the pull-based procedure discussed above [IBS08], yields top-k results. We provide the following Theorem to capture this:

Theorem 3.5. *Given a query Q, the data G and a predefined parameter k, an integrated query plan consisting of rank operators produces a sorted list of k Steiner graphs $\{G_{S_1}, \ldots, G_{S_k}\}$ for Q s.t. there exist no other Steiner graph G_{S_i} in G with $Score(G_{S_i}) > Score(G_{S_k})$.*

Proof Sketch. The integrated query plan can be decomposed into a number of subplans, each representing a different join order for the keywords in Q. Processing every plan using the top-k procedure in [IBS08] based on rank join yields a sequence of Steiner graphs $\{G_{S_1}, G_{S_2}, \ldots\}$, such that $Score(G_{S_i}) \geq Score(G_{S_{i+1}})$. The last operator of the integrated query plan is a union operator that reports a top-k result only when its score equals or is higher than the maximum of the thresholds of the underlying rank join operators, i.e. when no results can be produced by another subplan that have a higher score. □

The proof for this essentially exploits the top-k property of the underlying rank operators. The intuition is this: the integrated query plan can be decomposed into a number of subplans, each represents a different join order for the keywords in Q. Because every such subplan corresponds exactly to the notion of query plan used previously [IBS08], the established top-k property holds in this case, providing the guarantee that every subplan yields the k best Steiner graphs (of one particular structure reflected by the join order). The rank union operator reports a top-k result only when its score equals or is higher than the maximum of the thresholds of the underlying rank join operators (subplans). This maximum threshold can be seen as a global threshold applied to results of all subplans. The top-k property is preserved because by definition, no subplan can produce further results with scores exceeding this global threshold.

Push-based Architecture. The pull-based architecture [IBS08] is "driven" by the final results. When called by the *next* method, each operator consumes its inputs until it is able to produce one result. Such an architecture is problematic in keyword query processing, as some operators of the integrated query plan may produce no results, which can only be determined after completely reading at least two base inputs. Detecting and avoiding these "broken operators" (and the subplans resulting from them) can improve efficiency. To this end, we propose a push-based architecture, which is "driven" by the data access operators instead of the results. These operators *push* their outputs into the join operators they are connected to, from where keyword graphs propagate upwards through the query plans. In contrast to pull-based architectures, control and data flow are in the same rather than opposite direction.

Operator Ranking. Using such a push-based architecture, we can apply operator ranking to accommodate knowledge related to which operators are broken, which ones produce more results, or which ones produce results earlier than others. The ranking of operators determines its order during execution. That is, we propose not only to rank inputs and (partial) results, but also the join operators themselves. We associate rank join operators with a global score, which is estimated based on current results (R), and upper bound estimates for subsequent join operations to be performed on the remaining base inputs (NB_k).

Definition 3.9 (Operator Rank). *Given the results R of a $\bowtie_{Rank}$ operator and the remaining set NB_K of keyword neighborhoods not included in the inputs to $\bowtie_{Rank}$, the* global score *of $\bowtie_{Rank}$ is defined as $S = max\{Score(G_K)|G_K \in R\} + \sum_{NB_k \in NB_K} max\{Score(P)|P \in NB_k\}$.*

Query Execution. The global score is used to guide query execution. When a join operator has results that can be pushed to the next operator, it is associated with an (updated) global score and becomes active. If there are no active join operators, the lower level data access operators are activated in a round-robin fashion, each pushing a path entry into all rank $\bowtie_{NB}$ operators they are connected to. If there are active operators, the operator with the highest global score pushes its results to subsequent operators until its result stack is empty, or another join operator has a better global score.

Detailed Algorithms. Alg. 3.2 shows the query execution algorithm. First, the keyword elements N_k for all $k \in Q$ are retrieved and their keyword neighborhoods are created. Priority queue J keeps track of all currently active join operators, sorted by their global scores. While the number of results is lower than k, the algorithm gets the best result (via the *topR* method) from the topmost push rank join (PRJ) operator *op* in the queue J. By calling the *push* method of every connected operators (retrieved via *nextLevelOps*), this result is propagated to the next level. Now we check if the second best result (the one not been pushed yet) passes the threshold to determine if *op* is still active, and add it back to the queue if this is the case. If no active operators are available, the base inputs are activated until at least one operator becomes active or all inputs are exhausted.

The employed PRJ shown in Alg. 3.3 is based on the hash rank join [IAE02]: it also maintains a hash table for each input (H_1, H_2) for efficient lookup and computation of the join results J, and a threshold T (updated via the *threshold* method). Additionally, the PRJ operator also maintains the global score S. As previously defined, S is computed from the score of the currently best result and

---

Algorithm 3.2: EvaluateQuery(Q, I_{PE}, k)

Input: Keyword query Q, number of results k

Data: Queue J of active join operators, the integrated query plan IQP.

1   Retrieve N_k for all $k \in Q$

2   Retrieve $NB_k \in NB_K$ for each N_k

3   **while** *number of final results* $< k$ **do**

4   **if** $|J| > 0$ **then**

5          $op = J$.pop()

6          $NOps = IQP$.nextLevelOps(op)

7   **foreach** $nop \in NOps$ **do** nop.push (op.topR)

8   op.active $= \exists op.secR(Score(op.secR) > op.T)$

9   **if** $op.active$ **then** Add op to J

10   **else**

11   Select next input NB_k

12         $NOps = IQP$.nextLevelOps(NB_k)

13   **foreach** $nop \in NOps$ **do** nop.push (NB_k.topR)

14   Add all active operators to J

---

the maximum score of the combination of remaining base inputs that have not been joined during the process, i.e. are not part of the current results.

Example 3.8. *Fig. 3.9 shows a PRJ operator at level l, joining neighborhoods of ex:Mary and ex:Steve. The inputs, i.e. path entries (ex:Mary, 0.5, ex:Berlin), (ex:Mary, 0.5, ex:ACME) from one operator and inputs (...) from other operators, are pushed from operators at level l − 1. The two hash tables contain 4×2 elements already processed. One output with score 2.5 has been pushed to the next level. A candidate result with score 2.0 is in the queue. Because the last seen score is 0.5, $T = 2.0 + 0.5 = 2.5$. As the result has a score less than threshold T, it cannot be pushed to subsequent operators yet (is thus inactive). This may change subsequently because T may decrease when lower input scores are processed. The query execution controls the push operation: an operator is only activated to push its results if its global score S is the highest among all active operators.*

Note that the proposed modifications to the basic strategy, i.e. push-based execution in combination with operator-ranking, only aims at improving the

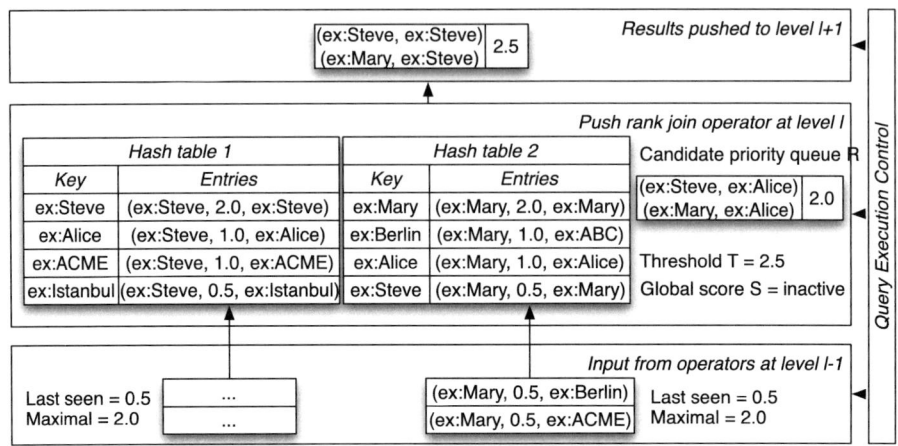

Figure 3.9: Example instance of the PRJ operator for the join between the neighborhoods of *ex:Steve* and *ex:Mary*.

Algorithm 3.3: PRJ: Push(r)

Input: Pushed input element r

Data: Queue R of sorted results, hash tables H_1, H_2 for inputs, global score S

```
// Use m,n to identify hash tables and inputs
```

1 **if** r *is left input* **then** $m = 1$, $n = 2$

2 **else** $m = 2$, $n=1$

3 Insert r into hash table H_m

4 T = threshold()

5 J = probe H_n for valid joined results with keys of r

6 **forall the** $j \in J$ **do** insert j into R

7 **if** $|R| > 0$ **then**

8   **if** $Score(this.topRes) > T$ **then**

9         $this$.active = true

10   Update S

---

efficiency. It has no effect on the top-k property. Essentially, because the same threshold checks are carried out, Theorem 3.5 must also hold in this case.

3.4 Related Work

We discussed research work on neighborhood indexing [STW04, CY09] and join processing [IBS08, IAE02] that underlies our approach. We also provided an overview of existing keyword search solutions, which can be categorized into the categories of (1) schema-based [HGP03, LYMC06, LLWZ07, QYC09, QYC10] and (2) schema-agnostic [KPC+05, HWYY07, LOF+08] approaches. A similar distinction was made in a recent survey of keyword search in relational databases [YQC10]. The capabilities of the underlying database engine can be fully utilized by the former approaches, while the applicability of the latter approaches is not limited to structured data that have well defined schemas. Our work follows the line of schema-agnostic approaches, aiming at providing keyword search support for different types of data, from structured to semi-structured up to unstructured data [LOF+08]. In particular, we compute Steiner graphs by operating directly on the data graph [LOF+08, KPC+05, TWRC09]. We make two kinds of contributions that are substantially different from previous work along this line: (1) previous strategies for searching Steiner graphs load the data graph into memory, and then find Steiner graphs by traversing graph edges [KPC+05], or pruning them [LOF¹08]. Instead, we propose the use of join operations for this. (2) Further, for efficient data access, we propose an index that stores materialized paths in the neighborhoods of graph elements. While the concept of neighborhood is conceptually similar to the notion used by EASE [LOF+08], the data structure to implement it is more efficient because the employed strategies for neighborhood pruning is based on the more fine-grained notion of paths, instead of graphs. Further, this implementation enables us to conceive a neighborhood as a set of paths, enabling the search for Steiner graphs to be conducted via path-based join operations.

3.5 Evaluation

Systems. We compare our approach with an implementation of EASE [LOF+08], a state-of-the-art native keyword search solution. We also implemented the bidirectional search algorithm (BDS) [KPC+05]. We used two variants of our approach: the first features operator ranking (KJ) and the second one does not (KJU).

For all approaches, a Lucene keyword index is used to retrieve the top 300 matching keyword elements for each keyword of the query. The time needed for

	Triples	I_{PE}	I_P	EASE
BTC	10M	237	890	7933
DBLP1	1M	42	76	234
DBLP5	5M	250	452	2201
DBLP10	10M	559	1004	7435

Table 3.3: Dataset and index statistics (index sizes in MB).

this is not counted as it is the same for all systems. For BDS, the exploration is performed directly on the data graph to obtain top-k Steiner graphs. For EASE, first all maximal 2-radius graphs, which contain at least one keyword element for every keyword, are identified. The union of these graphs computed for all query keywords is then loaded into memory, and pruned successively to obtain Steiner graphs.

All systems were implemented in Java 1.6 on top of Oracle Berkeley DB (Java Edition). Experiments were performed on a Linux system with two Intel Xeon 2.80GHz Dual-Core processors, a Samsung HE322HJ SATA 320GB disk and 8GB of main memory, 4GB of which were assigned to the Java VM. Operating system caches were cleared after each query run.

Data and Queries. We used a crawl of the Billion Triple Challenge 2009[1] (BTC) dataset, and 3 DBLP datasets from the SP2Bench benchmark [2] (DBLP) that vary in size, which we employ for the scalability experiment. Tab. 3.3 shows detailed statistics about the datasets and the size of the indexes for KJ (path entry index I_{PE} and path index I_P) and EASE. For each dataset, we created nine keyword queries of length 2 ($Q_1 - Q_3$), 3 ($Q_4 - Q_6$) and 4 ($Q_7 - Q_9$). Table 3.4 shows example queries for both datasets. All queries used in this evaluation can be found in Appendix A.1.

Index Statistics. For each dataset we created the path entry and path indexes with $d = 2$ for our approach and an index containing maximal 2-radius graphs for EASE. As discussed, the scale-free nature of Web data graphs makes values $d > 2$ impractical because neighborhoods become as large as the entire data graph. Note that unlike EASE, this is not such a strong limitation because paths between 2 keyword elements can still have lengths up to $|Q| - 1 \times d$ (instead of $2 \times d$).

---

[1]http://vmlion25.deri.ie/, retrieved 2013-01-18
[2]http://dbis.informatik.uni-freiburg.de/index.php?project=SP2B, retrieved 2013-01-18

DBLP	BTC
"miller journal"	"event movie"
"press article 1988"	"album queen magic"
"journal medical article 1979"	"document iswc owl semantic 2009"

Table 3.4: Example queries for DBLP and BTC datasets.

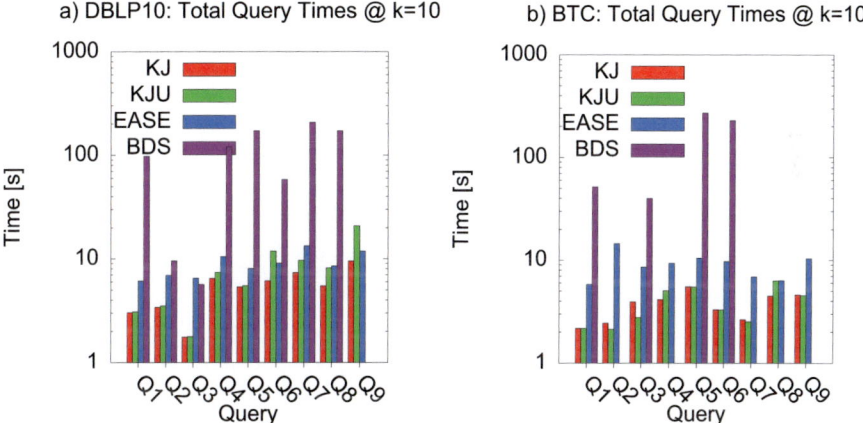

Figure 3.10: Overview of query processing times of all queries for a) DBLP10 and b) BTC (both at $k = 10$).

Due to more fine-grained pruning, the KJ indexes were much smaller than the EASE indexes: for the DBLP datasets, the size of the KJ indexes was between 50% (DBLP1) and 21% (DBLP10) the size of the corresponding EASE indexes. For the BTC dataset, the difference was even larger: the KJ index was only 14% the size of the EASE index.

Overall Performance. Fig. 3.10a+b show total query times for all queries on the DBLP10 and BTC datasets (missing values indicate timeouts). The performance of BDS was worse than all other systems on average (up to one order of magnitude for some queries). This suggests that the materialization strategies employed by other systems largely improve online performance. For both datasets, the performance of KJ was better than EASE for all queries. For DBLP10, and $k = 10$, the average total query times for KJ and EASE were 5.4s and 8.9s, respectively (BDS: 105.5s). On the BTC dataset with $k = 10$, the total

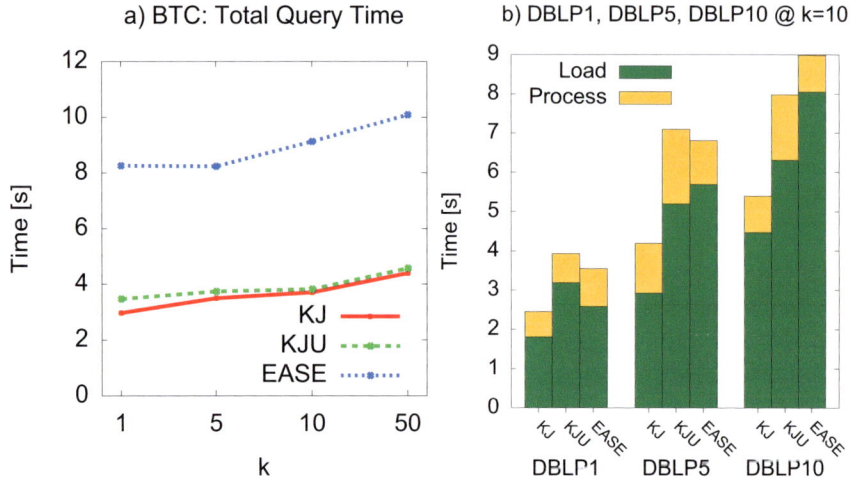

Figure 3.11: Query processing times for a) different values of k on the BTC dataset, and b) for different sizes of the DBLP dataset.

times were 3.7s and 9.1s (BDS: 147.9s). This represents an improvement of 39% and 59%, respectively. However, the performance advantage of KJ compared to EASE decreases with longer queries. Whereas for $|Q|=2$ on DBLP10 with $k=10$, EASE was on average 2.39 times slower than KJ, this factor decreased to 1.53 and 1.51 for $|Q|=3$ and $|Q|=4$, respectively. We will show later that the reason for that lies in the increased number of joins needed to process the search space resulting from the standard semantics of keyword search results that is larger than the one of EASE.

Top-k Processing. Fig 3.11a shows query performance for different values of k for the BTC dataset. Clearly, query times for all systems increase with higher values of k.

Operator Ranking. We compare KJ and KJU to examine the effect of operator ranking. Fig 3.11a shows that, on average, KJ with operator ranking was faster than KJU without operator ranking. We can see that the difference in query time between KJ and KJU decreases with larger values of k. For $k=1$ KJU took 17% longer than KJ, whereas for $k=50$ the difference was only 4%. This shows that operator ranking enables faster early result reporting, but also that the benefit decreases when more results are requested, which can be explained by the additional overhead introduced by operator ranking during query execution.

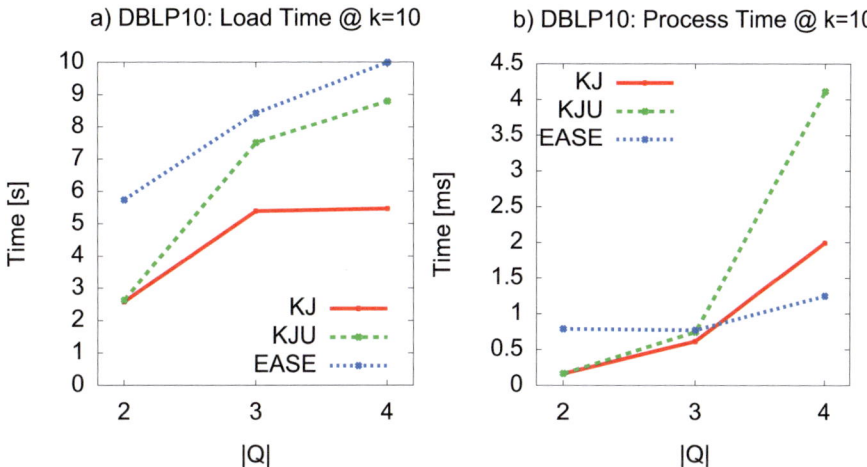

Figure 3.12: Evaluation results: load and process times for different keyword
query lengths.

Scalability. Fig. 3.11b shows overall query times for the three different DBLP
datasets. The query time is split into the time for data access (load) and the
time for join processing (process). We can see that data access makes up the
main share of total time. For all datasets, KJ outperforms EASE. With respect to
scalability, we found that the difference in performance between EASE and our
system increases with larger datasets. On DBLP1, the smallest dataset, EASE
was worse by a factor of 1.44. This increases with larger versions of the DBLP
dataset, e.g. EASE was worse by a factor of 1.66 on DBLP10.

For an examination of the separate impact of data access (load) and data
processing (process), Figure 3.12 illustrates a decomposition of query time.

Data Access. Fig. 3.12a shows access times at different query lengths $|Q|$ for
DBLP with $k = 10$. For all systems, access times increase with longer queries.
Again, we can see the positive effect of operator ranking, as access times for
KJ do not increase as sharply as for KJU. For $|Q| = 2$, both KJ and KJU exhibit
similar access times, whereas for $|Q| = 4$ KJU is 1.6 times worse than KJ. Access
times for EASE are worse than KJ for all query lengths. This confirms that
the more fine-grained path-level pruning implemented by KJ helps to focus on
smaller neighborhoods. Further, this efficiency gain can also be attributed to the
fact that instead of loading all entire neighborhoods (i.e. all matching 2-radius
graphs), KJ only loads path entries necessary to compute top-k results.

Data Processing. Fig. 3.12b shows processing times at different values for $|Q|$. Clearly, processing times increase for larger values of $|Q|$. However, this effect is more pronounced for KJ and KJU than for EASE. From $|Q| = 2$ to $|Q| = 4$, KJ's processing times increase by a factor 12.2 where EASE's times increase only by 1.6. This result is not surprising, given our approach supports the standard semantics whereas EASE assumes a center node. With more complex queries, the search space for KJ becomes larger. This is reflected in a higher number of query plans and join operators that have to be processed. Regardless of query length, EASE always operates on the union of the 2-radius graphs, and obtain results using the same pruning procedure.

Here, we can more clearly see the benefit of operator ranking: KJU's processing times are higher than KJ's times; this difference increases with $|Q|$, indicating that operator ranking is beneficial when the queries are more complex.

3.6 Conclusion

We proposed a native keyword search database solution based on the basic operations data access and join. We introduced the d-length 2-hop index and a top-k procedure for implementing this database style processing. In experiments using large scale datasets, we showed that our solution consistently outperformed state-of-the-art solutions, i.e. it reduced storage requirement up to 86%, improved scalability by several factors, and improved performance by more than 50% on average. Further, our approach exhibits two main qualitative advantages. (1) While the existing solution requires large graphs to be loaded entirely into memory at once, the database style processing we propose can operate on data streams that are loaded successively. (2) Also, the semantics of the results supported is more general, leading to more results formed by longer paths. Whereas this work focuses on the efficiency of top-k keyword search processing, the question of how differences in semantics and scoring functions affect the quality of results is considered as main future work.

Chapter 4

Stream-based Linked Data Query Processing

4.1 Introduction

In recent years, the amount of *Linked Data* on the Web has been increasing rapidly. Datasets made publicly available on the Web as Linked Data cover different domains, including life sciences, geographic locations, media and entertainment. There are also cross-domain encyclopedic datasets such as Freebase and DBpedia (the structured data counterpart of Wikipedia). Besides enterprises, such as media companies like BBC and Last.FM, several governments recently started to make data of public interest available to citizens, including CO_2, Mortality, Energy and Postcodes.

Many such data providers follow the *Linked Data principles* [BHBL09], which dictate how to publish and access Linked Data and how to establish links between them. According to these principles, structured data about an entity can be made available as Linked Data essentially by publishing an "entity Web page", called *Linked Data source*, that has a URI. Dereferencing this URI via HTTP should return structured data about that entity. This data may contain other URIs representing links to related entities (related Linked Data sources). Thus, as an alternative to managing structured data through federated endpoints, Linked Data represents a simple mechanism for publishing, accessing and linking structured data on the Web just like Web pages.

In this chapter, we focus on the problem of processing structured SPARQL queries directly over Linked Data instead of using SPARQL endpoints or materializing Linked Data in a warehouse. As introduced in Section 2.3.3 this type of query processing is associated with new challenges. We discuss this problem in a systematic fashion, propose new query operators and plans designed to tackle

67

these challenges and discuss our solution in detail. In particular, we make the following contributions:

- For Linked Data query processing, we identify the challenges, discuss concrete tasks, and derive three main strategies. There is a *top-down strategy* corresponding to the approach implemented by [HHK+10], a *bottom-up strategy* implemented by [HBF09], and a *mixed strategy* that as opposed to [HHK+10], does not assume complete but only partial knowledge about the sources and unlike [HBF09], have to discover only some but not all sources at run-time.

- We propose an implementation of the mixed strategy that is able to use run-time information for *run-time refinements of the query plan* based on a ranking scheme that determines the relevancy of data sources. The proposed ranking scheme can deal with different types of source descriptions containing knowledge at varying levels of granularity.

- As an alternative to the pull-based non-blocking iterator [HBF09], we propose the use of *push-* and *stream-based query processing* where source data is treated as finite streams that can arrive at any time in any order. This approach is better suited to deal with network latency as it is driven by incoming data and does not require temporary rejection of answers.

- We propose a new join operator called Symmetric Index Hash Join (SIHJ) that is non-blocking, pushed-based, stream-based, and in particular, is able to process both remote and local linked data.

- We propose a cost model that can be used to analyze this operator given only remote data, only local data, or a combination of them. Further, we provide a cost model for the proposed non-blocking iterator join (NBIJ) [HBF09]. These two cost models can be used for query optimization, and allow us to compare the mechanisms underlying these operators in a systematic fashion.

- In an experimental comparison, we evaluate the proposed strategy and compare it to the previously proposed strategies and show that the mixed strategy improves early result reporting. Further, we compare the performance of SIHJ and NBIJ in more detail on real-world datasets and a synthetic dataset to more systematically analyze the impacts of the individual components captured by the proposed cost models.

In this chapter, we use the definitions of Linked Data and BGP queries first given in Section 2.3. For ease of reading, we repeat the important definitions here:

Definition 2.10 (Linked Data Source / Graph). *A Linked Data source, identified by an HTTP URI d, is a set of RDF triples $\langle s,p,o \rangle$, denoted as T^d. There is a link between two Linked Data sources d_i, d_j if d_j appears as the subject or object in at least one triple of d_i, i.e. $\exists t \in T^{d_i}, t = \langle d_j, p, o \rangle \vee t = \langle s, p, d_j \rangle$ or vice versa, $\exists t \in T^{d_j}, t = \langle d_i, p, o \rangle \vee t = \langle s, p, d_i \rangle$. With D as the set of all Linked Data sources, the* Linked Data *graph is constituted as $T^D = \{t | t \in T^{d_i}, d_i \in D\}$.*

Definition 2.11 (Basic Graph Pattern). *Let $\mathcal{V}$ be the set of all variables. A triple pattern (TP) $\langle s,p,o \rangle \in (\mathcal{V} \cup \mathcal{U}) \times (\mathcal{V} \cup \mathcal{U}) \times (\mathcal{V} \cup \mathcal{U} \cup \mathcal{L})$ is a triple where the subject, predicate, and object can either be a* variable *or a* constant *(an RDF term). A* basic graph pattern *(BGP) is a set of triple patterns, $Q = \{t_1, \ldots, t_n\}$. Two TPs that share a variable form a* join pattern.

Definition 2.12 (BGP Result). *Let G be an RDF graph, Q be an BGP query, and $\mathcal{V}$ be the set of all variables. Let μ' be the function that maps elements in Q to elements in G:*

$$\mu' : \mathcal{V} \cup \mathcal{U} \cup \mathcal{L} \to \mathcal{U} \cup \mathcal{L} \begin{cases} v \mapsto \mu(v) & \text{if } v \in \mathcal{V} \\ t \mapsto t & \text{if } t \in \mathcal{U} \cup \mathcal{L} \end{cases}$$

where the mapping $\mu : \mathcal{V} \to \mathcal{U} \cup \mathcal{L}$ is employed to map variables in Q to RDF terms in G. A mapping μ is a result *to Q if it satisfies $\langle \mu'(s), \mu'(p), \mu'(o) \rangle \in G$, $\forall \langle s,p,o \rangle \in Q$. We denote the set of all result bindings for query Q over graph G as $\Omega_G(Q)$ (we omit G if clear from context), i.e. $\mu \in \Omega_G(Q)$. The set of all bindings for a single triple pattern $t \in Q$ is $\Omega_G(t)$.*

In the examples in this chapter we use the example data and query first shown in Section 2.3. We therefore repeat Fig. 2.3 that shows five Linked Data sources and Fig. 2.4 that shows an example BGP query.

4.1.1 Source Discovery and Ranking

There are multiple ways for sources to be discovered: Sources can be explicitly set in the *query* using special syntax or can be part of a triple pattern (e.g. the example query in Fig. 2.4 references source *ex:Mary*). The query engine can maintain a list of *known sources*. This list can either be entered manually

Src. 1: http://example.org/Mary

```
ex : Mary
    ex : name  ' Mary Smith '  ;
    ex : knows  ex : Richard  ;
    ex : knows  ex : Alice  ;
    ex : worksAt  ex : ABC  .
```

Src. 2: http://example.org/Alice

```
ex : Alice
    ex : name  ' Alice Smith '  ;
    ex : knows  ex : Mary  ;
    ex : knows  ex : Steve  ;
    ex : worksAt  ex : ACME  .
```

Src. 3: http://example.org/ABC

```
ex : ABC
    ex : name  ' ABC Corp '  ;
    ex : locatedIn  ex : Berlin  .
```

Src. 4: http://example.org/ACME

```
ex : ACME
    ex : name  ' ACME Corp '  ;
    ex : locatedIn  ex : Istanbul  .
```

Src. 5: http://example.org/Richard

```
ex : Richard
    ex : name  ' Richard Miller '  ;
    ex : knows  ex : Mary  ;
    ex : worksAt  ex : ABC  .
```

Figure 2.3: Example Linked Data sources containing data from Fig. 2.1.

Figure 2.4: Example BGP query that asks for the names of companies people known by *ex:Mary* work at.

or be compiled from previously executed queries. Sources can be *discovered* during query processing by following links mentioned in the content of retrieved sources.

In the first two cases, sources are known before the execution of the query. Compile-time optimization decisions concerning source ranking and query optimization (discussed in the following) are based exclusively on information derived from these sources. In the last case, sources are dynamically added at run-time. New information derived from these sources has an impact on the compile-time optimization plan. This information might render the plan no longer optimal. It is used in our work for run-time adaptation of query plans.

A source is *relevant* if it contains data that can contribute to the final answers. The standard optimization goal is to (1) obtain all results as fast as possible. However, given the volume and dynamic of the Linked Data collection, it is often infeasible to retrieve and process all sources. It is important to rank sources by their relevancy to the query and more fine-grained optimization goals. In particular, it might be desirable to (2) report results as early as possible, (3) to optimize the time for obtaining the first k results, or (4) to maximize the number of total results, given a fixed amount of time.

Source ranking uses available source descriptions that may vary in quality and completeness, i.e. they may lack information important for ranking. This means that it is essential to incorporate not only a priori available knowledge, but also knowledge obtained during query execution.

4.1.2 Evaluation Strategies

Previous works tackle the challenges from two directions:

Top-Down Query Evaluation. Linked Data comprises heterogeneous data that comes from different sources. Typically, a federated database system is used to integrate multiple sources and systems into one single federated database. The goal is to obtain a fully-integrated virtual database that provides transparent access to data of all its constituent sources.

Typically, sources and databases are geographically decentralized in a federated system. However, a system, which discovers, retrieves and stores Linked Data sources centrally, also falls into the category of a federated system. In fact, no matter the physical location (and other characteristics) of the sources, a source is considered if and only if the federated system knows about it. The federated system assumes that *all source descriptions are available* and based on that, compiles a *query evaluation plan* that specifies the relevant sources, and the order for retrieving and processing these sources. Thus, query planning and optimization is a one-off process performed in a top-down fashion based on complete information.

Harth et al. [HHK+10] implement this top-down evaluation. The main focus is on using a data structure capturing rich statistics that can be used to improve query planning and optimization. In approaches that fall into this category, source discovery is performed offline and source ranking is not part of the process. In order to deal with the large amount of sources, source ranking based on approximate triple and join pattern cardinality estimation is used to consider only a fixed number of top-ranked sources.

Bottom-Up Query Evaluation. As opposed to top-down query processing, this strategy does not assume source descriptions to be available beforehand and computes results in a bottom-up fashion. Without planning and optimization, it directly evaluates the query. During this process, it (1) retrieves the sources that are mentioned in the query, (2) discovers further sources based on source URIs and links found in the data of the retrieved sources, (3) incorporates the content of these discovered sources into query evaluation and (4) terminates when all sources found to be relevant have been processed.

Systems that implement this strategy do not rely on sources or source descriptions being managed centrally but discover and retrieve sources from external locations. *Source discovery* and *retrieval* are an integral part of the online process. These online tasks make this approach to query processing different from traditional database approaches. They might be needed due to the Linked Data specific challenges we have discussed. The large volume and the dynamic of the sources and source collection render the traditional top-down approach impracticable. In particular, it cannot be applied when there are sources that are not known beforehand and can only be discovered during online processing.

Another aspect distinct to this approach is *completeness* [HS12, Har12]. As opposed to traditional query processing, it might not be possible to obtain complete knowledge about all sources. In particular, processing queries against Linked Data where sources have to be discovered online might not yield all results. Results to the query cannot be found when they are part of sources that are unknown and cannot be discovered during online processing. This is the case when a link between two sources is only stored in one of the sources, meaning that the link cannot be discovered from the other source.

The bottom-up strategy is implemented in [HBF09, Har11], using non-blocking iterators to avoid blocking due to network delay.

Example 4.1. *Let Q be the example query in Fig. 2.4, to be evaluated over the example Linked Data shown in Fig. 2.3.*

Suppose that all sources of the example data are indexed in a source index, such that looking up a query triple pattern $t \in Q$ returns a list of sources that contain triples matching t. A top-down query engine would then, for example, first lookup pattern $\langle ?x, ex{:}worksAt, ?y \rangle$ and obtain source URIs $\{ex{:}Mary, ex{:}Alice, ex{:}Richard\}$, because all these sources contain triples matching t and are indexed as such in the source index. By dereferencing the source URIs, their contained data can be retrieved and processed (i.e. joined). The *remaining triple patterns are processed in the same manner until all query results have been found.*

In contrast, a bottom-up query engine does not have a source index, and can therefore only start by dereferencing sources mentioned in the query, i.e. only ex:Mary. After the source has been retrieved via an HTTP lookup, the query engine can discover new links to other sources, such as ex:knows links to ex:Alice and ex:Steve, from which further sources can be discovered. By traversing links in this manner and retrieving sources, all query results can be obtained. However, note that the completeness depends on the availability of (back-)links. For example, ex:ACME can be discovered from ex:Alice, but not ex:Alice from ex:ACME as there is no link to ex:Alice in the content of ex:ACME.

4.1.3 Remote and Local Linked Data Query Processing

While all approaches proposed so far assume remote data, in realistic scenarios, some Linked Data may be available locally. Conceptually, local data can be seen as yet another source. Thus, a *basic solution* to integrate locally stored data is to treat them just like a remote source and process them in the same way.

However, the availability of local data makes a great difference in practice, because while remote Linked Data sources have to be retrieved entirely (only URI lookup is available), local data can be accessed more efficiently using specialized indexes. Typically, local data are managed using a triple store, which maintains different indexes to directly retrieve triples that match a given pattern, i.e. relevant bindings Ω_t of a local source d can be directly obtained for triple pattern $t \in Q$.

Given such querying capabilities for local data, we will show in this work that remote and local Linked Data with different access options can be processed using a single join operator. Instead of loading all local data, this operator retrieves only triples matching a given pattern. Further, we observe that there are non-discriminative triple patterns such as $\langle ?x, rdf{:}type, ?y \rangle$, which produce a large number of triples that do not contribute to the final results. To alleviate this problem, we take advantage of the available indexes to further instantiate query triple patterns with data obtained during query processing to load only triples that are guaranteed to produce join results.

4.2 Overview

In this section we present our approach to Linked Data query processing that seeks to address the challenges C1-C4 presented in Section 2.3.3.

4.2.1 Mixed Query Evaluation Strategy

Our approach starts with (1) "best-effort" query planning, and based on this plan, evaluates the query. During this process, (2) sources are retrieved, (3) new sources are discovered, (4) source data is incorporated into evaluation and in a continuous fashion, (5) new source descriptions arc used for adaptive source re-ranking. The evaluation proceeds with the continuously refined plan and (6) terminates when all relevant sources have been processed. This processing represents a "*mixed*" strategy in two different aspects. One the one hand, it combines top-down and bottom-up query evaluation in a setting where information (obtained from previous runs) about some sources is available (the source data itself is not assumed to be available locally), and more information can be obtained during online query processing. Then, compile-time query planning is performed to reduce the number of sources to be considered while at query time, relevant source data is retrieved to discover new sources and fresh results as well as more information about sources for adaptive refinement of the initial query plan (C3,C4). It also combines the use of Linked Data accessible via URI lookups and Linked Data available in local RDF stores or through SPARQL endpoints (C1,C2).

The novelties of this approach can be summarized as follows: (1) It employs a *framework for planning and optimizing* Linked Data queries, which in addition to the standard operators such as union and join needed to process the data, captures special operators for processing sources. It recognizes that source processing is critical in Linked Data query processing and thus, is treated as an integral part of the optimization process. (2) It uses dynamic programming for *compile-time query planning* and further, incorporates newly discovered source information into an *adaptive source re-ranking* process that continuously refines the plan. (3) It is based on a *symmetric index hash join* that combines stream-based processing of Linked Data sources with index-based access to data managed by local RDF stores or even remote SPARQL endpoints.

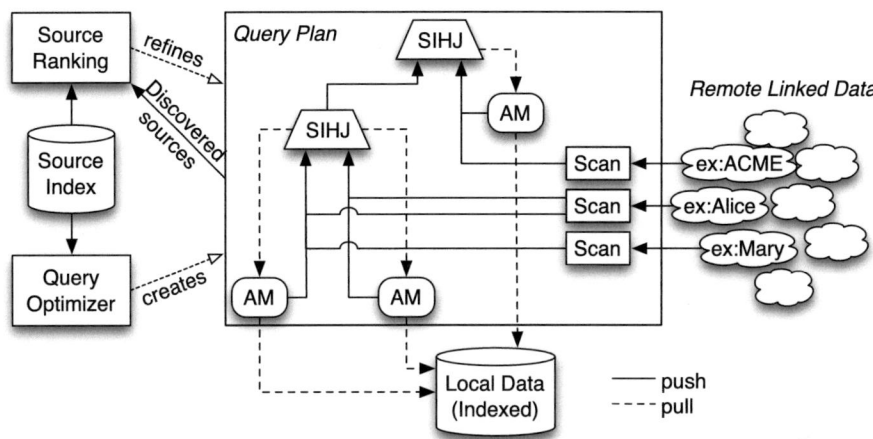

Figure 4.1: Architecture overview of Stream-based Linked Data Query Processing

4.2.2 Architecture

We will now give an overview of the architecture of the system implementing the mixed query evaluation strategy. Fig. 4.1 shows an overview over the components of the system. Structured queries, such as the example query in Fig. 2.4, are executed as follows.

First, the *query optimizer* constructs a best-effort query plan. Depending on available source descriptions, basic information or detailed statistics stored in the *source index* can be used to select an initial set of sources and plan the order of operators to be executed, and to perform other kinds of database optimizations that might consider indexes, materialized views, or the concrete join implementations [NW08]. The retrieval of Linked Data sources is captured as *source scan* operators that are responsible for retrieving sources and pushing them into the query operators. A detailed description of Linked Data query operators and plans is given in Section 4.3.

After the construction of the query plan, the query execution is started by retrieving Linked Data sources. During this process, we also *discover sources* that were unknown to the system by following links in retrieved sources. The identifiers of discovered sources are collected by the *source ranking* component that determines the relevancy of newly discovered sources, but also of already known sources. The query plan is refined at run-time in order to incorporate

75

source scans for newly discovered sources and to determine the order in which source scan operators are executed, i.e. according to the relevancy of their source. The source ranking and the run-time refinement of query plans are described in Section 4.4.1 and Section 4.5, respectively.

In addition to data retrieved via source scan operations from remote Linked Data sources, the system also takes advantages of data stored in local indexes, such as RDF stores. We use *access modules* (AM) to capture the pull-based access to such indexed data in order to decouple index access from data processing and thereby avoid blocking. Access modules are part of the *symmetric index hash join* (SIHJ) operator, an extension of the symmetric hash join operator. The SIHJ operator is described in Section 4.3.2.

Several *termination conditions* can be configured: (1) maximum discovery distance, (2) maximum number of sources to load and (3) number of results to produce. If any of these conditions are reached, the source ranker notifies the join operators so that query execution is terminated as soon as all remaining intermediate results have been processed.

4.3 Linked Data Query Operators and Plans

Given a BGP query, sources containing data for every triple pattern have to be retrieved and processed.

4.3.1 Linked Data Query Plans

The main difference to traditional query processing is that while some relevant sources can be determined using descriptions in a source index, their entire contents have to be retrieved (as opposed to only the parts matching the query when SPARQL endpoints are available). This is similar to a *table scan*, with the difference that sources have to be retrieved from remote sites. Moreover, several sources may contain answers for one single triple pattern, and vice versa, one single source may be used for several patterns. This is captured by the source scan operator:

Definition 4.1 (Source Scan). *The input of a source scan operator, $scan_d$, is the source URI d. Executing this operator outputs all triples in d, i.e. $scan_d = T^d$.*

Given the source data T^d, a selection $\sigma_{T^d}(t)$ is performed to output triples in T^d that match the triple pattern t. The outputs of two triple patterns t_i and t_j that share a common variable are joined, $t_i \bowtie t_j$. The union operator can be used to combine results from different sources for one pattern:

Definition 4.2 (Source Union). $\bigcup(I_1, \ldots, I_n)$ *outputs the union of its inputs* I_i, $1 \leq i \leq n$, *where every input* I_i *may stand for results for one triple pattern,* $I_i = \Omega(t)$, *or subexpression, e.g.* $I_i = \Omega(Q')$ *with* $Q' \subseteq Q$. *Because a triple pattern can match several sources,* I_i *may also capture partial results for a pattern t such that the union* $\bigcup(\sigma_{T^{d_1}}(t), \ldots, \sigma_{T^{d_n}}(t))$ *combines results from several selection operators.*

Query plans for relational databases consist of access plans for individual relations whose outputs are then processed by join and other operators. Here, we create an access plan for every triple pattern:

Definition 4.3 (Access Plan). *Given a query Q, let* $t \in Q$ *be a triple pattern in Q and* $D = source(t)$ *be the set of sources for t. An access plan* $p(t)$ *for t is a tree-structured query plan constructed in the following way: (1) At the lowest level, the leaf nodes of* $p(t)$ *are source scan operators, one* $scan_{d_i} = T^{d_i}$ *for each* $d_i \in D$; *(2) the next level contains selection operators, one for processing the output of every scan operator, i.e. we have* $\sigma_{T^{d_i}}(t)$ *for every* $d_i \in D$; *(3) the root node is a union operator* $\bigcup_t(\sigma_{T^{d_1}}(t), \ldots, \sigma_{T^{d_{|D|}}}(t))$ *that combines the outputs of all selection operators for t.*

At the next levels, the outputs of access plans' root operators are successively joined to process all triple patterns of the query, resulting in a *tree of operators*. However, in Linked Data query processing, it is often the case that a single Linked Data source contains data matching several triple patterns. It is therefore possible that a data source is used for more than one query triple pattern. In this case it is detrimental to execute the scan operator more than once as this will incur network costs that can be avoided. We therefore employ *operator sharing*, where the output of a source scan operator is used as input for more than one selection operator, i.e. the output is shared. This means that access plans may overlap and the query plan is no longer a tree, but has the form of a directed acyclic graph (DAG) [Neu05].

In a DAG-shaped plan the outputs of shared operators are read multiple times. There are several possible strategies for executing DAG-shaped plans [Neu05]. One strategy is based on *push-based execution*, where operators push their outputs to subsequent operators in the DAG. The shared operator simply pushes its output to several consumers, thereby avoiding temporary materializations. We employ this push-based execution in our approach.

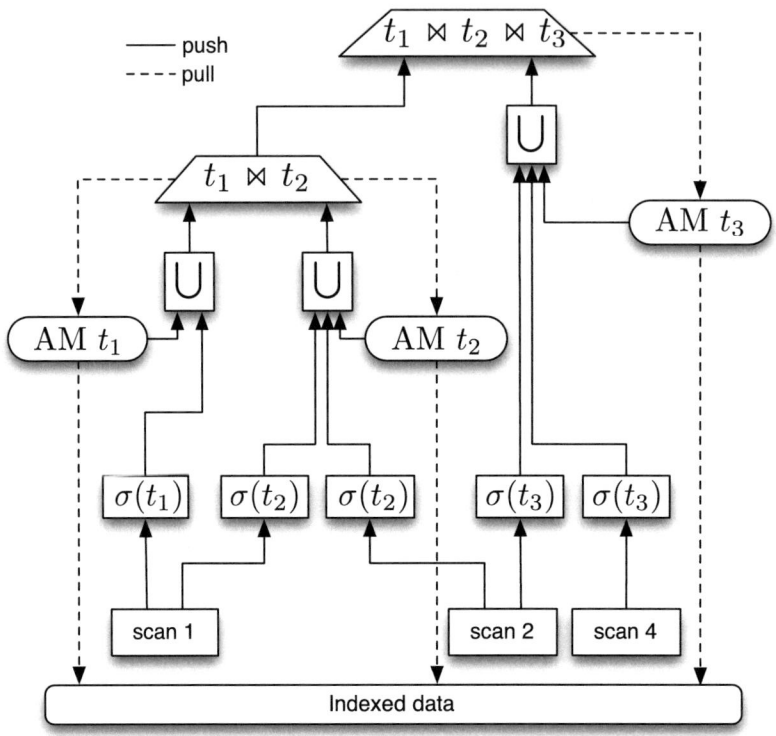

Figure 4.2: Query plan with source scans, access plans, access modules (AM)
and SIHJ operators.

Example 4.2. *Fig. 4.2 shows a query plan for the example query with three relevant sources. The sources are represented in the plan by their source scan operators. The output of source scans 1 and 2 are shared for triple patterns t_1, t_2 and t_2, t_3, respectively. Selection operators then select data matching the triple patterns and pipe their output through union operators into the corresponding join operators. This query plan also shows the combined use of Linked Data retrieved from Linked Data sources (via the source scans) and data retrieved from local indexes. The access to local indexes is encapsulated in* access modules (AM) *that receive requests from their associated symmetric index hash join (SIHJ) operators. After retrieving data from local indexes, the access modules push the data via the union operator back into the join operator where it is then further processed to obtain join results.*

4.3.2 Symmetric Index Hash Join

Query processing in highly distributed environments, where data is often stored at remote locations, requires flexible scheduling. That is, operators should not block so that progress can still be achieved even when some necessary inputs are delayed [IT08]. For this purpose, we adopt a stream-based approach where source data is treated as a (finite) stream that can arrive in any order. While data retrieved via URI lookups (source scans) is processed as streams, data from local RDF stores or remote SPARQL endpoints are considered as an index, which can be used to selectively retrieve only those triples that match a particular pattern.

To process such streams, pipelined operators are employed that produce results even before the whole input has been read, i.e. no intermediate results are materialized. One such operator is the *symmetric hash join* (SHJ), which, in contrast to hash joins, does not have to wait until one of the input has been completely read but can report results as soon as input tuples arrive [WA93]. The SHJ operator employs a pull-based execution model in that starting from the root operator, higher-level operators in the plan invoke the next method of lower-level operators to obtain their inputs. The SHJ operator maintains two hash tables, one for each input. Pulled tuples on either input are first inserted into their respective hash table and then used to probe the other hash table to find valid join combinations. A SHJ would block until it can produce at least one result. Instead of pulling from the root, a *push-based SHJ* is driven by its inputs, which are fed from lower operators (such as source scans). After inserting and probing its hash tables the push-based SHJ then actively pushes its results to higher level operators by invoking their push methods. Thereby, results can be produced as soon as input tuples arrive.

4.3.2.1 Query Processing based on SIHJ

We propose to extend the push-based SHJ operator to obtain the *symmetric index hash join* (SIHJ) that supports access to indexed data. SHIJ takes advantage of the structured querying capability of SPARQL endpoints. When the capability to return results for a given triple pattern is conceived as an index-based lookup, SIHJ is similar to the index nested-loop join, where a tuple of one input is used to formulate a lookup query that retrieves matching tuples from the index available for the other input. As opposed to that, it is a *non-blocking* operator that employs both *push- and pull-based* execution. Without access to indexed data, the SIHJ is essentially a push-based SHJ. Otherwise, it combines pull and push, i.e. while processing tuples that have been pushed to either one of its inputs, it also supports pulling data from indexes available for one of its inputs using data of the other input.

For a query with three triple patterns, Fig. 4.2 shows a left-deep query plan consisting of SIHJ operators and access modules for loading data. In a left-deep plan, the left input of all join operators is connected to the output of a join operator lower in the query plan, while the right input is connected to data sources, which in our case, might comprise both remote and local data. The exception is the lowest join operator, whose left input is not connected to another join operator but to data sources. Data arriving from remote sources are retrieved by a source scan operators that are scheduled on dedicated retrieval threads (see Sections 4.2.2 and 4.3.1) and their data is pushed directly into the corresponding operators, whereas the access modules pull data from local indexes on request and then push them into the join operators.

Algorithm. In particular, we designate the left input of SIHJ as the "driving" input. All bindings that arrive on the left are used to perform lookups on local data to load only bindings into the right input that produce join results. This is achieved by instantiating the triple pattern on the right input with bindings for the join variable obtained from the left input:

Definition 4.4. *Let t_i, t_j be two triple patterns of Q, v the join variable shared by t_i and t_j and Ω_{t_i} be the set of bindings for t_i. The results of the join of t_i and t_j on v is then calculated as $\Omega_{t_i} \bowtie_v \Omega_{t_j}$, where $\Omega_{t_j} = \bigcup_{u \in \Omega_{t_i}(v)} \{b \mid b \in \Omega_{t_j(v,u)}\}$, where $t_j(v,u)$ is an instantiated triple pattern obtained by substituting constant u for variable v.*

For local data we use separate *access modules* [RDH03] (AM) that encapsulate access to local indexes. The load method for the AM is specified in Alg. 4.1. For every SIHJ operator, one access module is created and connected to its right input. The access module accepts requests from the join operator *in* for loading the bindings Ω_t from triples matching a triple pattern t using the index I (line 1). All access to local storage is executed asynchronously by the access module so that operations in other parts of the query plan can still progress. Bindings loaded by an access module are pushed into its join operator (line 2).

This use of local data via the access module is shown in Alg. 4.2. All inputs of the "driving" left input are also pushed into this operator. When a binding b arrives on the left input, the corresponding hash table H_i is first probed to determine if it already contains the binding $b(v)$ for the join variable v captured

---

Algorithm 4.1: AM: *load*(*in*,*t*)

Input: Operator *in*, which requests data inputs for pattern *t*

1   $\Omega_t = I.\text{lookup}(t)$ `// lookup in local index`

2   **foreach** $b \in \Omega_t$ **do** *in*.push(this,*b*)   `// push bindings to join`
      `operator`

Algorithm 4.2: SHJ: *push*(*in*,*b*)

Input: Operator *in* from which input binding *b* was pushed

Data: Hash tables H_i and H_j; current operator *this*; subsequent operator *out*;
         join variable *v*; t_i is the left and t_j the right triple pattern

1   **if** *in is left input* **then**

2   **if** $b(v) \notin H_i$ **then** *AM*.load(this,$t_j(v,b(v))$)

3      $H_i[b(v)] \leftarrow H_i[b(v)] \cup b$

4      $J \leftarrow H_j[b(v)]$

5   **else**

6      $H_j[b(v)] \leftarrow H_j[b(v)] \cup b$

7      $J \leftarrow H_i[b(v)]$

8   **forall the** $j \in J$ **do** *out*.push(this,merge(j,b))

---

by *b* (line 2). If this is not the case, i.e. this binding has not been processed before, a request to load triples from the local index using the instantiated triple pattern $t_j(v,u)$ is sent to the access module (line 2). Then, *b* is inserted into the corresponding hash table H_i and H_j of the right input is probed to obtain valid join combinations (line 3 - 4), which are then pushed to operator *out* (line 8). Bindings arriving on the right input (i.e. from remote sources or those pushed from the AM) are processed in a similar manner, except that no requests are sent to the access module (line 6 - 7), which is not necessary as all bindings are stored in hash table H_j and are therefore available when a matching input arrives on the left input.

Note that bindings on the right or left input may be both local or remote data. Both remote and local data may be pushed into the left input. Remote data may also be pushed into the right input, and through explicit pulling using the AM (line 4), this input might also contain local data.

Example 4.3. *Fig. 4.3 illustrates the operation of a SIHJ operator. An input containing bindings for two variables* ?*x*,?*y is received and then inserted into*

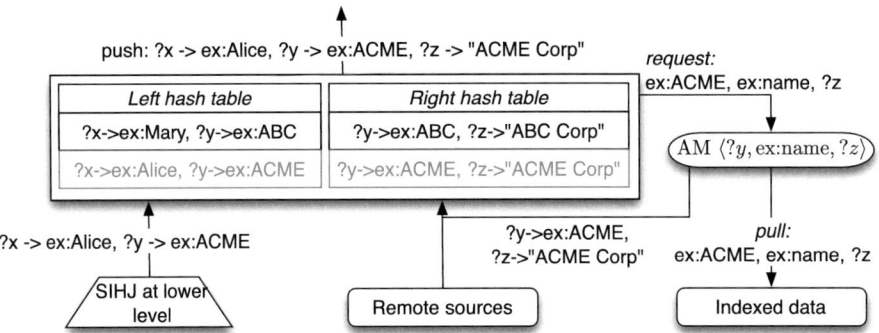

Figure 4.3: Operation of an SIHJ operator. After a binding was accepted on the left input, the access module pulls bindings for the instantiated triple pattern from the indexed data and then pushes the results back into the join operator.

the left hash table. Then a request for $\langle ex{:}ACME, ex{:}name, ?z \rangle$ is sent to the access module. After loading the data from the index, the binding for $?y, ?z$ is inserted into the right hash table. In combination with the binding in the left hash table a join result is finally created and pushed to the subsequent operator.

4.3.2.2 Cost Model

We use a unit-time-basis cost model that captures the operator cost in terms of the tuples that are accessed and the cost of the physical operations needed [KNV03]. All costs are defined in an abstract manner, independent from the concrete implementation and data structures being used.

The cost of a SIHJ with two inputs A and B is the sum of three components: the cost for joining tuples arriving on the left and the right input and the cost of the access module:

$$C_{A \bowtie B} = C_{A \times B} + C_{A \ltimes B} + C_{AM}$$

The operation carried out for tuples on the left input are: insertion into hash table for A, probing of hash table for B, creating join results and finally, sending a request to the access module. Accordingly, the cost $C_{A \times B}$ is defined as follows:

$$C_{A \times B} = |A| (I_h + P_h + \varphi \cdot |B| \cdot J \cdot \frac{|A|}{|A| + |B|} + R)$$

with: weight factors I_h, P_h for hash table insert and probe; join selectivity φ; weight factor J for creating result tuples; weight factor R for request to access module; the fraction $\frac{|A|}{|A|+|B|}$ of inputs arriving on the left input.

The term $I_h + P_h$ represents the cost of inserting an incoming tuple and then probing the other hash table. Given a join selectivity φ, the number of results for $A \bowtie B$ is $\varphi|A||B|$. Multiplied by the weight factor for creating results, this yields the term $J \cdot \varphi \cdot |A||B|$. Further, it is multiplied with $\frac{|A|}{|A|+|B|}$ to consider join cost only for tuples that actually arrive in A. For each tuple in A, a request is sent to the access module, whose cost is captured by R.

The cost $C_{A \bowtie B}$ for the other input is defined in a similar fashion, except that no requests to the access module are needed:

$$C_{A \bowtie B} = |B|(I_h + P_h + J \cdot |A| \cdot \varphi \cdot \frac{|B|}{|A|+|B|})$$

The cost C_{AM} for the access module is defined as $C_{AM} = |A| \cdot P_l + |B_l| \cdot L_l$, where the input B is split into tuples from remote sources B_r and local tuples loaded from disk B_l (i.e. $B = B_r \cup B_l$ and $B_r \cap B_l = \emptyset$). The cost for probing the local index, which has to be done for all tuples arriving in A, is represented by $|A| \cdot P_l$. When matching tuples are found, they have to be loaded from disk, the cost of which is given by $|B_l| \cdot L_l$.

Using the Cost Model for Query Optimization. The cost model developed in the previous section abstracts from concrete implementations and hardware by using weight factors. To use the cost model for query optimization these weight factors have to be known. The weight factors can be determined by running the operator on known input and then measuring the CPU time of the operations represented by the individual weight factors. Note that the weight factors are dependent on the characteristics of the data being used, in particular on the input size (both remote and local) and join selectivity. For example, the higher the join selectivity, the higher the relative weight of join result creation. Thus – as always the case of query optimization in practice – weight factors shall be derived from the underlying data.

In particular, measurements shall be taken for different combinations of input size and join selectivity. These measurements shall aim at covering a large space of possible combinations. At query compile-time, the weight factors precomputed for the combination that best fit the input size and join selectivity estimated for the given query are used to estimate join operator cost.

4.3.2.3 Batching

When an access module receives a request for loading data matching an instantiated triple pattern from local storage, all matching triples will have the same binding for the join variable because it has been used to instantiate the triple pattern in the first place. Sending each binding one by one to the join operator will incur an unnecessary overhead because they all will be inserted into the same hash bucket; and subsequently, the same hash bucket has to be probed several times when using these bindings. It is therefore beneficial to process data loaded from local indexes in *batches*, where the hash tables of the join operator are accessed only once for a batch of bindings.

4.3.2.4 Comparison to Non-Blocking Iterator

In [HBF09], the Non-Blocking Iterator Join (NBIJ) was proposed to deal with high network latency in the Linked Data context and the resulting issue of blocking. We now study this operator, extending previous work [HBF09] with a completeness analysis and cost model.

Query Processing based on NBIJ. NBIJ is based on a traditional pull-based mechanism, i.e. each operator in the query plan has a next method that is called by operators higher in the query plan tree. It is also used in left-deep plans, where all inputs consist only of data from remote sources.

During query processing an in-memory list G of data sources is maintained. Each downloaded source is indexed and then added separately to G. When the next method receives a result from a lower operator on the left input, first the following requirement is checked:

Requirement 1. *Let t_i, t_j be two triple patterns of Q, v the join variable shared by t_i and t_j and $b \in \Omega_{t_i}(v)$ a binding received on the left input. Then b can only be further processed if the following condition holds: $\forall u \in \{s(t_j(v, b(v))), p(t_j(v, b(v))), o(t_j(v, b(v)))\}$: if u is an URI then $ID(u) \in G$.*

This requirement ensures that all sources identified by URIs in the instantiated triple pattern have been retrieved and added to the list of in-memory sources. If the requirement is not fulfilled, the sources are marked for asynchronous retrieval, the binding is *rejected* by calling the reject method of the lower join operator, and the operator calls next again to retrieve further inputs. Otherwise, all sources in G are successively queried for the instantiated triple pattern $t_j(v, b(v))$ using in-memory indexes to construct join results.

When the reject method of a NBIJ operator is called, the rejected binding is added to a separate list maintained by the operator. On subsequent calls to its next method, the operator randomly decides between returning a previously rejected binding from the list or a new one. The rejection mechanism ensures that query processing can proceed even when sources for a particular pattern are not yet available.

Completeness. A disadvantage of NBIJ is that the obtained results are not necessarily complete w.r.t. downloaded data, i.e. it is not guaranteed that all possible results that can be derived from downloaded data are actually computed [HBF09]. While Requirement 1 does ensure that all sources mentioned in an instantiated triple pattern are retrieved before processing the pattern, it is possible that data matching that pattern is contained in other sources *retrieved later* during query processing. This is possible because Linked Data sources can contain arbitrary data and therefore not all data matching a particular triple pattern is necessarily contained in the sources mentioned in the pattern. As the NBIJ works in a pull-based fashion (and not push-based), this data will be disregarded if it is never requested again.

In contrast, a query plan based on SIHJ operators is guaranteed to produce all results. Requirement 1 is not necessary, because the operation of the SIHJ operator is completely symmetrical and push-based, i.e. incoming data can arrive on both inputs and in any order and its operation is driven by the incoming data instead of the final results. When an input tuple arrives on either of its input, the SIHJ operator is able to produce all join results of that tuple with *all previously seen inputs*, because these are kept track of in the hash table of the SIHJ operator. This ensures that it does not matter at which point during query processing a particular input for a triple pattern arrives, the final result is always complete with respect to the data in the sources that were retrieved.

Cost Model. Since the randomness of the rejection mechanism cannot be accurately captured in a cost model, we simply assume that all incoming bindings on the left input are first rejected and then processed on the second try. The cost for the NBIJ operator can then be calculated as follows:

$$C_{A\bowtie_{NBIJ}B} = |A|(P_G + T + |G| \cdot L) + \varphi |A||B| \cdot J$$

with: weight factor P_G for checking Req. 1; number of sources $|G|$; weight L for probing in-memory graph; weight T for tracking rejected bindings.

The term P_G gives the cost for checking whether the corresponding sources for a binding have been retrieved. The cost for rejecting a binding is T. Both these operations are performed for all bindings of the left input. For each binding from A all available graphs (in the worst case all sources) are consecutively probed for join combinations, yielding the term $|A||G| \cdot L$.

We now compare the cost models of the SIHJ and NBIJ operators. As the NBIJ operator only operates on remote data, we disregard the costs of SIHJ for requests sent to the access module. The cost of SIHJ is then:

$$C_{A \bowtie_{SIHJ} B} = |A|(I_h + P_h) + |B|(I_h + P_h) + \varphi|A||B| \cdot J$$

Assuming that both operators operate on the same inputs (i.e. we disregard the completeness issue discussed earlier), the results produced by both operators are the same and therefore the cost $\varphi|A||B| \cdot J$ for creating results is the same. The SIHJ might incur higher overhead for maintenance of its hash tables as all incoming tuples require insertion into and probing of a hash table. Compared to this, NBIJ incurs cost for checking the requirement, rejecting bindings and maintaining rejected bindings. However, NBIJ further incurs cost for probing all in-memory sources $|A||G| \cdot L$, which depends on the number of available sources. That means that the more sources are retrieved during processing, the higher the cost of the operator, whereas the SIHJ operator incurs no such cost and is independent from the number of retrieved sources.

4.4 Query Planning and Optimization

Traditional optimization is typically geared towards reporting all query results as fast as possible. However, since the number of Linked Data source is large, it is often infeasible to process all sources and to follow all links in the sources. Instead of result completeness, we therefore focus on *early result reporting*. To this end, two tasks are performed during compile time. (1) Sources with larger contribution to the final results are retrieved and processed earlier than sources with smaller contribution. This is accomplished by a *source ranking* mechanism. By employing push-based execution and pipelined operators, results become available as soon as data from high ranked sources are pushed into the query plan. (2) While this ranking is concerned with source scan operators, the execution order of other operators is determined based on standard *cost-based optimization*. Intuitively, while source ranking ensures that promising inputs are selected for early result reporting, the optimizer makes sure they are processed efficiently.

4.4.1 Source Ranking

In this section, we elaborate on the source features that are taken into account, concrete metrics derived from them, the indexes used to compute the metrics, newly discovered information used to refine and correct previously computed metrics, and how they are incorporated into source ranking.

4.4.1.1 Source Features and Metrics

The ranking of sources is calculated according to several source relevance metrics, which we will now present.

A source is more relevant if it contains data that contributes to final answers of the query. Thus, it is relevant when it contains triples matching a query triple pattern.

Definition 4.5 (Triple Pattern Cardinality). *The* triple pattern cardinality $card(d,t)$ *gives the number of triples in source d that match the triple pattern t.*

Clearly, the higher the cardinality, the more relevant is a source matching that pattern. However, this metric alone is yet no good indicator for the relevance of a source. Given Web data follows a power-law distribution [GCHQ10], some triple patterns might have a high cardinality for many sources. These patterns do not discriminate sources, just like words that frequently occur in all documents of a collection. One example is $\langle ?x, rdf{:}type, ?y \rangle$, which can be found in most Linked Data sources. To alleviate this problem, we adapt the TF-IDF concept to obtain weights for triple patterns that capture their importance. The importance of a triple pattern positively correlates with how often bindings to this pattern occur in a source as measured by its cardinality, and negatively correlates with how often its bindings occur in all sources of the collection: Higher weight is thus given to discriminative triple patterns.

Definition 4.6 (TF-ISF). *Given a source d and a triple pattern t, the* triple frequency - inverse source frequency *(TF-ISF) is* $\text{TF-ISF}(d,t) = card(d,t) \cdot \log \frac{|D|}{|\{r \in D | card(r,t) > 0\}|}$ *where, $r \neq d$ and D is the set of all sources.*

Join Pattern Results. A source containing data matching larger parts of the query is more relevant. Thus, a source that contains data matching a join pattern is considered highly relevant. However, not containing data for a join does not render a source irrelevant as its data might be joined with data from other sources. The join pattern cardinality estimates the results of a join pattern.

Definition 4.7 (Join Pattern Cardinality). *Given the join pattern* $t_i \bowtie_v t_j$ *on the shared variable v, the* join pattern cardinality *of a source s denoted* $card(s, t_i, t_j, v)$ *gives the number of results a join on the variable v between triples retrieved from s for* t_i *and* t_j *produces.*

Retrieval cost. Sources are more useful the faster they can be retrieved.

Definition 4.8 (Retrieval Cost). *The* retrieval cost *of a source s is a monotonic aggregation of the* size *of s and the* bandwidth *of a host h, defined as* $cost(s) = Agg(size(s), bandwidth(h))$.

Source size is available in the source description. Bandwidth is approximately derived for a particular host based on past experiences or, when available, average performance recorded during the process for sources retrieved from this host.

4.4.1.2 Metric Computation

In the mixed strategy, some of the source metrics are available locally. We store these metadata in specialized indexes (1) to select relevant sources and (2) to compute cardinalities for these sources.

Indexes for Source Selection. Given a triple pattern, these indexes return a set of sources that contain triples matching the pattern. The only "interesting" patterns are those with one or two variables. Patterns with no variables match only themselves and pattern with no constants match all triples and thus, match all sources. Three indexes are sufficient to support all patterns with one variable. In particular, we create the indexes SP, PO and OS (where S, P, O stand for subject, predicate and object). Each maps the indexed pattern to a set of sources. For example, to find sources for $\langle ?x, rdf{:}type, foaf{:}Person \rangle$, we use the PO index to retrieve relevant sources. Using prefix lookup, the same indexes can be used to cover all patterns with two variables.

Index for Cardinality Computation. In [HHK⁺10], a probabilistic index structure is used to support triple and join pattern cardinality estimation of individual sources. A different technique based on aggregation indexes is presented in [NW09]. We adopt this method, but extend it to support lookup of triple pattern cardinalities and estimation of join cardinalities for individual sources. Instead of calculating the statistics and indexes for the whole dataset, we treat each source as its own dataset and create the aggregation indexes accordingly. While we lose the ability to perform selectivity and cardinality estimation over the indexed data as a whole, we can now calculate estimates for individual sources, which is what is necessary for source ranking.

4.4.2 Estimating Cost and Cardinality of Plans

While source ranking determines the number and order of source scan operators, i.e. the leaf nodes of the query plan, the query optimizer decides how data from the sources are processed, i.e. the operators in the upper levels of the query plan. A dynamic programming optimizer is adapted to take operator sharing into account. The optimizer relies on cost estimates.

For the presented structure of a Linked Data query plan and its operators, many techniques for estimating the cost of operators in the RDF setting [SSB$^+$08, NW09] are applicable. We will present how these techniques are applied to this case to obtain both cost and cardinality estimates. We focus on basic estimates needed in this work and refer the reader to more specific work on join size estimation for more advanced techniques [SSB$^+$08, NW09, HL11].

Operators. We first define the output cardinality, i.e. the number of produced outputs, for each operator in Linked Data query plans:

Definition 4.9 (Cardinality). *The output cardinality of the source scan operator is the same as the size of the source, i.e.* $card(scan_d) = |T^d|$. *For union, cardinality is the sum of the cardinalities of its inputs:* $card(\cup(I_1, ..., I_n)) = \sum_{i=1}^{n} card(I_i)$. *The cardinality for selection and join depends on selectivity estimates* $sel(\cdot)$, *i.e.* $card(\sigma_{T^d}(t)) = sel(t) \times |T^d|$ *and* $card(t_i \bowtie t_j) = sel(t_i \bowtie t_j) \times card(t_i) \times card(t_j)$, *respectively.*

This source size statistics can be directly obtained from the source index discussed before. The calculcation of operator cost is directly based on the output cardinality:

Definition 4.10 (Cost). *Typically cost is assumed to be proportional to cardinality, which is captured as* weights $h_s, h_\sigma, h_\cup,$ *and* $h_\bowtie$ *for scan, selection, union and join, respectively. The costs for scan, selection, union and join are then* $cost(scan_d) = h_s \times |T^d|$, $cost(\sigma_{T^d}(t)) = h_\sigma \times |T^d|$, $cost(\cup) = h_\cup \times card(\cup)$, *and* $cost(\bowtie) = h_\bowtie \times card(\bowtie)$, *respectively.*

Typically, the weight parameters are tuned based on performance results observed from previous workloads and the availability of indexes and algorithms. For instance, $h_\bowtie$ depends on the join algorithm employed. The cost model for the SIHJ operator is specified in Section 4.3.2. In case of operator sharing, separate cost models for the first source scan (when the data is retrieved over the network) and subsequent scans (when the data has already been retrieved) are used. We use $cost_2(scan_d) = (1 - b) \cdot cost_1(scan_d)$, where $cost_1$ denotes first time cost,

$cost_2$ stands for cost for each subsequent scan, and b is a parameter to control the benefit achievable through operator sharing.

Atomic Plan. The cardinality of an access plan $p(t)$ is captured by its root node, i.e. $card(p(t)) = card(\cup_t)$. Its cost is calculated as the sum of the cost of its nodes. Source scan operators are marked after first time usage so that the right cost model can be determined for this calculation.

Composite Plan. Composite plans capture the joins between results obtained for several triple patterns (outputs of access plans). For an expression $T = t_i \bowtie t_j$, $card(p(T)) = card(t_i \bowtie t_j)$ and $cost(p(T)) = cost(t_i \bowtie t_j)$.

4.5 Run-time Adaptation of Query Plans

Compile time optimization as discussed before is based on knowledge from previous runs. In order to take advantage of new knowledge that becomes available during query processing, the query plan is adaptively changed at run-time.

4.5.1 Run-time Source Discovery

A central tenet of our query evaluation strategy is online source discovery, i.e. discovering sources at run-time through link traversal [HBF09]. When new sources are discovered by the query engine, we modify the query plan by adding new source scan operators and also, compute relevance metrics. While information such as triple pattern cardinality could be collected for sources processed in previous runs, no information is available for new sources. The number and type of links through which these sources were discovered (or could be reached, in general) are used for estimating relevance. A source containing many links coming from relevant sources is more useful. The relevance of such sources is even higher when these links match query predicates. Note that unlike triple pattern results that can be computed given a source, links can only be discovered by processing several sources. A source at first considered irrelevant based on triple pattern results might become relevant during the process.

Definition 4.11 (Links to Results). *Let S be the set of sources already processed, $links(s_i, s_j)$ be a function that returns all links between a source $s_i \in S$ and the source s_j, the* links to results *of s_j is defined as $links(s_j) - \bigcup_{s_i \in S} links(s_i, s_j)$.*

After these sources have been processed, cardinality of triple patterns are collected for them in an offline process and stored in the source index that is exploited for subsequent runs.

4.5.2 Run-time Refinement

For known sources from previous runs, we estimate join pattern cardinality, which is yet another metric employed for ranking. This information is obtained at run-time and is then used to refine the ranking of sources. The technique used for estimation is similar to how SIHJ accesses indexed data. In particular, to obtain join cardinality estimates, a triple pattern of a join is instantiated with intermediate results to obtain more specific triple patterns. Then, the cardinality of these triple patterns is looked up from the source index and aggregated to obtain an estimate for the size of the join. In order to reduce the cost of this process, sampling is performed to instantiate the triple pattern with only a subset of the triples:

Definition 4.12 (Join Pattern Cardinality Estimate). *Let t_i, t_j be two triple patterns joined on variable v, $\Omega_{Td}(t_i)$ and $\Omega_{Td}(t_j)$ the set of triple bindings for t_i and t_j in the source d, and $\Omega_{Td}(t_i^v)$ the specific elements in the triple bindings $\Omega_{Td}(t_i)$ that match the variable v. A cardinality estimate of a join $t_i \bowtie_v t_j$ is calculated as $card(d, t_i, t_j) = \sum_{u \in \Omega_{Td}(t_i^v)} card(d, t_j(v, u))$, where $t_j(v, u)$ denotes the instantiation of the variable v of the triple pattern t_j with the binding u, and $card(d, t_j(v, u))$ is the cardinality of the triple pattern $t_j(v, u)$.*

Example 4.4. *Let t_1, t_2 be the triple patterns from the example query that are joined on variable ?x. Let $\Omega_{Td}(t_1^{?x}) = \{ex{:}Richard, ex{:}Alice\}$ be bindings for ?x in t_1 obtained at some point during query processing. In order to obtain a cardinality estimate for $t_i \bowtie_v t_j$ for a Linked Data source d, we instantiate variable ?x in t_j with bindings from $\Omega_{Td}(t_1^{?x})$ and lookup their cardinalities in d with the source index. For example, with $d = ex{:}Alice$, the instantiated triple pattern is $t_j(?x, ex{:}Alice) = \langle ex{:}Alice, ex{:}worksAt, ?y \rangle$. For this pattern, the source index returns $card(d, t_j(?x, ex{:}Alice)) = 1$ (cf. Def. 4.5), For the other binding ex:Richard the cardinality in d is zero as there are no matches for the instantiated triple pattern $card(d, t_j(?x, ex{:}Richard))$ in ex:Alice. The cardinalities of individual bindings are then summed up to obtain the final estimate, which is 1 in this case.*

While new source scans are operations are continuously added as a result of source discovery, the re-ranking of sources is performed only when "necessary" as it also represents an overhead. For this, we employ heuristics, such as the the number of sources with outdated scores and the score confidence (the latter is dependent on the quality of cardinality estimates, which in turn is determined by the sample size).

In our implementation we prioritized early result reporting, i.e. producing results as early as possible is the optimization goal. First, for every indexed source, we calculate the TF-ISF measure for all query triple patterns. In order to produce early results the join cardinality is important. We employ both methods for join cardinality estimation: using join pattern indexes and sampling from join states obtained during query processing. Less information is available for sources that are not indexed and were only discovered during query processing. No join cardinality estimation is performed for these sources. For all sources, however, the count and type of incoming links are available. In particular, we follow *owl:sameAs* and *rdfs:seeAlso* links as well as links that have a predicate that occurs in a query triple pattern. Links with query predicates receive a higher weight than others as these are more likely to deliver results. Finally, all scores are normalized separately and then combined using a monotonic aggregation function, in this case a weighted summation.

We define several parameters that are used to influence the behavior and cost of the ranking process:

- *Invalid Score Threshold*: the score of a source is invalid if it has not been calculated before, or if new information about the source is available. A ranking is performed when the number of invalid scores passes a threshold.

- *Sample Size*: using larger samples for join size estimation will give better estimates, but are also more costly to use.

- *Resampling Threshold*: results of previous join size estimates are cached for each indexed source. Only when the corresponding hash table maintained by the join operator grows over a given threshold, join size re-estimation is performed using a new sample.

4.6 Related Work

Seminal work on Linked Data query processing [HBF09, HHK$^+$10] and some concrete techniques related to our work have been discussed throughout the chapter. Here, we summarize the relation between the proposed corrective ranking and stream-based processing techniques to database work on query optimization and processing in an distributed environment.

Federated Query Processing. Closely related to Linked Data query processing are approaches for federated query processing [SVHB04, SHH+11, GS11, AVL+11], also known as SPARQL endpoint federation. Here, source indexes are also employed to determine whether a particular federation member can answer a query or a part of a query [SVHB04, GS11]. The set of federation members is usually fixed or at least known at compile-time, similar to the top-down query evaluation strategy for Linked Data query processing. However, there is no run-time source discovery as is the case for the bottom-up and mixed strategies. Further, federation members are not only simple data sources, but usually also have query processing capabilities, meaning that less data has to be transferred over the network. In the case of Linked Data query processing, only complete sources are retrieved, making an effective source ranking mechanism much more important.

Query Optimization. One main problem of query optimization is finding the optimal join order. To do that, it is necessary to estimate their selectivity. Histograms [SSB+08] and more complex probabilistic data structures have been suggested to store and estimate selectivity information of RDF triples. In [NW09], aggregation indexes are used to improve the accuracy of selectivity estimation for joins between triple patterns. As discussed in Section 4.4.1.2, we extend these indexes to estimate the cardinality of joins for individual sources (instead of the entire source collection).

Compared to these approaches, [KBMvK10] does not perform compile-time join ordering, but optimizes the query at run-time by using chain sampling to estimate the selectivity of joins that were not yet performed. In our work, we use sampling combined with triple pattern cardinality indexes to estimate the cardinality of joins given data in a particular source.

Sideways information passing has been employed to complement compile-time optimization with a run-time decision-making technique for reusing intermediate states from one query part to prune and reduce computation of other parts [IT08, NW09]. The feedback process between query execution and source ranking employed in our approach for run-time metric refinement can be seen as a case of sideways information passing.

Query Processing in Distributed Environments. In distributed environments data is often stored in remote locations, causing delays in data access. Much research has been focused on compensating for these delays. Widely used for this are pipelineable query operators that operate on streams. As discussed in Section 4.3.2, the symmetric (index) hash join is one such operator. Another aspect of stream-based query processing is adaptivity. Query processing techniques have been proposed to adapt the query plan at run-time to deal with changing characteristics of the data. One technique is to switch among query plans at run-time [IHW04]. Other techniques use special operators, such as Eddies [AH00] and STAIRs [DH04] that adaptively route incoming tuples through a series of query operators.

Join Operators. In the database community a lot of research has been done on join operators that can produce results as soon as inputs become available without blocking and are therefore suited to high latency environments and stream processing. The symmetric hash join [WA93] was the first of a new generation of such operators. To deal with the high memory requirements of the SHJ, the XJoin operator [UF00] flushes tuples to disk if memory becomes scarce (during the arriving phase). During a reactive phase, when inputs are blocked, XJoin uses previously flushed tuples to produce further join results. During the final cleanup phase after all inputs have been consumed, the XJoin operator joins the remaining tuples that were missed during the previous phases. An important observation is that the output rate is heavily influenced by which tuples are flushed to disk, as some tuples might produce more results than others. This lead to the introduction and subsequent improvement of a flushing policy [MLA04, TYP+05, BVKD09].

The SIHJ operator proposed in this work is also based on the symmetric hash join. The memory consumption of the SIHJ could be addressed using concepts proposed for the XJoin; but this topic was not the focus of this work. Similar to XJoin, SIHJ does access locally stored data, but the purpose is different: SIHJ treats local data as an additional data source whereas XJoin and the mentioned work based on it use the disk as a cache and focus on the problem of how to use it for tuple storage when memory becomes scarce.

Adaptive Query Processing. Access Modules [RDH03] were proposed to be used in conjunction with an Eddy [AH00] to provide different data access methods (scan, index) and switch between them at run-time. Probe tuples are sent from the Eddy to the access module to request a particular subset of the data. The access module then pushes the data into the Eddy, marking the end with a special tuple. In our work we adopt the notion of an Access Module to provide access to local indexes in an asynchronous fashion.

Stream Databases. Fjords [MF02] support push- and pull-based operators and combine push-based stream processing with pull-based processing. Fjords provide a bounded queue between operators that buffers tuples between two operators so that push- and pull-based operators can be used in the same query plan. Because the queues are bounded, tuples may have to be discarded. The SIHJ operator also uses push- and pull- based processing, but in a single operator.

In all, some concepts underlying SIHJ overlap with ideas from related database work. However, there is no single operator that can be used for remote and local data where the latter is not considered as cache but an additional independent source – especially in the Linked Data setting. SIHJ fills this gap and presents a means to incorporate local data into Linked Data query processing.

Comparison. Our work is the first to provide a systematic overview of Linked Data query processing. The specific techniques proposed extend related work in database research to deal with the specific aspects of Linked Data. In particular, whereas selectivity information has been used for query optimization [NW09, SSB+08, HHK+10], it is incorporated in this work into a framework for source ranking, a task that is novel and specific to Linked Data query processing. Likewise, the ideas behind stream-based and adaptive processing [IHW04] and sideways information passing techniques [IT08] are adopted to address the specific challenges of Linked Data, to refine the query plan at run-time as new sources are discovered and the score of known sources is recalculated.

4.7 Evaluation

The evaluation consists of two parts. We first compare the proposed mixed strategy to the previously proposed top-down [HHK+10] and bottom-up [HBF09] evaluation strategies and show that the mixed strategy improves early result reporting. Second, we compare the performance of SIHJ and NBIJ in more detail on real-world datasets and also create several synthetic datasets with different characteristics to study the performance based on the proposed cost models

4.7.1 Comparison of Evaluation Strategies

In these experiments, we systematically compare the top-down, bottom-up, and mixed strategies and examine the impact of various parameters on corrective source ranking.

Queries and Data. We create a set of eight queries that can all be executed using a discovery-only approach (i.e. results can be discovered by exploring from sources mentioned in the query). These queries use popular datasets from the Linked Open Data Project, such as DBpedia, Geonames, DBLP, Semantic

Web Dog Food, data.gov, Freebase and others. Overall, during answering these queries, 6200 sources were retrieved containing 500k triples in total. All queries used in this part of the evaluation can be found in Appendix A.2.1.

Systems. We compare the approaches proposed in [HBF09] for bottom-up evaluation (BU), [HHK+10] for top-down (TD), and our implementation of the mixed (MI) strategies. All approaches were implemented on top of the same stream-based query engine. We randomly chose 25% of the sources from the complete index of TD to construct a partial index for MI. Note that these indexes are used for obtaining source descriptions, but the actual data used for query processing comes from remote hosts.

Setting. To obtain a controlled environment to systematically investigate different aspects of the discussed strategies, we simulate the Linked Data environment by creating a local and configurable cache of relevant sources as follows. We executed all queries against real Linked Data sources available on the Web, recorded all HTTP accesses and their responses (200 OK, 404 Not Found, 30x Redirect), and locally stored the obtained RDF documents. Next, we set up a proxy server on the local network that uses the previously recorded data to respond to requests by the query engine. All requests for unknown URIs were answered with a Not Found response. Because local access has lower latency than remote, we applied a configurable delay to the proxy server. This enables us to control the impact of network latency. For this evaluation we used a latency of 2s, whereas in real condition this can be much higher. The evaluation was executed on a quad-core system with Intel Xeon 2.8GHz CPUs and 8GB memory, 2GB of which were assigned to the Java VM.

The strategies under investigation vary with regard to completeness of results. The bottom-up strategy finds only sources and results that can be discovered by following links, the mixed strategy usually finds some more, and the top-down strategy finds all of them. To make the approaches comparable, we restrict the sources to those that can be considered by all strategies, i.e. those discovered by the BU strategy.

Comparison of Strategies. Table 4.1 shows the evaluation results for all queries, capturing the times needed to obtain (some percentage of the) results, and the specific times needed for source selection and ranking. The results show that for all queries, the MI and TD approaches report results earlier than BU. The benefit lies in the use of prior knowledge about sources, which helps to retrieve more relevant sources first. Less expected, MI outperformed TD in some cases (Q1,Q3,Q5,Q6,Q7,Q8) in terms of early reporting. The cause lies in the higher source selection times resulting from the use of a larger index. On average the

	BU	MI	TD	BU	MI	TD
		Q1			Q2	
25% res. [ms]	24810.5	10300.0	11038.0	10464.5	10162.0	8096.5
50% res. [ms]	43464.5	40782.0	15787.0	13080.5	17974.5	8327.0
Total [ms]	84066.5	86895.5	44323.5	21623.5	23273.0	21428.0
Src. sel. [ms]	0.0	853.0	1444.5	0.0	805.0	1280.0
Ranking [ms]	25.5	2404.0	411.0	32.5	358.0	196.5
#Sources	622.0	612.0	154.0	120.0	120.0	67.0
		Q3			Q4	
25% res. [ms]	9207.0	7900.0	11166.0	56800.5	26025.5	10969.5
50% res. [ms]	10568.0	8048.5	11391.5	56804.5	26047.0	13605.0
Total [ms]	22711.0	21944.0	21733.5	98129.0	98931.0	91352.0
Src. sel. [ms]	0.0	1211.0	1717.0	0.0	270.0	351.0
Ranking [ms]	32.0	575.5	523.0	31.0	3173.5	1358.5
#Sources	134.0	134.0	67.0	392.0	390.0	342.0
		Q5			Q6	
25% res. [ms]	16837.5	6580.5	4177.0	8222.5	4743.5	5545.0
50% res. [ms]	21578.5	11855.5	9186.0	10961.5	7650.5	5634.0
Total [ms]	29562.0	30603.5	20074.0	24086.0	20711.0	16469.0
Src. sel. [ms]	0.0	203.0	292.0	0.0	1331.0	1863.5
Ranking [ms]	25.5	283.5	414.5	23.5	292.5	335.0
#Sources	119.0	117.0	70.0	236.0	92.0	49.0
		Q7			Q8	
25% res. [ms]	7164.0	3636.5	3710.5	42029.0	33740.0	14929.0
50% res. [ms]	9578.5	6503.5	3753.0	61726.5	34704.5	14943.0
Total [ms]	24250.0	20630.0	6780.5	91405.5	91093.0	90360.5
Src. sel. [ms]	0.0	287.5	333.0	0.0	1242.0	1821.0
Ranking [ms]	25.0	281.5	181.0	25.0	2751.0	1354.5
#Sources	119.0	98.0	16.0	368.0	365.0	332.0

Table 4.1: Evaluation results for all evaluation queries: query time for producing 25%, 50% and all results, time spent performing source selection and ranking, and the total number of sources retrieved during processing.

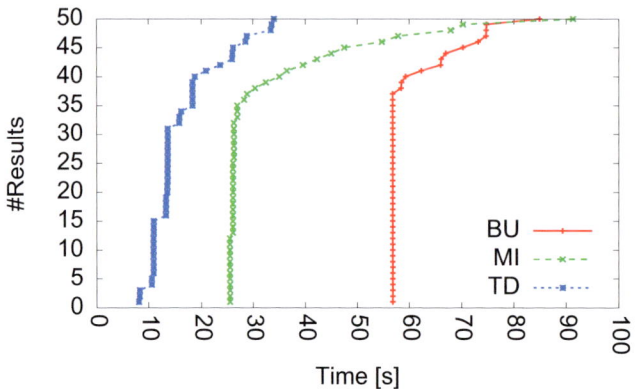

Figure 4.4: Result arrival times for query Q4. Each data point shows many results at a particular time since start of query processing.

time to retrieve 25% and 50% of the results was 8.7s and 12.8s for MI and 15.1s and 22.0s for BU, respectively. This is an improvement of about 42% in both cases, which may increase with higher, more realistic latencies where the impact of ranking will be higher.

In terms of total execution time, MI and BU are comparable, while TD is significantly faster in most cases. While TD incurs more overhead for the initial source selection because of the larger index, it enables the exclusion of sources. Due to the high network cost, not retrieving irrelevant sources results in a significant performance gain. Using only a partial index, MI is not able to restrict the number of sources that have to be retrieved. This means that in the end MI processes almost the same sources, same data and thus does the same work as BU. The additional overhead incurred by source selection, ranking and sampling lead to execution times worse than BU in some cases (Q1,Q2,Q4,Q5). However MI was able to process more useful sources and results earlier.

To better illustrate the behavior of the different approaches, Fig. 4.4 shows the arrival of results over time for query Q4. The first result for TD was produced after less than 10s and all results were reported after 33s. The difference to overall execution time of about 90s given in Table 4.1 is due to the fact that even after the final result was reported other relevant sources had to be processed, but did not contribute to the final result. This indicates that early result reporting resulting in better responsiveness is very important in some cases, where processing all sources might be very costly and not needed. Clearly, TD produced results

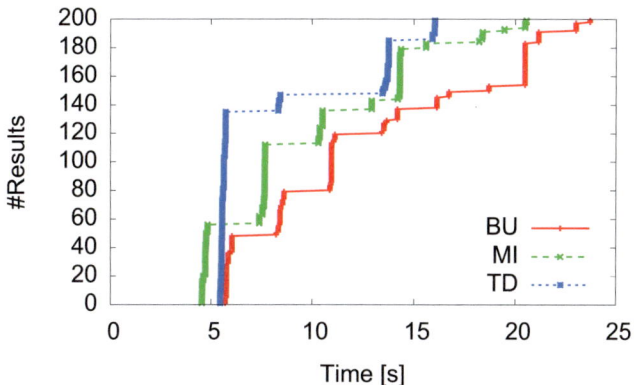

Figure 4.5: Result arrival times for query Q6. Each data point shows many results at a particular time since start of query processing.

earlier than MI, which was better than BU. A similar pattern can be seen for Q6 (Fig. 4.5), except that MI started reporting results earlier than TD, because of the lower overhead of the smaller index.

Run-time Refinements. In this part we examine the influence of various parameter configurations on sampling and ranking at run-time, as presented in Section 4.5. To separate the effect of each parameter, we vary one while setting the other parameters to default values 40% for invalid score threshold, 3 for resampling and 50 for sample size.

Invalid Score Threshold. Fig. 4.6 shows average query times for computing 5% and 25% of the results and for sampling at different invalid score thresholds from 10%-80%. With increasing threshold, ranking is performed less often, and correspondingly, times for ranking decreased. The effect of performing ranking less often was positive for computing 5% results, but no clear trend could be observed for 25% results, where the best time was observed for a threshold of 40%. Ranking is beneficial as query execution is more guided and sources that directly contribute to join results are preferred, especially by using join cardinality estimation with sampling.

Resampling Threshold. Fig 4.7a shows that times for sampling decrease with higher resampling thresholds, as sampling is performed less often. Times for 5% and 25% results are best for a threshold of 1.5 and 3, respectively. Clearly, sampling is better than no sampling, because the time to reach 25% of results is the highest when sampling is off.

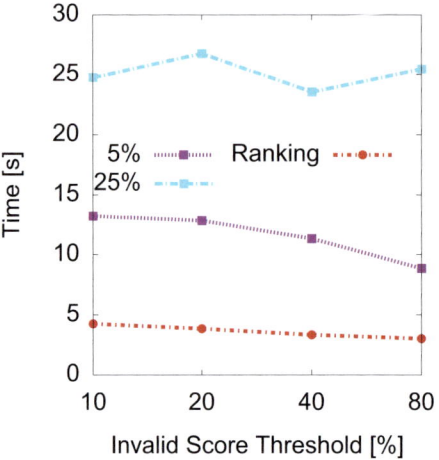

Figure 4.6: Effect of the invalid score threshold on ranking time and the average time to report 5% and 25% of all results.

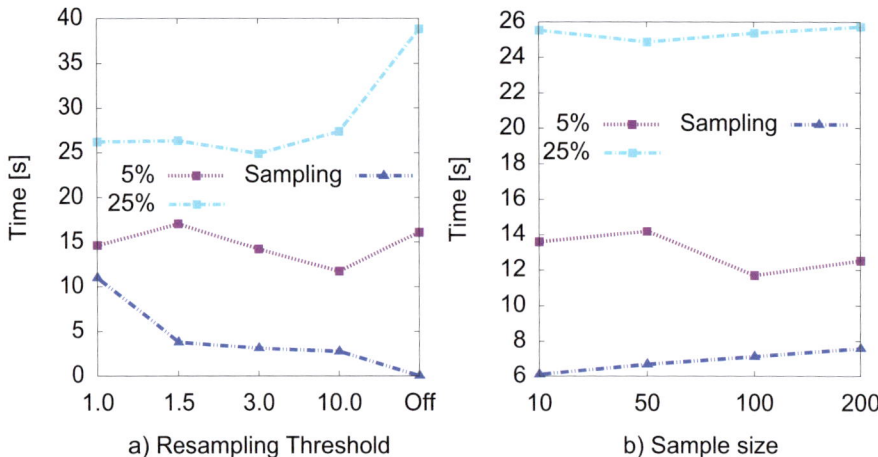

Figure 4.7: Effects of a) resampling threshold and b) sample size on sampling time and the average time to report 5% and 25% of all results..

Sample Size. Fig 4.7b shows that times for sampling increased as the sample grows larger. While sampling creates an overhead, it also provides benefits. Larger sample sizes can lead to more accurate cardinality estimates. Thus, total effect on result computation times varies. While the time for 25% results stayed largely the same, time for 5% results was clearly best for a sample size of 100.

4.7.2 Stream-based Linked Data Query Processing

In this part of the evaluation, we first use real-world datasets to compare SIHJ with NBIJ. Second, we create several synthetic datasets with different characteristics to study the performance based on the proposed cost models.

4.7.2.1 Overall Performance

Setting. In this part, we first show the benefits of stream-based query processing in comparison to non-blocking iterators. We compare an SHJ-based (i.e. SIHJ without data in local indexes) implementation (*SQ*) with the implementation of the NBIJ-based query processing (*NBI*) in the reference implementation SQUIN[1]. Both systems do not use local data and run without query optimization, and thus are comparable. Second, we compare three implementations of stream-based query processing over local and remote data to study the push- and pull-based mechanism. One is the baseline, which is a configuration of SIHJ that does not pull from the local data indexes but simply pushes all able query operators that operate on streams. As discussed in Section 4.3.2, the symmetric (index) hash join is one such operator. Another aspect of stream-based query processing is adaptirelevant data into the query plan (*SQ-L*), i.e. this corresponds to the basic solution described in Section 4.1.3. This is compared with the configuration using indexes as proposed in this work, where *SQ-I* ran without and *SQ-IB* ran with batching.

All experiments were run on a server with two Intel Xeon 2.8GHz Dual-Core CPUs and 8GB of main memory. SQUIN is a Java implementation of NBIJ, whereas the SQ systems are implemented in Scala. Both systems employ multithreading and were configured to use five threads to retrieve sources.

Dataset. The data consists of several popular Linked Data datasets, among them DBpedia, Geonames, New York Times, Semantic Web Dog Food and several life science datasets. In total, the data consists of ca. 166 million triples.

---

[1] http://www.squin.org, retrieved 2013-01-18

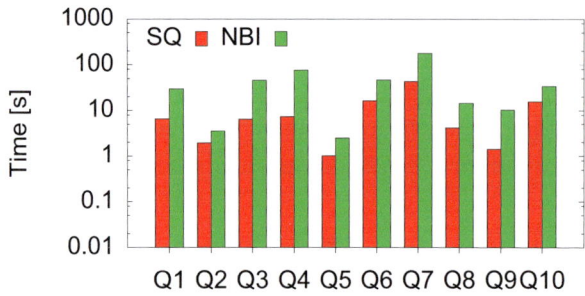

Figure 4.8: Comparison of overall query times for SQ and NBI.

For the experiments with approaches using local data, the dataset was split into remote and local data, where the randomly chosen local data accounted for 10% of the total dataset. Remote data were deployed on a CumulusRDF[2] Linked Data server on the local network so that data can be accessed using URI lookup, whereas local data were indexed using our triple store [WLP+09].

Queries. We created 10 BGP queries that cover different complexities w.r.t. query size and the number of sources retrieved during query processing. All queries used in the evaluation can be found in Appendix A.2.2. For example, Q1 retrieves the names of authors of demo papers at ISWC 2008:

```
SELECT * WHERE {
  ?p sw:isPartOf <http://data.semanticweb.org
         /conference/iswc/2008/poster_demo_proceedings> .
  ?p swrc:author ?a .   ?a rdfs:label ?n .
}
```

Results. Fig. 4.8 shows query times of the SQ and NBI systems for all ten queries. The SIHJ-based system was faster for all queries, in some cases up to an order of magnitude. On average, queries took 9699.18ms for SQ and 41704.27ms for NBI, corresponding to an improvement of 77%.

Query times for SQ-I, SQ-IB and SQ-L are presented in Fig 4.9. In all cases, SQ-I and SQ-IB outperformed SQ-L and also here, improvements were up to an order of magnitude in some cases. Note that for Q8, SQ-L ran out of memory because the amount of local data to be loaded was too large. On average, query times were 9366.39ms for SQ-IB, 9396.18ms for SQ-I and 28448.7.98ms for SQ-L. This yielded an improvement of 67% of SQ-IB over SQ-L, clearly showing

---

[2]http://code.google.com/p/cumulusrdf/, retrieved 2013 01 18

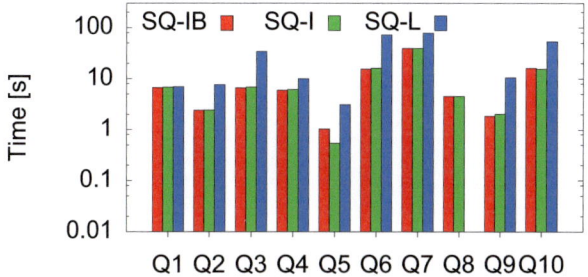

Figure 4.9: Comparison of overall query times for SQ-IB, SQ-I and SQ-L.

that using locally available indexes is beneficial. It reduced the amount of data that is loaded from disk, especially for queries with less selective triple patterns. The improvement achieved through batching could also be observed, and will be examined in more detail in the next section.

4.7.2.2 Join Operator Performance in Detail

Setting. Previously, the operators were incorporated into plans for processing entire BGP queries. Here, we focus on *join processing* using SIHJ and NBIJ. Synthetic datasets that have known characteristics are used to examine the performance of these operators in detail. We evaluated three SIHJ-approaches: SQ-IB, SQ-I and SQ. For the NBIJ operator, we used our own implementation in order to instrument the code with detailed measurement points.

  Datasets. The synthetic datasets for these experiments consist of separate sets of triples for the left and right input. The right input is split into local and remote parts, where the remote part is distributed among a number of sources. Here, we want to focus on the weight factors of the cost models and therefore keep "remote" data in memory and push it into the operator, instead of performing network access, which might lead to inconsistencies in the performance measurements. The data were generated with the following parameters: the size of the left and right input is given by a, b, respectively; ρ is the fraction of the right input that is local data; φ is the join selectivity; the number of sources for the remote part of the right input is s (the source sizes follow a normal distribution). We create several sets of datasets, where one of the parameters is changed while the others are fixed in order to examine the influence of each parameter.

  Results. We examine the parameters' effect on the weights of the cost model:

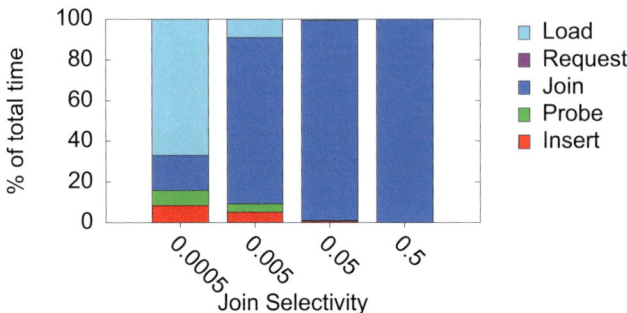

Figure 4.10: Results for varying join selectivity ($b = 10000, \rho = 0.2, s = 200, a = 10000$).

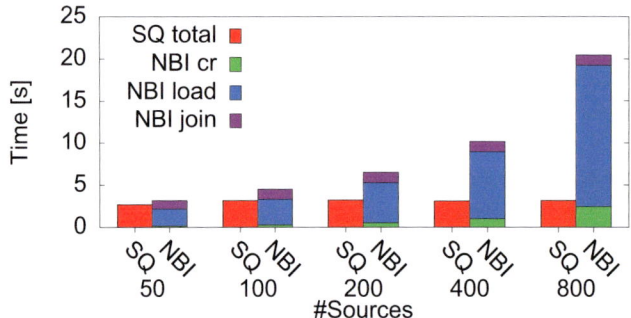

Figure 4.11: Results for varying number of sources ($b = 500000, \varphi = 0.0002, \rho = 0.2, a = 10000$).

Join Selectivity. Fig. 4.10 shows the influence of join selectivity on the different weight factors of the SIHJ cost model in terms of their relative fraction of total time measured for SQ. For joins with high selectivity ($\varphi = 0.0005$), i.e. only a small number of input tuples match other tuples to form join results, loading of local data took the largest part of total processing time. For low selectivity joins ($\varphi = 0.5$), the creation of result tuples dominated query processing. Using the cost model, this can be explained by the observation that join selectivity has impact only on the term $J \cdot \varphi |A||B|$, meaning that only the weight of result creation increases with lower join selectivities.

Number of Sources. Fig. 4.11 shows processing times for various number of sources $|G|$ for SQ and NBI. Overall, times for SQ were largely the same for all source counts, whereas the times for NBI increased with larger a number of

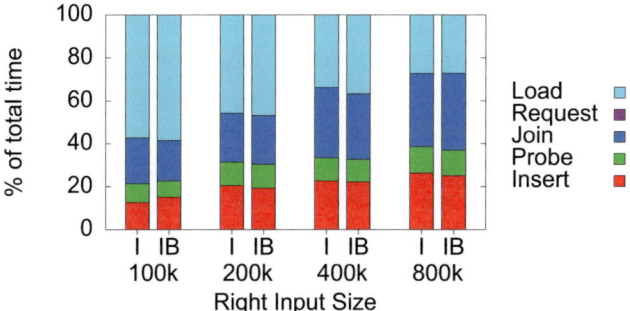

Figure 4.12: Results for varying input size ($\varphi = 0.2, \rho = 0.2, s = 200, a = 10000$).

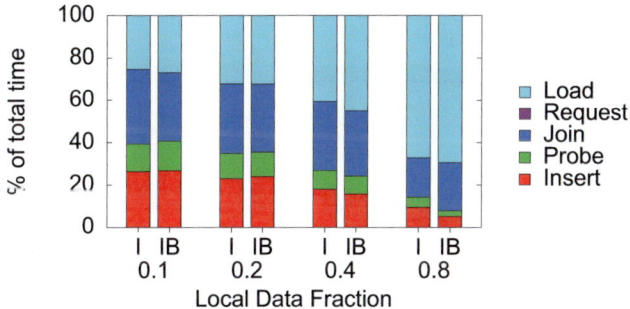

Figure 4.13: Results for varying local data fraction ($b = 500000, \varphi = 0.0002, s = 200, a = 10000$).

sources. The times for NBI were split into times for checking the requirement (cr), loading data from the in-memory graphs (load) and creating result tuples (join). Clearly, results show that both cr and load times were dependent on $|G|$. This is accounted for by the cost model, i.e. the term $|A|(P_G + |G| \cdot L)$ indicates that cost depends on P_G and $|G|$. Join times were the same because the number of results does not change with $|G|$.

Input Size. Fig. 4.12 presents the effect of input size (on the right input) on processing times of SQ-I and SQ-IB. We can see that for larger inputs, the relative time spent on loading local data decreased and the relative weights of hash table insertion and increased. This is probably due to the larger hash tables that were required for larger input sizes, introducing more overhead for rehashing when the hash tables need to be expanded.

Local Data Fraction. We examined processing times for various local data sizes. The overall number of inputs on the right input was the same, only the ratio between remote and local data changed. A value of $\rho = 0.1$ means 10% of the data is local data. Fig. 4.13 shows processing times for SQ-I and SQ-IB. With higher local data fractions, the impact of loading on total processing times is more pronounced. Whereas for a local fraction of 0.1 loading accounted for about 22% of total time, at 0.8 it accounted for over 60%. This is because with more local data, more effort was spent on using the local indexes to find triples that produce join results. Thus, less effort was needed for join, probe as well as insert. Note that as remote data were actually in-memory data, access to local data was slower than for "remote" data. Thus, loading here essentially means loading local data. In the standard setting, network access is usually slower than disk access. This means that loading would have an even larger impact.

This experiment also shows the benefits of batching, which are more pronounced for larger amounts of local data, as reflected by the smaller amounts of time spent on inserting and probing hash tables.

4.8 Conclusion

We provided a systematic analysis of the challenges and tasks, and discussed concrete strategies for linked data query processing. We proposed an implementation of the mixed strategy that mimics a realistic Linked Data scenario where some partial knowledge of Linked Data sources are available. The implementation exploits different types of knowledge available beforehand, and also, incorporates information gained during query processing to perform run-time refinements of the query plans based on a source ranking scheme. The proposed ranking scheme specifies various types of metrics, which can be combined to reach different optimization goals.

A stream-based processing technique is adopted to deal with the unpredictable nature of Linked Data access. For this, we propose a new operator, the Symmetric Index Hash Join (SIHJ) for processing queries over local and remote Linked Data in a stream-based and non-blocking fashion. We provide cost models for SIHJ and the Non-Blocking Iterator (NBIJ) previously proposed for dealing with remote Linked Data. A detailed comparison shows that while SIHJ might have larger overhead for accessing its hash tables, its cost does not depend on the number of data sources processed. The number of sources however has a large impact on the performance of NBIJ. Further, as opposed to NBIJ, SIHJ guarantees complete results w.r.t. the data retrieved during query processing.

Experiments showed that the proposed implementation leads to early reporting of results and thus, more responsive query processing. On average early results were reported 42% faster than for the bottom-up strategy. In the Linked Data scenario where response times are very high due to the large number of sources and network latency, the capability to produce early results is essential.

We performed an evaluation of the SIHJ and NBIJ operators on a real-world dataset and several synthetic datasets. We show that stream-based query processing using push-based SHJ performs on average 77% better than NBIJ-based query processing w.r.t. overall query execution time. The experiments show that using available indexes to access local data is beneficial, resulting in an average improvement of 67% compared to a baseline that simply loads all data matching query triple patterns. Detailed analyses using the synthetic datasets further shed light on the weights of the proposed cost models.

Chapter 5

Multi-Objective Query Optimization

5.1 Introduction

Existing works on Linked Data query processing, such as the work presented in the previous chapter, focus on the ranking and pruning of Linked Data sources [LT10, HHK$^+$10], or on the efficient processing of data while it is retrieved from Linked Data sources [HBF09, LT11b], i.e. joins and traversal algorithms for retrieving and processing data from sources. However, there exists no *systematic approach for query plan optimization*, especially the kind that considers both the problems of source selection and data processing in a holistic way. Further, we observe that due to long execution times resulting from the large number of sources and their high processing cost, result completeness is often no longer affordable. Instead of assuming completeness and optimizing exclusively for cost, other criteria such as relevance, quality and cardinality of results, and trustworthiness of sources may be considered. This is problematic because these criteria are not always complementary. For instance, there is an inherent trade-off between output cardinality and cost: to produce more results, we have to retrieve more sources, which in turn increases processing cost. Taking this trade-off into account, we propose a *multi-objective optimization* framework. The contributions presented in this chapter can be summarized as follows:

- Solutions related to Linked Data query processing include (a) query processing strategies [HBF09, LT10] and (b) using Linked Data summaries [HHK$^+$10] and heuristics for adaptive ranking to select only the few best sources [LT10]. However, there exists no works that systematically study the problem of query optimization, i.e. consider different query processing strategies as query plans, establishes optimality criteria for these plans, and find the optimal ones. We propose the first solution *towards a systematic optimization of Linked Data query processing* that holistically considers query processing and ranking.

- In particular, we propose an optimization framework for Linked Data query processing, which incorporates *both standard query operators* and *source selection*. That is, we propose to extend the scope of query optimization from how to process data to also include which data to process. This is to reflect the nature of Linked Data query processing, where source selection and scanning become an essential part. Further, this framework supports the *joint optimization of several objectives*, cost and output cardinality in particular.

- We propose a *dynamic programming (DP) solution* for the multi-objective optimization of this integrated process of source selection and query processing. It produces a set of Pareto-optimal query plans, which represent different trade-offs between optimization objectives. The challenge of using DP here is that after retrieval, sources can be re-used in different parts of the query, i.e. the source scan operators can be shared. Depending on the reusability of these operators, the cost of subplans may vary such that the cost function is no longer monotonic with regard to the combination of subplans. We provide a tight-bound solution, which takes this effect into account.

In this chapter we refer to concepts and definitions first introduced in Chapter 4, mainly concerning the structure of Linked Data query plans and their cost and cardinality estimation. For ease of reading, we repeat important definitions here:

Definition 4.3 (Access Plan). *Given a query Q, let $t \in Q$ be a triple pattern in Q and $D = source(t)$ be the set of sources for t. An access plan $p(t)$ for t is a tree-structured query plan constructed in the following way: (1) At the lowest level, the leaf nodes of $p(t)$ are source scan operators, one $scan_{d_i} = T^{d_i}$ for each $d_i \in D$; (2) the next level contains selection operators, one for processing the output of every scan operator, i.e. we have $\sigma_{T^{d_i}}(t)$ for every $d_i \in D$; (3) the root node is a union operator $\bigcup_t (\sigma_{T^{d_1}}(t), \ldots, \sigma_{T^{d_{|D|}}}(t))$ that combines the outputs of all selection operators for t.*

Definition 4.9 (Cardinality). *The output cardinality of the source scan operator is the same as the size of the source, i.e.* $card(scan_d) = |T^d|$. *For union, cardinality is the sum of the cardinalities of its inputs:* $card(\cup(I_1, ..., I_n)) = \sum_{i=1}^{n} card(I_i)$. *The cardinality for selection and join depends on selectivity estimates* $sel(\cdot)$, *i.e.* $card(\sigma_{T^d}(t)) = sel(t) \times |T^d|$ *and* $card(t_i \bowtie t_j) = sel(t_i \bowtie t_j) \times card(t_i) \times card(t_j)$, *respectively.*

Definition 4.10 (Cost). *Typically cost is assumed to be proportional to cardinality, which is captured as weights* $h_s, h_\sigma, h_\cup$, *and* $h_\bowtie$ *for scan, selection, union and join, respectively. The costs for scan, selection, union and join are then* $cost(scan_d) = h_s \times |T^d|$, $cost(\sigma_{T^d}(t)) = h_\sigma \times |T^d|$, $cost(\cup) = h_\cup \times card(\cup)$, *and* $cost(\bowtie) = h_\bowtie \times card(\bowtie)$, *respectively.*

5.2 Overview

A BGP query is evaluated by first obtaining bindings for each of its constituent triple patterns $q \in Q$ and then performing a series of joins between the bindings. This is done for every two patterns that share a variable, forming a *join pattern* (that variable is referred to as the *join variable*). In the Linked Data context, BGP queries are not evaluated on a single source, but, in order to obtain all results, they have to be matched against the combined Linked Data graph T^D, where relevant sources in T^D have to be retrieved on the fly.

Previous work proposes exploration-based *link traversal* [HBF09, Har11] for obtaining relevant sources. These approaches take advantage of links between sources and discover new sources at run-time by traversing these links. For this, the query is assumed to contain at least one constant that is a URI. This URI is used for retrieving the first source, representing the "entry point" to the Linked Data graph. Triples in this entry point represent links to other sources. By following these links, new sources are discovered and retrieved. When retrieved sources contain data matching the query triple patterns, they are selected and joined to produce query results.

Given the large number of Linked Data sources and their high retrieval costs, it is often not practical to process all relevant sources. Thus, existing work does not guarantee *result completeness* but instead, ranks and processes the few best sources [HHK+10, LT10]. The on-the-fly source exploration mentioned above has been combined with compile-time [HHK+10] and adaptive ranking of sources [LT10] (see also Chapter 4). The idea is that, whenever statistics about sources are available, they can be exploited to find sources more effectively than zero-knowledge on-the-fly exploration. The most common statistics used is a *source index*, which maps a triple pattern t to URIs representing sources that contain results for t, i.e. $source(t) = \{d | d \in D \land, \Omega_{T_d}(t) \neq \emptyset\}$. Often, the source index used by existing work not only returns the URIs but also selectivity information for triple and join patterns. These statistics are collected from previously explored sources or catalogs such as the Data Hub[1].

These existing works address the subproblems of (a) how to process SPARQL BGP queries in the Linked Data setting [HBF09, LT10], i.e. when only URI lookups are available, and (b) how to obtain Linked Data summaries and statistics to select relevant sources [HHK+10, LT10]. We focus on the *compile-time optimization of Linked Data query processing*, given the statistics acquired and stored in the source index. Compared to these works, we propose a holistic solution to optimization that considers both the subproblems of (a) and (b), i.e. selecting and retrieving data from the sources as well as matching the query against this data to produce results. Further, this optimization is performed w.r.t. multiple objectives, which is solved through a novel DP solution. The optimization performed is done at compile-time, which as future work, can be integrated with adaptive optimization [LT10] that may also considers the exploration and retrieval of additional sources and computing their statistics on-the-fly.

5.3 Pareto-optimal Query Plans

In standard cost-based optimization, completeness is assumed such that all results have to be computed. Optimality in this case is defined with respect to processing cost, and the goal is to find plans that are cost-optimal, i.e. to produce all results at lowest cost. Completeness is often not practical in Linked Data query processing and existing approaches select only a few best sources [HHK+10, LT10] to terminate early. Not only cost but also the number of results and other aspects such as the trustworthiness of sources and the quality of data may play an important role. This is especially the case when Linked Data query processing is used in batch mode to crawl for data that meets certain criteria.

Multi-objective optimization can be used to support this. For a query Q, the goal is to compute the Pareto-optimal set of query plans that represents different trade-offs between multiple objectives. For clarity of presentation, we will focus on the two main objectives of maximizing output cardinality, $card(\cdot)$, and

---

[1] http://datahub.io/, retrieved 2013-01-18

processing cost, $cost(\cdot)$. The Pareto-optimal set of solutions is defined using a *dominance* relation that incorporates the multiple objectives. A query plan is considered to dominate another plan, if it is at least as good in all objectives and better in at least one objective:

Definition 5.1 (Dominance). *Given two query plans p_1 and p_2, p_1 dominates p_2 ($p_1 > p_2$) if both the cost and cardinality of p_1 are "better" or equal to the cost and cardinality of p_2, and either the cost or cardinality is strictly "better" than the cost or cardinality of p_2, i.e. $cost(p_1) \leq cost(p_2) \wedge card(p_1) \geq card(p_2) \wedge ((cost(p_1) < cost(p_2)) \vee card(p_1) > card(p_2)) \Rightarrow p_1 > p_2$.*

Definition 5.2 (Pareto Optimal Plans). *Given a query Q and a set of query plans $P(Q)$ for Q, the Pareto-optimal set $P^*(Q) \subseteq P(Q)$ comprises all plans that are not dominated by any other plan in $P(Q)$, i.e. $P^*(Q) = \{p_i \in P(Q) | \neg \exists p_j \in P(Q), p_j > p_i\}$. We denote the set of dominated plans as $P^-(Q) = P(Q) \setminus P^*(Q)$.*

5.4 Dynamic Programming-based Solution

In this section we propose a solution to the multi-objective Linked Data query optimization problem based on the original dynamic programming (DP) algorithm [SAC$^+$79]. The original DP algorithm for query optimization works in a bottom-up fashion, constructing the query plan from the leaves, which are table scan operators to access relations. DP is used to deal with the exponentially large search space of possible query plans. It takes advantage of the *optimal substructure* of the problem, i.e. the optimal plan can be constructed from optimal subplans such that non-optimal subplans can be discarded during the process to reduce the search space.

For optimizing Linked Data query processing, we propose to construct access plans $P(t)$ for every triple pattern $t \in Q$. These *atomic plans* are then successively combined using join operators to create *composite plans* for larger subexpressions $T \subseteq Q$. For instance, to construct a query plan for the expression $T = t_1 \bowtie t_2$, the optimizer may consider all possible pairs $\{(p_1, p_2) | p_1 \in P(t_1), p_2 \in P(t_2)\}$ as possible combinations of plans. When combining two plans p_1, p_2 to form a new plan p, we write $p = \text{cmb}(p_1, p_2)$. At each stage, the optimizer reduces candidate subplans by discarding those that cannot be part of an optimal solution. That is, before constructing plans for larger subexpressions the optimizer creates $P^*(T) \subseteq P(T)$ for every subexpression T.

In the following, we firstly discuss how to use existing techniques to estimate the optimality of subplans for any expressions $T \subseteq Q$. We note that the focus of this work is not to obtain accurate cost and cardinality estimates but a DP solution that produces optimal plans by combining subplans (given their estimates). We discuss the main problems that arise when using DP for our problem. Firstly, we need to establish the *comparability of plans*, given there are multiple objectives. Further, because query plans are no longer required to produce all results, a *relaxation of the comparability constraint* is needed. Also, there is the effect of *operator sharing*. We will establish tight bounds on subplans' costs to deal with this effect and prove that the resulting multi-objective query optimization problem still has optimal substructure such that the proposed solution yields the Pareto-optimal solution.

5.4.1 Comparability

Comparability is defined as an equivalence relation $\sim$ over plans. It determines which plans are comparable, based on which the optimizer decides which plans are suboptimal and then prunes all but the optimal plans for each equivalence class induced by $\sim$.

In the traditional setting, atomic operators and plans are *comparable when they produce the same results*. This comparability relation is applicable there because input relations are fixed given the query such that operators used to process them produce the same output and vary only with regard to cost, i.e. plans are compared only w.r.t. cost because they produced the same results. The optimizer only chooses how to process data (e.g. table or index scan) based on cost estimates. In Linked Data query processing, however, the selection of sources (represented by source scan operators) is part of query optimization. Thus, the optimizer decides both what and how data shall be processed, i.e. plans have to be compared w.r.t. cost and the results they produce. If we apply the comparability concept as defined previously, each unique combination of source scan operators may yield different results and thus, constitutes a separate equivalence class of query plans. This limits the number of comparable plans and hence, those that can be pruned.

However, we note that given the objectives here are cardinality and cost, we are not interested in which results but how many results will be produced. Accordingly, a relaxation of this comparability relation can be employed that enables the optimizer to prune plans more aggressively.

Definition 5.3. *Two query plans* p_i, p_j *are* comparable *if they produce results for the same expression, i.e.* $p_i(T_i) \sim p_j(T_j)$ *if* $T_i = T_j$.

This relaxation means that plans can be compared even when they do not produce exactly the same results. The equivalence class of comparable plans is enlarged to include all plans that produce the same type of results (bindings for the same pattern). As a consequence, the query can be decomposed into subpatterns, and plans constructed for subpatterns can compared w.r.t. the objectives.

5.4.2 Monotonicity and Dominance

Every objective can be reflected by a scoring function. When combining plans for subpatterns to successively cover a larger part of the query, the scores of these subplans have to aggregated. For pruning suboptimal plans, a central requirement for the DP solution is that the scoring function must be *monotonic* with respect to plan combination. Only then, it can be guaranteed that some subplans can be safely pruned because they cannot be part of optimal plans. We now discuss monotonicity w.r.t. the scoring functions for the objectives of cost and cardinality, and show under which conditions pruning is possible.

Cardinality. Atomic plans are combined to capture joins between results. The monotonicity of the cardinality scoring function can be established because the cardinality function for join is monotonic:

Lemma 5.1. *Given a query* Q, *let* $T, T' \subset Q$ *be two subexpressions of* Q, *such that* $T \cap T' = \emptyset$. *Let* $p_1, p_2 \in P(T)$ *and* $p' \in P(T')$ *be plans for* T *and* T'. *Then we have* $card(p_1) \leq card(p_2) \Rightarrow card(\text{cmb}(p_1, p')) \leq card(\text{cmb}(p_2, p'))$.

Proof. The combination above captures the expression $T \bowtie T'$. Based on the definition of $card(T \bowtie T')$, we write the condition in the lemma as $card(p_1) \leq card(p_2) \Rightarrow card(p_1) \times card(p') \times sel(T \bowtie T') \leq card(p_2) \times card(p') \times sel(T \bowtie T')$. This is true due to monotonicity of multiplication. □

Cost. For cost estimation, operator sharing is taken into account. Because the costs of first and subsequent scans vary, the cost of the source scan operator changes when a plan is combined with another plan that shares that operator. Suppose we have two plans p, p' for the subexpression $T \subset Q$ and $cost(p) > cost(p')$, and a plan p_t for a triple pattern t such that $Q = T \cup t$. The optimizer would consider p' to be the optimal plan for T and discard p to form $P^*(T) =$

$\{p'\}$. Now, due to operator sharing it is possible that the cost of the combination of two plans is less than the sum of the cost of the two combined plans, i.e. it is possible that $cost(\text{cmb}(p, p_t)) < cost(\text{cmb}(p', p_t))$ if p and p_t share the same source such that the cost of p_t when combined with p is much lower than the cost of p_t that is combined with p'. In this case, p' is not part of $P^*(T)$.

Cost Bounds for Partial Plans. In order to take this effect of operator sharing into account when calculating the cost of a partial plan p, we define upper and lower bounds for p based on larger plans that use p as subplans:

Definition 5.4 (Lower and Upper Bound Cost). *Given a query Q, the subexpressions $T \subset Q$, $T' = Q \setminus T$, a plan $p \in P(T)$, and let $P^p(Q) \subseteq P(Q)$ be the set of all plans for Q that are constructed as combinations of p and plans in $P(T')$: $P^p(Q) = \{\text{cmb}(p, p') | p' \in P(T')\}$. Then, we have* lower bound cost *for p as $cost_L^Q(p) = MIN\{cost(\text{cmb}(p, p')) | \text{cmb}(p, p') \in P^p(Q)\}$ and* upper bound cost *for p as $cost_U^Q(p) = MAX\{cost(\text{cmb}(p, p')) | \text{cmb}(p, p') \in P^p(Q)\}$.*

Intuitively, a plan p_i for a subexpression T of Q is "worse" in terms of cost than another plan p_j for T, if all plans for Q that are based on p_i have higher cost than all plans for Q that are based on p_j, i.e. if $cost_L^Q(p_i) > cost_U^Q(p_j)$. Based on these bounds, we can establish the monotonicity of plan cost with respect to plan combination as follows:

Lemma 5.2. *Let $T, T' \subset Q$ be two subexpressions of Q such that $T \cap T' = \emptyset$, and $p_1, p_2 \in P(T)$ and $p' \in P(T')$ be plans for T and T', respectively. We have*

$$cost_U^Q(p_1) \leq cost_L^Q(p_2) \Rightarrow cost_U^Q(\text{cmb}(p_1, p')) \leq cost_L^Q(\text{cmb}(p_2, p'))$$

Proof. Any plan for Q that is constructed as the combination $p_1' = \text{cmb}(p_1, p')$, i.e. any plan in $P^{p_1'}(Q)$, is also a p_1-combination (because p_1' is constructed based on p_1) such that $P^{p_1'}(Q) \subseteq P^{p_1}(Q)$ and thus, $cost_U^Q(p_1') \leq cost_U^Q(p_1)$. Analogously, for p_2 and $p_2' = \text{cmb}(p_2, p')$, we have $cost_L^Q(p_2') \geq cost_L^Q(p_2)$. Hence, $cost_U^Q(p_1) \leq cost_L^Q(p_2) \Rightarrow cost_U^Q(p_1') \leq cost_L^Q(p_2')$. $\qquad\square$

Based on these results for cardinality and cost monotonicity, we now refine the dominance relation to make it applicable to subplans, i.e. plans for strict subexpressions of Q:

Theorem 5.1. *Given a query Q, a subexpression $T \subset Q$ and two comparable plans $p_1 \sim p_2$ for T, $p_1 > p_2$ if $card(p_1) \geq card(p_2) \wedge cost_U^Q(p_1) \leq cost_L^Q(p_2) \wedge (card(p_1) > card(p_2) \vee cost_U^Q(p_1) < cost_L^Q(p_2))$.*

This is the main result needed for pruning. A subplan is suboptimal and thus can be pruned if it is dominated in the sense specified above.

Cost Bound Estimation. A basic strategy to compute the lower and upper bounds of a plan p is to construct all plans based on p. This is of course very cost intensive and defeats the purpose of pruning. Observe that for pruning, we need only to compare the upper and lower bounds between pairs of plans p_1, p_2 for the subexpression $T \subset Q$. Given p_1, p_2 can be pruned if it has higher cost when used to process T, and further, when its *benefit* that may arise when processing other parts of the query cannot outweigh this difference in cost. If such a benefit exists, it can be completely attributed to operator sharing. Hence, for the efficient estimation of bounds, we propose to focus on the maximal benefit that is achievable through operator sharing. As the source scan is the only shareable operator, we derive the maximal benefit of one plan p_2 compared to another p_1 through a comparison of their source scan operators. In particular, only those source scans captured by p_2 and not covered by p_1 (i.e. the additional benefit achievable with p_2) have to be considered:

Definition 5.5 (Maximal Benefit). *Given a query Q and two query plans $p_1, p_2 \in P(T), T \subset Q$, let D_{p_1}, D_{p_2} be the sets of sources (respectively the source scan operators) used by p_1 and p_2, respectively, D'_{p_2} be the set of sources used by p_2 not covered by p_1, i.e. $D'_{p_2} = D_{p_2} \setminus D_{p_1}$ and Q' be the set of triple patterns not covered by p_1 and p_2, i.e. $Q' = Q \setminus T$, the maximal benefit of p_2 given p_1 is $mb(p_2|p_1) = \sum_{t \in Q'} \sum_{d \in source(t), d \in D'_{p_2}} (1 - b) \cdot cost_1(scan_d)$, where b is the sharing benefit and $cost_1(scan_d)$ is the cost for the first scan of d (see Section 4.4.2).*

Lemma 5.3. *Given a query Q, a subexpression $T \subset Q$ and two plans p_1, p_2, if $cost(p_1) \leq cost(p_2) - mb(p_2|p_1)$ then $cost_U^Q(p_1) \leq cost_L^Q(p_2)$.*

Proof. As plans p_1, p_2 are both in $P(T)$ they both can be combined with the same set of plans for $P(Q \setminus T)$, meaning that the only difference in final plans built for p_1 and p_2 lies in the shared source scan operators. If we now know that p_1 has lower cost than p_2 even when the maximal benefit for p_2 obtainable from operator sharing is considered, then the upper bound cost $cost_U^Q(p_1)$ is also lower than $cost_L^Q(p_2)$. □

Based on these bounds defined w.r.t. the maximal benefit, we finally obtain the following dominance relation:

Theorem 5.2. *Given a query Q, a subexpression $T \subset Q$ and two plans $p_1 \sim p_2 \in P(T)$, $p_1 > p_2$ if $card(p_1) \geq card(p_2) \wedge cost(p_1) \leq cost(p_2) - mb(p_2|p_1) \wedge (card(p_1) > card(p_2) \vee cost(p_1) < cost(p_2) - mb(p_2|p_1))$.*

5.4.3 Pareto-optimality

The goal of the optimizer in Linked Data query processing is to find the Pareto-set of query plans, while pruning as many plans as possible at each step. We now show that pruning suboptimal plans based on the comparability and dominance relations established previously yields the complete Pareto set $P^*(Q)$, i.e. the proposed multi-objective optimization still has optimal substructure. Given the decomposition of Q into the subproblems $T \subset Q$, we construct $P^*(Q)$ as a combination of optimal subsolutions $P^*(T)$. This means a non-optimal solution for a subproblem T must not be part of an optimal solution for Q:

Theorem 5.3. *Given a query Q and two subexpressions $T_1, T_2 \subseteq Q$ with $T_1 \cap T_2 = \emptyset$, the set of optimal plans for $T_1 \cup T_2$ can be constructed from optimal plans for T_1, T_2, i.e. $P^*(T_1 \cup T_2) \subseteq \{\text{cmb}(p_1, p_2) | p_1 \in P^*(T_1), p_2 \in P^*(T_2)\}$.*

Proof. We prove this by contradiction: Let $p^* \in P^*(T_1 \cup T_2)$ be a plan that is a combination of a dominated plan for T_1 and a non-dominated plan for T_2, i.e. $p^* = \text{cmb}(p_1^-, p_2^*), p_1^- \in P^-(T_1), p_2^* \in P^*(T_2)$. This means, there must be a non-dominated plan $p_1^* \in P^*(T_1)$ that dominates p_1^-, but the combination of p_1^* with p_2^* is dominated by the combination of p_1^- and p_2^*:

$$\exists p_1^* \in P^*(T_1) : \text{cmb}(p_1^-, p_2^*) \text{ dominates } \text{cmb}(p_1^*, p_2^*)$$

Given p_1^* dominates p_1^- and $\text{cmb}(p_1^-, p_2^*)$ dominates $\text{cmb}(p_1^*, p_2^*)$, it follows from the established dominance relation that (without loss of generality, we use strictly lesser/greater relations):

$$card(p_1^-) < card(p_1^*) \wedge card(\text{cmb}(p_1^-, p_2^*)) > card(\text{cmb}(p_1^*, p_2^*))$$
$$cost_L^Q(p_1^-) > cost_U^Q(p_1^*) \wedge cost_U^Q(\text{cmb}(p_1^-, p_2^*)) < cost_L^Q(\text{cmb}(p_1^*, p_2^*))$$

However, this contradicts with the monotonicity property for cost, because $cost_L^Q(p_1^-) > cost_U^Q(p_1^*)$, but $cost_U^Q(\text{cmb}(p_1^-, p_2^*)) < cost_L^Q(\text{cmb}(p_1^*, p_2^*))$. Analogously, a contradiction also follows from the monotonicity of cardinality. With regard to our original proposition, this means that there is no plan $p^* \in P^*(T_1 \cup T_2)$, such that p^* is a combination of a dominated plan p_1^- and a non-dominated plan

p_2^*. This obviously also holds true when p^* is a combination of two dominated plans. Thus, all $p^* \in P^*(T_1 \cup T_2)$ must be combinations of non-dominated plans in $P^*(T_1)$ and $P^*(T_2)$ and therefore $P^*(T_1 \cup T_2)$. $\qquad\square$

5.4.4 Optimizer Algorithm

In this section we present a DP algorithm that exploits the previously established theoretical results to perform multi-objective Linked Data query optimization. The proposed solution shown in Alg. 5.1 takes the proposed structure of Linked Data plans into account and uses Pareto-optimality to prune plans according to the optimization objectives.

Algorithm 5.1: PLANGEN(Q)

Input: Query $Q = \{t_1, \ldots, t_n\}$
Output: Pareto-optimal query plans $P^*(Q)$

1 **foreach** $t \in Q$ **do**
2 $\quad$ $S \leftarrow \{\cup(\{\sigma_{T^d}(t)|d \in D\})|D \in \mathcal{P}(source(t))\}$
3 $\quad$ $P^*(t) \leftarrow \{p \in S | \nexists p' \in S : p' > p\}$
4 **for** $i \leftarrow 2$ **to** $|Q|$ **do**
5 $\quad$ **foreach** $T \subseteq Q$ such that $|T| = i$ **do**
6 $\quad\quad$ **foreach** $t \in T$ **do**
7 $\quad\quad\quad$ $S \leftarrow S \cup \{cmb(p_1, p_2)|p_1 \in P^*(t), p_2 \in P^*(T \setminus t)\}$
8 $\quad\quad$ $P^*(T) \leftarrow \{p \in S | \nexists p' \in S : p' > p\}$
9 **return** $P^*(Q)$

In the first step, access plans for single triple patterns are created (lines 1-3). For each triple pattern t in Q, relevant sources are determined using the source index. As we need to consider all possible combinations of sources, we create the power set $\mathcal{P}(source(t))$ of all sources (line 2). For each member D of the power set, we create an access plan, consisting of a scan and a selection operator $\sigma_{T^d}(t)$ for each source $d \in D$ and a single union operator $\cup$ that has the selection operators as input. S then contains a set of access plans, one for each combination of relevant sources. From this set of comparable plans (they cover the same pattern t), we then select only the non-dominated access plans and store them in $P^*(t)$ (line 3).

During the next iterations (line 4-8), previously created plans are combined until all query triple patterns are covered. For iteration i, we select all subsets $T \subseteq Q$ with $|T| = i$. For each $t \in T$ the algorithm creates all possible combinations between the Pareto-optimal plans for t and $T \setminus t$ (line 7). All these plans are stored in S. They are comparable since they cover the same triple patterns T. Finally, only the non-dominated plans from S are selected and stored in $P^*(T)$ (line 8). After the last iteration, $P^*(Q)$ contains all the Pareto-optimal plans for Q (line 9).

Complexity. The join order optimization problem has been shown to be NP-complete [VM96] and the classic DP algorithm for query optimization has a time complexity of $O(3^n)$ [KS00], where n is the number of relations (triple patterns in the case of Linked Data queries) to be joined. Our approach for multi-objective query optimization adds the dimension of source selection to the query optimization problem. Given a set of $|D|$ sources, we can think of the problem as, in worst case, creating a query plan for each unique combination of sources, of which there are $2^{|D|}$, leading to a complexity of $O(2^{|D|} \cdot 3^n)$. This theoretical worst case complexity does not change in the multi-objective case. However in practice, the number of plans that can be pruned at every iteration can be expected to be much larger in the single-objective case, compared to the multi-objective case. One strategy to deal with that is to approximate the bounds that we have established. In the experiment, we study one basic approximation, which instead of the cost bounds, use actual cost for pruning. That is, it ignores the bounds and accepts the discussed cases where subplans, which become non-optimal through operator sharing, may be part of the final result.

5.5 Related Work

We have reviewed works in the area of *Linked Data query processing* and showed that the proposed solution is the first work towards optimizing the entire querying process, from source selection to processing data retrieved from sources. Also, the differences to *federated query processing* have been discussed: there are no endpoints that can answer parts of the structured query such that the problem here is not the composition of views [PH01] or joined results retrieved from endpoints but the selection of sources and the processing of the entire sources' content. We will now discuss other directions of related work.

Source Selection. The problem of selecting relevant sources has been a topic in data integration research [LRO96]. In this setting, sources are described not only by their content, but also their capabilities. Algorithms have been proposed to efficiently perform source selection by using the source characteristics to prune the search space. However, in these approaches, source selection here is a separate step that is decoupled from query optimization. In [NK01] the authors recognize that the decoupling of source selection and query optimization leads to overall sub-optimal plans and propose a solution that optimizes not only for cost but also coverage. A (weighted) utility function is proposed to combine them into a single measure. Then, classic query optimization algorithms, such as DP, can be applied. Finding the right utility function is generally known to be difficult, especially when many objectives have to be considered. Instead, we follow a different direction, employing multi-objective optimization to produce Pareto-optimal plans that represent different trade-offs between the objectives.

Query Optimization and Processing. There is a large amount of database research on query optimization. The dynamic programming solution was first proposed in [SAC$^+$79] and remains a popular approach for query optimization [MN08]. There is also work on approximating the DP approach to increase run-time performance in the context of distributed query processing [KS00]. Efficiently generating optimal DAG-shaped query plans when performing operator sharing has been addressed in [Neu05]. In our work we also uses operator sharing for dealing with Linked Data sources. However, the effect of this is different in our multi-objective optimization problem, where we introduce special bounds needed for pruning. The efficient execution of DAG-shaped plans was discussed in [Neu05], where several approaches were proposed, including the push-based execution that is used in our implementation.

Top-k Processing. Top-k query processing focuses on the most important (top-k) answers to a given query [IBS08]. It has been studied from different angles, resulting in different techniques for joins and query optimization and indexing methods [IBS08]. Multi-objective optimization is different from top-k processing in that instead of a fixed number of results, a range of plans representing different trade-offs is computed.

Multi-objective Query Optimization. To the best of our knowledge, [PY01] is the only work addressing multi-objective query optimization, where it is studied in the context of Mariposa [SAL$^+$96], a wide-area database. The optimizer splits the query tree into subqueries and then obtains bids from participating sites that specify a delay and cost for delivering the result of a subquery. The goal of the proposed multi-objective optimizer [PY01] is to obtain the Pareto optimal set of plans with respect to cost and delay. While dynamic programming is also employed to show that the Pareto set can be computed in polynomial time, it is not based on the classic DP algorithm [SAC+79]. The problem studied there is different because there is only a single query operation tree and for each operation node, the optimizer has a list of alternatives for implementing the operation. In contrast, the classic DP algorithm does not consider only a single query tree (i.e. a single order of operations), but considers all possible query trees to construct optimal plans in a bottom-up fashion and. Our work extends the classic DP algorithm to support multi-objective query optimization.

Skyline Queries. The skyline operation finds the Pareto set from a potentially large set of points and is used in conjunction with standard relational algebra [BKS01]. While our approach also aims at the Pareto set, the problem is not computing results but query plans. As a result, the relaxed comparability, the conditions under which the scoring functions are monotonic, the estimation of bounds as well as the proposed DP algorithm are specific to our problem setting.

5.6 Evaluation

Existing works in data integration [LRO96] and Linked Data query processing [HHK+10, LT10] perform source ranking without joint optimization. We implement source ranking to select sources first and then use the proposed DP solution to optimize cost. This baseline implements single-objective optimization where source selection and query processing is decoupled. Based on this, we study the effect of the holistic treatment of source selection and query processing and the multi-objective optimization. The experiment shows that compared to our work, the baseline yields only a small fraction of Pareto-optimal plans, and the resulting suboptimal plans lead to much higher cost when producing the same number of results.

5.6.1 Systems

Our Approach. We implemented three versions of our approach. The first version (DP) implements all the proposed techniques to produce the complete set of Pareto-optimal plans. The second version (DPU) also uses operator sharing. However, it uses directly the cost instead of the lower and upper bounds that have been established to guarantee monotonicity of cost in the case of operator sharing. Thus, while DPU might compromise Pareto-optimality, it can prune more aggressively and thus, is expected to exhibit better performance than DP. In fact, DPU can be seen as an approximate version of DP that simply uses actual cost as an approximate estimate for bounds. With this baseline, we aim to study the positive effect of using the proposed bounds on Pareto-optimality, and to find out whether the proposed technique for estimating the bounds is effective in reducing the overhead resulting from that. The third version (DPS) does not use operator sharing at all, i.e. if a source is used for more than one triple pattern it is retrieved multiple times. We use DPS to study the effect of operator sharing. We use different settings for b to study the effect of operator sharing. For example, with $b = 0.8$ the optimizer assumes that 80% of the source scan cost is saved, i.e. subsequent reads cost only 20% of the first read.

Baselines. Existing Linked Data approaches implement ad-hoc source ranking to select few best sources [HHK+10, LT10], and then process these sources without joint query optimization. This processing represents one single plan, whose optimality is unknown. We implement existing source ranking strategies [HHK+10, LT10] (RK) and a random source selection strategy (RD). Then, given the selected sources, we apply our DP solution on top but only to optimize the cost. Instead of one single cost-optimized plan, our approach yields a Pareto-set of query plans. Thus, to make systems comparable, we extend these baselines to obtain cost-optimized plans for different combinations of sources.

Both baselines first retrieve all relevant sources D for a query Q from the source index, i.e. $D = \bigcup_{t \in Q} source(t)$. Then, a set $\mathcal{D}$ containing $|D|$ different subsets of D, each with size in the range $[1, |D|]$ is created. The baselines differ in how these subsets are selected.

- Baseline RD randomly selects the $|D|$ subsets.

- Baseline RK first ranks sources in D by the number of contained triples that match query triple patterns, calculated as $score(d) = \sum_{t \in q} card_d(t)$. The subsets are created by starting with the highest ranked source and then successively adding sources in the order of their rank to obtain $|D|$ subsets in total.

Each element in $\mathcal{D}$ represents a combination of sources. For each of them, a cost-optimized query plan is created. As a result, we have a set of plans, which vary in the number of results as well as cost.

Note that our approach not only selects sources (source scan operators) but also for which triple patterns these sources are used (selection operators), while the sources selected for the baselines are used for all triple patterns. In order to

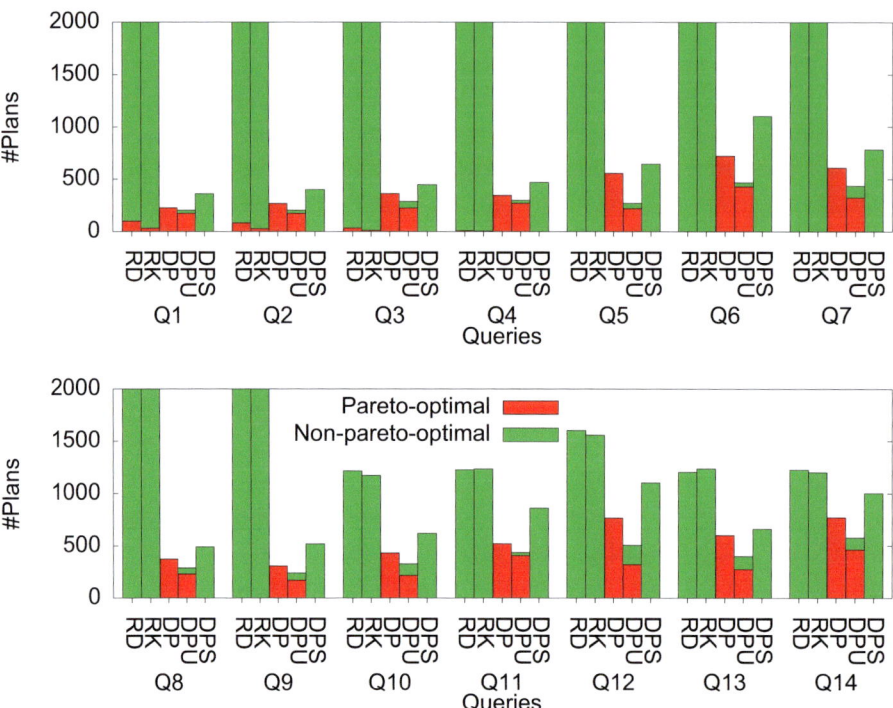

Figure 5.1: Number of Pareto-optimal and non-pareto-optimal plans for all queries and systems ($b = 0.8, m = 2000$).

obtain even more plans that further vary in the selection operators used, we create an additional set of m plans for each previously created plan of the baselines RK and RD by randomly removing a subset of the inputs (selection operators) from their access plans. In particular, to create a new plan from an existing plan, for each union that is root of an access plan, we remove a random subset of its input (selection) operators. If the source scan operator that is input for a removed selection operator is not shared it is also removed from the plan. Any invalid plans that are constructed in this way (e.g., all inputs of an union might have been) are discarded. In the end, each baseline has at most $m \cdot |D|$ plans that vary in terms of results (of which only $|D|$ sets of plans vary in cost).

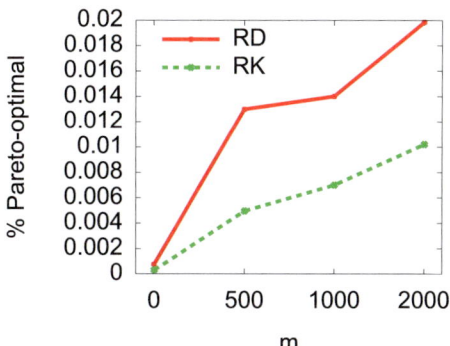

Figure 5.2: Pareto-optimal fraction for RD, RK for different value of m ($b = 0.8$).

5.6.2 Setting

Extending the Linked Data query set published in the recent benchmark [SGH$^+$11], we obtain 14 BGP queries that have non-empty results. The result size is in the range from 1 to 836. We use queries that largely differ in the number of results to discuss the effect of Pareto-optimality on the cost-cardinality trade-off in detail. These queries belong to different classes of complexity, which is reflected in the number of triple patterns. For the classes of 3, 4 and 5 patterns, we have 4, 5, and 5 queries, respectively. All queries used in the evaluation can be found in Appendix A.2.3.

As data, we use real-world Linked Data on the Web. Processing the 14 queries against Linked Data sources on the Web involves a total of 1,909,109 triples from 516,293 sources capturing information from popular datasets such as DBpedia, Freebase, and New York Times.

This dataset was then indexed in a source index and used for the evaluation. As the source index contained too many sources for the multi-objective optimization approach to deal with, we randomly aggregated sources during the creation of access plans into a set of $k = 5$ virtual sources. The size of the virtual sources follows a Zipf distribution with exponent 2. During this process, we observed that network latency greatly varies. In order to establish a controlled environment and ensure the repeatability of the experiments, we simulate source loading to obtain a fixed delay of 1.5s that was observed to be representative of real Linked Data sources [LT10]. We also experimented with different delays, but performance differences between systems were however not sensitive to these settings.

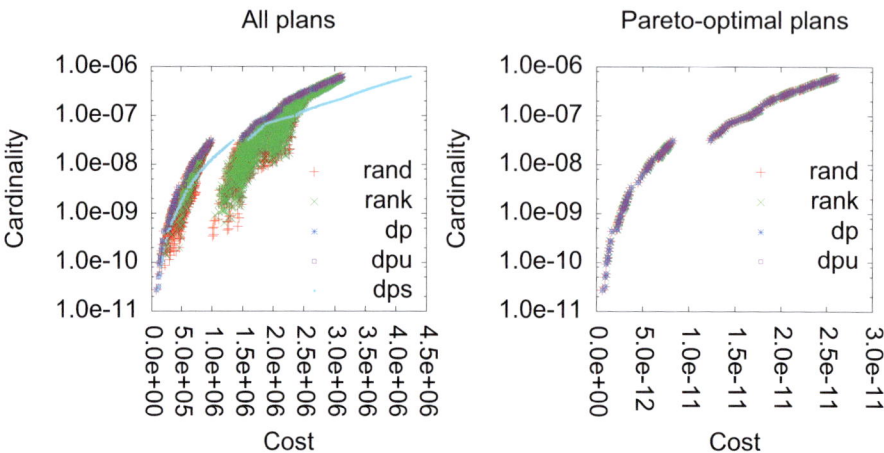

Figure 5.3: Plans for query Q1 on all systems: a) all plans and b) pareto-optimal plans ($b = 0.8, m = 2000$). Each data point represents the cardinality and cost of a query plan generated by the respective approach.

All systems were implemented in Java. All experiments were executed on a system with a 2.4 GHz Intel Core 2 Duo processor, 4GB RAM (of which 1GB was assigned to the Java VM), and a Crucial m4 128GB SSD.

5.6.3 Results

Pareto-optimality. Fig. 5.1 displays the number of plans that were generated by each system, categorized into Pareto-optimal and non-pareto-optimal (i.e. dominated) plans. The Pareto-optimal plans were determined by collecting all plans from all systems and then pruning all dominated plans. We can see that DP produces only Pareto-optimal plans and that there are many DPU plans that are part of the Pareto-optimal set (56% on average). However, the RD and RK baselines generate only small fractions of Pareto-optimal plans (1.9% and 1% on average). Also, DPS finds only few Pareto-optimal plans (less the 1%).

Fig. 5.2 shows the Pareto-optimal fraction for RD and RK for different values of m, i.e. the amount of additional generated plans. For larger values the Pareto-optimal fraction is higher, meaning that the larger plan space created by randomly removing source inputs is necessary to find Pareto-optimal plans.

Figs. 5.3a+b show plots of cost and cardinality of plans generated by all systems for query Q1. In these plots, a plan dominates all other plans that are to its lower right. We can see that many of the plans generated by the RD and RK baselines are dominated by other plans and that all DPS plans are also suboptimal. Fig. 5.3b shows for all systems only the plans that are part of the Pareto-optimal set. Here, the dominated DPS plans no longer appear and only few RD and RK plans remain.

Thus, ranking sources based on cardinality only does not help to produce Pareto-optimal plans. Further, this bias towards cardinality as reflected by the RK baseline actually leads to a smaller amount of optimal plans, compared to RD, the random strategy (Fig. 5.2). DPU optimizes for both objectives, thus is able to produce better trade-offs than RK and RD in most cases (Fig. 5.3a). However, because it only uses approximate estimates for cost, the resulting plans are relatively "good" but not always optimal.

Note that RD simply reflects the number of plans that are randomly generated. Out of the 3,154 random plans generated on average, only 1% are optimal. This suggests that the total space of plans is large, and a correspondingly large amount of plans have to be generated for RD to have higher coverage of optimal plans. Ranking sources based on cardinality only does not help to produce Pareto-optimal plans. In fact, we can see that this bias towards cardinality as reflected by the RK baseline actually leads to a smaller amount of optimal plans, compared to the random strategy (Fig. 5.2b). DPU optimizes for both objectives, thus is able to produce better trade-offs than RK and RD in most cases (Fig. 5.3a). However, because it systematically uses the wrong estimate for cost, the resulting plans are relatively "good" but rarely optimal.

Planning Time. On average, the fastest systems are RD and RK, while DP is more than one order of magnitude slower. This is to be expected because RD and RK randomly choose plans and use only simple source ranking, respectively, while DP requires computing precise bounds and finding Pareto-optimal plans using these bounds. Interestingly, the approximate version of DP, DPU, can be as fast as RD and RK, and is only 3 times slower on average. DPU is not only faster than DP but also DPS. Differences between DPS, DPU and DP are due to operator sharing. DPS is faster than DP because without operator sharing, it saves time for computing bounds. However, because operator sharing results in greater cost differences between plans, DPU could prune more plans compared to DPS (while the overhead it incurs for bound estimation is small). This is more obvious when we vary the sharing benefit, as discussed in the following.

Effect of Sharing Benefit. Figs. 5.4a+b show the planning time and Pareto-optimal fraction for different values of b. We see in Fig. 5.4a that planning times for systems without operator sharing (DPS, RD and RK) are not affected by b.

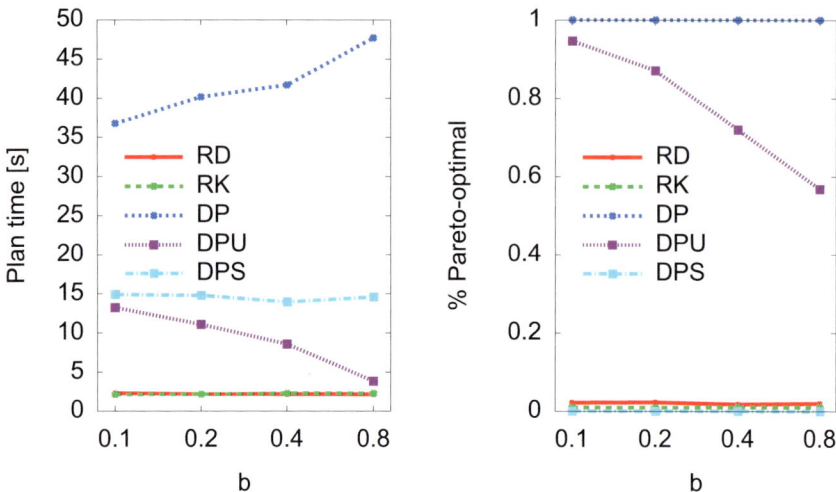

Figure 5.4: Effect of sharing benefit on a) planning time and b) pareto-optimal fractions ($m = 2000$).

For DP, planning time increases with higher sharing benefits, namely from 36.7s for $b = 0.1$ to 47.7s for $b = 0.8$. This is because cost bounds are more loose with increasing benefit, and thus less plans can be pruned. DPU's planning time exhibits the opposite behavior, decreasing from 13.2s ($b = 0.1$) to 3.8s ($b = 0.8$). Compared to DP, DPU does not incur the high cost of estimating bounds, and also, does not have the problem of loose bounds. Higher benefits only create steeper cost gradient between plans, thus resulting in more plans that can be pruned.

Not taking precise bounds into account however has a negative effect on the optimality of plans. Fig. 5.4b illustrates that DPU produces a smaller fraction of Pareto-optimal plans. This is because with higher sharing benefit, the deviation of DPU's bound estimates from the actual bounds increases.

In total, DPU however represents a reasonable trade-off between plan quality and time, producing 55 times more Parato-optimal plans while being only 3 times slower than the baselines RD and RK on average.

Effect of Query Complexity. Figs. 5.5a+b show time and Pareto-optimal fraction for different numbers of triple patterns. An increased number of patterns results in a larger search space for the query optimizer. As a result, both performance and quality decrease. Whereas for 3 triple patterns the baselines RD

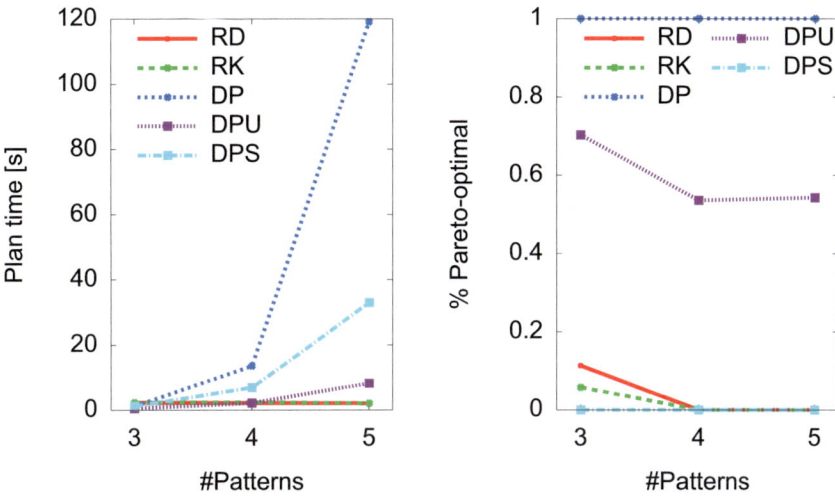

Figure 5.5: Effect of query complexity on a) planning time and b) pareto-optimal fractions ($b = 0.8, m = 2000$).

and RK are able to find 11% and 6% of the Pareto-optimal plans, few are found for 4 and 5 triple patterns ($< 1\%$). DPU provides 70% of the Pareto-optimal set for 3 triple patterns, and 54% for 4 and 5 triple patterns. For all systems, planning time increases with the number of patterns. From 3 to 5 triple patterns, the planning time of DP increases by a factor of 101.4, DPS increases by a factor of 28, while the planning time for DPU only increases by a factor of 18, and RD and RK are largely unaffected.

Cost-Cardinality Trade-off. We analyze the cost-cardinality trade-off by studying the times needed for producing different number of results. Different number of results can be obtained by using different plans. For every query, we randomly chose 20% of the plans generated by each system, execute all of them and record the total time of planning and processing. Fig. 5.6 shows the results for two extreme queries. While Q1 produces only 24 results, Q4 yields 836 results. Each point represents the average total time of all plans that produce a particular number of results. For example, all DP plans for query Q4 that produce 140 results have an average total query time of 7.1s.

First, we note that while DP and DPU varies in planning time, their total time performances are comparable. That is, while DP needs more time for planning,

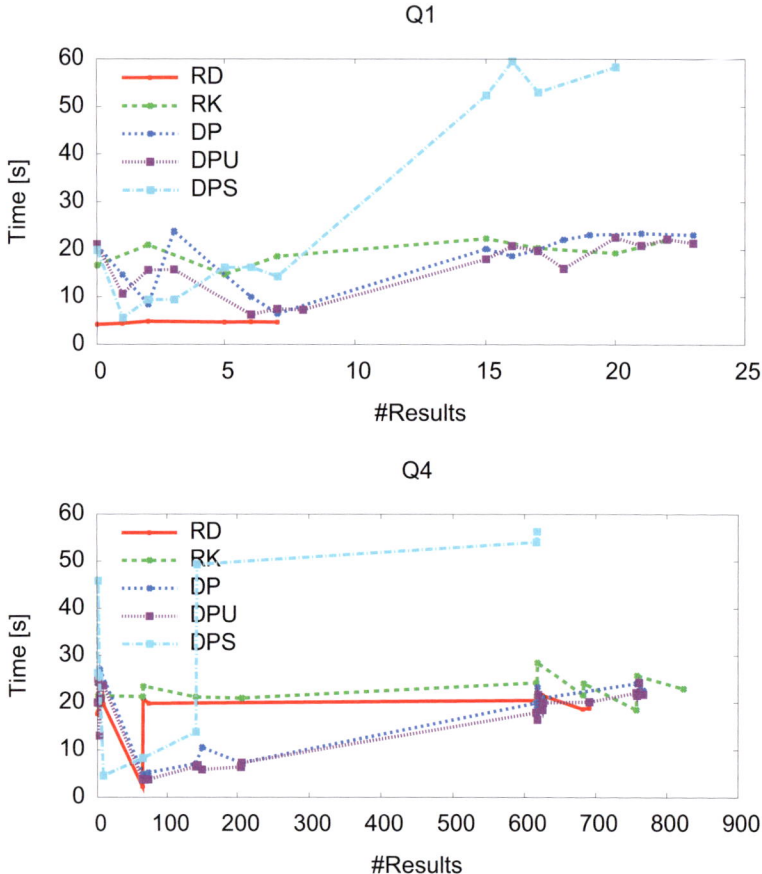

Figure 5.6: Execution times of query plans for queries Q1 and Q4. Each data point represents the average total time of all query plans for a query that produce a particular of results.

this overhead is compensated by the faster execution that could be achieved through more optimal plans.

Most importantly, our systems DP, DPU and DPS, which optimize for both objectives, indeed enable different trade-offs between the two, i.e. reduce total processing time, when fewer results are needed. We can see for both Q1 and Q4, there is a trend that total times increase with the number of results. These trade-offs are not possible with the baseline systems RK and RD. Because the plans they produce are not Pareto-optimal but cost-optimized, the time performance of RK and RD is rather constant and does not change or correlate with the number of results. RD is particularly cost-optimized: while it achieves best performance, the plans it employs do not yield the desired number of results, e.g. none of its plans produces more than 7 results for Q1.

Further, there are obvious differences between cardinality and cost estimated for the plans and the actual number of results produced and time required by them. Many of the plans that are Pareto-optimal according to estimates, actually produce no results. These plans however, take the longest time to finish. This explains while the trend mentioned above is not clear, i.e. fewer results require less time, but empty results require longest time.

Despite the simple estimates we employed in this work, the planning overhead can be outweighed by faster execution when the number of results is limited, i.e. DP and DPU provide better performance than the RK baseline. For example, to produce 7 results for Q1, DP and DPU require only 35% of the time RK needed to produce the same amount of result. Similarly, for Q4, DP and DPU requires only 28% of the total time of RK when 205 results have to be produced.

Summary. This experiment shows that compared to our work, the cost-based baselines produce only a small fraction of Pareto-optimal plans. The planning overhead incurred by our solution is relatively small compared to the gain in Pareto-optimality, e.g. 55 times more Pareto-optimal plans at the cost of 3 times higher planning cost for DPU. This Pareto-optimal planning has an effect on processing time and the actual results produced: using cost-optimized plans, the baselines cannot achieve the trade-off between cost and cardinality, while our solution reduces total processing time when fewer results are needed. This translates to about 4 times faster average performance than the RK baseline, when no more than 250 results are needed.

5.7 Conclusion

We propose the first solution towards a systematic optimization of Linked Data query processing, which considers both standard query operators and the specific characteristics of Linked Data source selection. The optimization result is the Pareto-set of optimal plans, representing different trade-offs between optimization objectives such as cost and cardinality. In experiments we compare our solution to cost-oriented baselines that independently optimize source selection and the processing of queries. Most plans computed by these baselines are sub-optimal such that the trade-off between different objectives is not adequately reflected. That is, while some baselines' plans achieve good time performance, they cannot produce the desired number of results; or they cannot help to improve time performance, given only a limited number of results are needed. Our solution provides different optimal trade-offs, enabling several times reduction of processing cost in some cases.

Chapter 6

Indexes for Hybrid Search

6.1 Introduction

Many databases today are *text-rich* in that they not only capture structured but also unstructured data, a combination called *hybrid data*. This is particular the case with RDF stores. Dealing with unstructured and structured data in an integrated fashion is a problem that is actively studied in the area of DB & IR integration [Wei07]. This research recognizes that while keywords are necessary for querying textual data and also, can be used as an intuitive paradigm to query structured data [HP02, LOF+08, TWRC09], requires query expressiveness that goes beyond keywords. For this, different types of *hybrid query languages* have been proposed, including content-and-structure queries for XML document retrievals, XQuery Full-Text [AYL06], and a combination of paths and keywords called FleXPath for XML data retrieval [AYLP04]. However, we note there exists no standard hybrid query language for the more general graph-structured RDF data.

As introduced in Section 2.4, we employ the notion of hybrid graph patterns to capture proprietary SPARQL full-text extensions employed by various RDF store vendors. In this chapter, we examine the problem of building indexes for hybrid data that allow for the efficient execution of hybrid graph patterns. To this end, we provide the following contributions:

- We first discuss the various types of queries that can be supported by the query model of hybrid graph patterns, i.e. from unstructured to structured to hybrid queries, from attribute to entity to full relational queries that involve several types of entities, and from schema-based queries that require schema knowledge (attribute and relation names) to schema-agnostic queries. We show in the experiment that most information needs studied in existing benchmarks can be expressed as queries belonging to one of these types.

- We propose a *general hybrid search index scheme* that can be used to specify access patterns needed to support these various query types and introduce *HybIdx* as one instance of this scheme.

- We perform a *comprehensive experiment* using several benchmark datasets and queries to systematically study existing solutions and HybIdx in several scenarios, from the text-centric retrieval of documents in Wikipedia and TREC[1] collections annotated with structured data to structure-centric retrieval of data in IMDB[2] and YAGO[3] up to "pure" hybrid data formed by combining Wikipedia and DBpedia.

- The main conclusions of this experimental study are: native solutions are faster than database extensions by up to an order of magnitude; native solutions that focus on one type of queries, i.e. entity queries, are fastest because of smaller index size. Compared to these, HybIdx provides superior performance for relational and document queries (outperforms the second best approach by up to three orders of magnitude) and yields results close to the ones achieved by the best "focused" solution for entity queries [DH07]. As opposed to these solutions, it is more complete regarding the types of hybrid search queries that can be supported.

In this chapter, we use the definitions of HGPs and their results first given in Section 2.4. For ease of reading, we repeat the important definitions here:

Definition 2.13 (Hybrid Graph Pattern). *Let $\mathcal{V}$ be the set of all variables. A hybrid triple pattern (HTP) $\langle s, p, o \rangle \in (\mathcal{V} \cup \mathcal{U} \cup \mathcal{K}) \times (\mathcal{V} \cup \mathcal{U} \cup \mathcal{K}) \times (\mathcal{V} \cup \mathcal{U} \cup \mathcal{L} \cup \mathcal{K})$ is a triple where the subject, predicate and object can either be a variable in $\mathcal{V}$ or a constant. The latter is either an RDF term in $\mathcal{U} \cup \mathcal{L}$ or a bag of keyword terms in $\mathcal{K}$. Two HTPs t_i and t_j that share a common variable v, establish the join condition (v^i, v^j), where v is called the join variable, and v^i and v^j denotes the variable v in t_i and v in t_j, respectively. A hybrid graph pattern (HGP) is a set of HTPs, $Q = \{t_1, \ldots, t_n\}$.*

---

[1]http://trec.nist.gov/, retrieved 2013-01-18
[2]Internet Movie Database (http://www.imdb.com), data and queries from benchmark in [CW10]
[3]http://www.mpi-inf.mpg.de/yago-naga/yago/, retrieved 2013-01-18

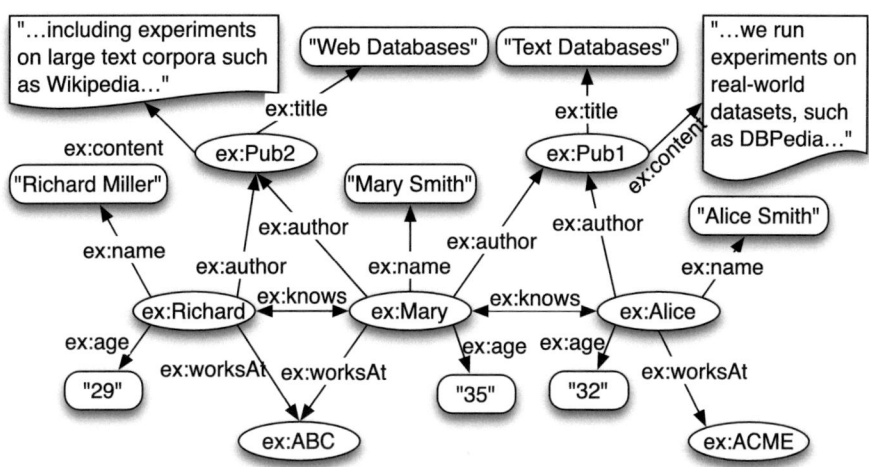

Figure 6.1: Excerpt of the example hybrid data from Fig. 2.1 used throughout this chapter.

Definition 2.14 (HGP Result). *Let $G = (G^R, text)$ be a hybrid data graph, Q be an HGP query, and $\mathcal{V}$ be the set of all variables and $\mathcal{K}$ the set of all bags of keyword terms. Let μ' be the function that maps elements in Q to elements G^R:*

$$\mu' : \mathcal{V} \cup \mathcal{U} \cup \mathcal{L} \cup \mathcal{K} \rightarrow \mathcal{U} \cup \mathcal{L} \begin{cases} (1)\ v \mapsto \mu(v) & \text{if } v \in \mathcal{V} \\ (2)\ K \mapsto t & \text{if } K \in \mathcal{K} \\ (3)\ t \mapsto t & \text{if } t \in \mathcal{U} \cup \mathcal{L} \end{cases}$$

where the mapping $\mu : \mathcal{V} \rightarrow \mathcal{U} \cup \mathcal{L}$ is employed to map variables in Q to RDF terms in G^R. A mapping μ is a result to Q if it satisfies $\langle \mu'(s), \mu'(p), \mu'(o) \rangle \in G^R$, $\forall \langle s, p, o \rangle \in Q$. We denote the set of all result bindings for HGP Q over G^R as $\Omega_{G^R}(Q)$ (we omit G^R if clear from context), i.e. $\mu \in \Omega_{G^R}(Q)$. The set of all bindings for a single hybrid triple pattern $t \in Q$ is $\Omega_{G^R}(t)$.

Fig. 6.1 shows an excerpt of the hybrid data example in 2.1 that is used in the examples throughout this chapter. Tab. 6.1 shows example queries over this data.

135

Name	Query
Q_1	$\langle ?s, ?p, dbpedia\ experiments \rangle$
Q_2	$\langle ?s, name, alice \rangle \langle ?s, ex{:}knows, mary \rangle$
Q_3	$\langle alice, age, ?o \rangle$
Q_4	$\langle ?x, works\ at, acme \rangle \langle ?x, ex{:}author, ?p \rangle \langle ?y, author, ?p \rangle$
Q_5	$\langle ?s, ex{:}title, databases \rangle \langle ?s, ?p, experiments \rangle \langle ?x, ex{:}author, ?s \rangle$

Table 6.1: Example HGP queries over the data in Fig. 6.1. Query Q_4 asks for people who work at ACME, publications they have authored and their co-authors. Q_5 asks for the authors of publications with 'databases' in the title that include experiments.

6.2 Processing Hybrid Queries

Existing solutions target specific types of queries. In this section, we show that the proposed hybrid search query model is sufficiently general to capture the main existing types of queries as particular kinds of HGPs.

6.2.1 Hybrid Query Types

6.2.1.1 Unstructured vs. Structured

Standard keyword queries are *unstructured*, which are sets of keywords, each of the form $K = \{k_1, \ldots, k_n\}$. As a HGP, every such query can be expressed as $\langle x_1, y_1, k_1 \rangle, \ldots, \langle x_n, y_n, k_n \rangle$ where x_i and y_i, $1 \leq i \leq n$, are variables. A HGP that is a fully *structured* BGP is simply a pattern that does not involve the use of keywords, i.e. it is of the form $\langle x_1, y_1, z_1 \rangle, \ldots, \langle x_n, y_n, z_n \rangle$ where x_i, y_i and z_i, $1 \leq i \leq n$, are variables or RDF terms.

6.2.1.2 Entity vs. Attribute vs. Relational

Entity queries, especially the kind that seeks for entities of the type document, capture a large fragment of real-world information needs commonly supported by standard IR solutions and Web search engines. Instead of searching for documents, Semantic Web search engines and recent IR solutions focusing on structured data, support the retrieval of entities in general. A HGP corresponding to this type is star-shaped, whose triple patterns share the same variable at their subject position, i.e. $\langle ?x, y_1, z_1 \rangle, \ldots, \langle ?x, y_n, z_n \rangle$ where y_i and z_i, $1 \leq i \leq n$, are variables, RDF terms or keywords, and the "center node" variable, $?x$, stands for the entities to be retrieved (see Q_1 and Q_2 in our example).

An *attribute* query $\langle x, y, ?a \rangle$ retrieves the attribute (or property) value for a given entity and attribute. That is, x and y are RDF/keyword terms representing the given entity and attribute and $?a$ is a variable that captures the attribute value (see Q_3). Note that while other types of queries typically involve a variable at the subject position, this one explicitly specifies the subject entity and seeks for information about that entity. Thus, the ability to specify the subject using simple keywords is crucial for this type.

A *relational* query is more complex in that it involves several entities and their relations. That is, it is composed of triple patterns that have different entities at their subject position, and these entities are connected through relations as captured by the query triple patterns, i.e. queries of this type are of the general form $\langle x_1, y_1, z_1 \rangle, \ldots, \langle x_n, y_n, z_n \rangle$ where x_i, y_i and z_i, $1 \leq i \leq n$, are variables, RDF terms or keywords (see Q_4, Q_5).

6.2.1.3 Schema-based vs. Schema-agnostic

Another dimension based on which queries can be distinguished is whether they involve schema information, i.e. attributes and relations. *Schema-agnostic* querying does not require users to precisely know the attributes and relations such that the query may contain variables or keywords at the predicate position: $\langle x_1, y_1, z_1 \rangle, \ldots, \langle x_n, y_n, z_n \rangle$ where y_i, $1 \leq i \leq n$, is a variable or a keyword (see Q_1-Q_5). As opposed to that, y_i is an RDF term in *schema-based* queries (e.g. see second triple pattern in Q_2). Standard queries supported by database engines (e.g. SQL) are schema-based while BGPs supported by RDF stores might be schema-agnostic. As opposed to BGPs, users can specify not only variables but also keywords in the predicate position of patterns in HGPs.

Given an HGP, the matches are computed using two main operations, (1) retrieving data and (2) combining partial results. We now discuss the main existing solutions addressing these two tasks, indexes and join processing techniques in particular. We show their limitations in terms of the types of queries they can support and other drawbacks with regard to the processing of general hybrid search queries.

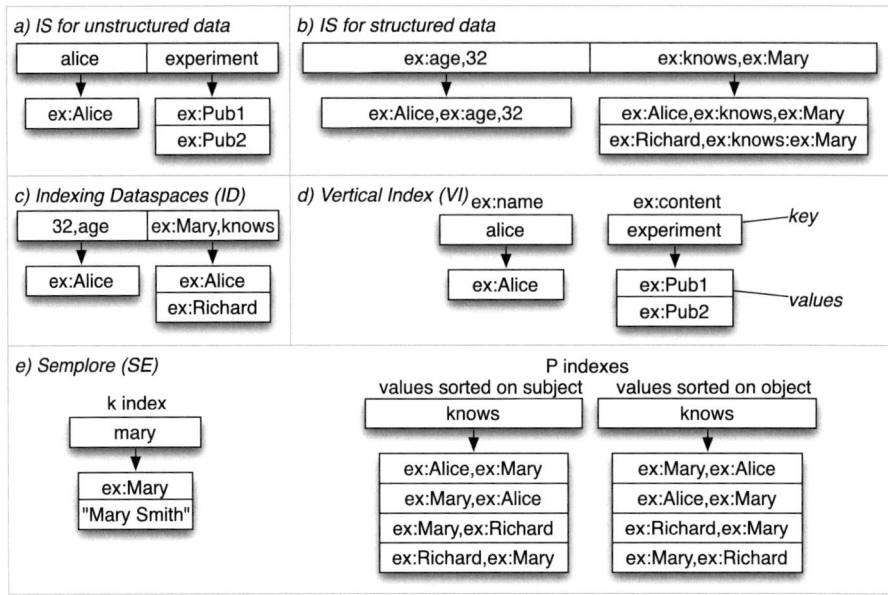

Figure 6.2: Index scheme examples for a) unstructured queries, b) structured queries, and hybrid queries: c) Indexing Dataspaces [DH07], d) Vertical Index [BMV11], e) Semplore [WLP+09].

6.2.2 Indexes

Indexes are employed to enable quick lookup of (partial) results, given a key. In Fig. 6.2, we provide several example indexes to illustrate the solutions discussed in the following. Traditional solutions can be distinguished in those targeting *structured queries* and those that deal with *keyword queries*. Regarding the former, there are many types of indexes for different types of structured data, e.g. special indexes for geo-spatial or multi-dimensional data [GMUW00]. For graph-structured data, such as RDF, many indexes are *triple-based* in that they return triples as results, given the constant(s) specified in the triple pattern as key. Since constants can be specified in different positions, there are different combinations of keys that can be supported (Fig. 6.2b shows an index supporting the combination of predicate and object as key). Different indexes are created to support these different access patterns captured by the keys [NW08]. As opposed to that, the latter focusing on keyword queries is *entity-based* because it returns entities, given a keyword in the query as key. Traditionally, these indexes return document entities. Recently, they are applied to structured data to support keyword-based object retrieval [CGQ08], e.g. to return RDF entities (see Fig. 6.2a). While these solutions focus on general structured queries or unstructured entity queries, there are also proposals targeting the *hybrid case*. Here, we distinguish native approaches from database extensions.

6.2.2.1 Native Approaches

(1) The *vertical index* (VI) [BMV11] supports hybrid triple patterns that have an RDF term at the predicate position and keyword at the object position. That is, it assumes the predicate is known and thus, employs one index for every attribute in the dataset, e.g. for *ex:name*. It is an entity-based index because instead of returning triples for the given attribute-value key, it provides matching entities as results (see Fig. 6.2d for results to the key *ex:name, alice* and *ex:content, experiment*). Thus, this index only supports *schema-based entity queries* (to be precise, schema-agnostic queries are possible but not manageable because they require lookups to be performed on all indexes). Another drawback is that a large number of indexes have to be created, depending on the number of predicates to be supported for hybrid search. In their experiment, the authors only index a predefined set of popular attributes [BMV11].

(2) The solution proposed for *indexing dataspaces* (ID) [DH07] supports hybrid triple patterns where keywords may occur both at the object and predicate position. The indexed keys are terms extracted from attribute values as well as combinations of terms extracted from both attribute names and values (see Fig. 6.2c). Just like VI, this solution takes advantage of the fact that the unit of retrieval is an entity, which is treated as a document such that existing inverted indexes originally built for documents are directly applicable. Thus, while it is *schema-agnostic*, it is limited to *entity queries*.

(3) *Semplore* (SE) [WLP$^+$09] is the only solution supporting the more general *relational queries*, employing three indexes. The first simply maps keywords to the RDF terms they appear in, i.e. URIs and literals (see k index in Fig. 6.2e). The others are to support hybrid triple patterns with keywords at the predicate position. They return objects and subjects of the matching triples. In order to enable fast merge joins (discussed next), the values are sorted on the subjects for one index and on the objects for the other (see P indexes in Fig. 6.2e). The limitation of this solution is that while it enables the use of keywords at predicate position, it is *not entirely schema-agnostic* because it still requires the predicate to be specified, i.e. it cannot be a variable. Further, it is an entity-based solution,

meaning that (partial) results returned are entities. As discussed in their paper, the authors show that when queries are indeed relational, i.e. contain patterns capturing relations, a relation expansion step involving a mass-union operator is needed, which "might lead to prohibitive I/O as it requires a large number of back-and-forth disk seeks" [WLP+09].

6.2.2.2 Database Extensions

While native approaches discussed before employ one single index solution, database extensions have separate indexes for dealing with structured and textual data [TSW05, KSI+08, HD05, AYLP04, BKO+11]. We identify two main types of indexes employed by database extensions. Many RDF stores for instance, such as OWLIM [BKO+11], can be configured to support either of these two types.

- (Type 1) The first [BKO+11] employs an indexing strategy that is analogous to the VI solution. It creates a separate index for every attribute. Thus, it shares VI's merits and drawbacks.

- (Type 2) Just like the *k* index illustrated for Semplore in Fig. 6.2e, the second type maps keywords to RDF terms containing them [HD05]. Solutions built upon this are similar to Semplore in that they are capable of supporting *relational queries* but also, suffer from large joins. We discuss this in detail in the following.

6.2.3 Join Processing

Given the indexes for retrieving results for hybrid triple patterns, the processing of HGPs is similar to the processing of BGPs supported by RDF stores. Consequently, query optimization techniques such as join ordering or sideways information passing [NW08, NW09] are applicable. Here, we focus the discussion on the aspects of join processing that are directly affected by the choice of indexes.

6.2.3.1 Entity-based vs. Triple-based

Note that the native solutions above employ the entity-based strategy. With this, entity queries, such as Q_2, can be efficiently processed by intersecting the lists of bindings for the variable $?s$ obtained for each of the patterns. Efficient bitset representations have been developed through the long history of IR research that allow for very fast intersection operations on lists of integers [ZM06].

With triple-based solutions, intersections are performed on lists of tuples instead of single values. For this, there is a large body of database solutions for join processing that are applicable. Semplore and the database extensions discussed above that aim at full relational queries (type 2), however, require a mixture of the two strategies. The results they obtain for the structured query parts are triples, while results for keywords are entities (RDF terms in general). This mismatch requires additional joins to be performed to combine the two types of results. These additional joins are even needed for processing single hybrid triple patterns. To evaluate the second pattern in Q_2 for instance, they use the k index to retrieve all RDF terms matching *mary*, and one of the two P indexes (or a similar index that supports this access pattern, in the case of the database extensions) to obtain all triples matching $\langle ?s, ex{:}knows, ?o \rangle$, and finally, join these results on the variable $?o$.

6.2.3.2 Top-k vs. No top-k

The index solutions mentioned above have not been studied in the top-k setting. Especially when the use of keywords is involved, it is often only necessary to obtain the top-k ranked results. Top-k processing techniques can improve performance through early termination after obtaining the top-k results, *rank join* in particular [IBS08]. The downside is that it requires inputs to be sorted on the score, which is usually achieved by indexing the data in a sorted fashion to avoid the high cost of online sorting. However, entries in the index are often sorted according to values instead of scores. Given sorted values, efficient *merge join* can be employed to obtain running times linear to input size. Further, employing rank join also means that the engine cannot take advantage of the indexes on the join variables, when available, to perform *index-based join*.

6.3 Hybrid Search Index

We propose a native indexing solution that fully supports the proposed query model. Compared to previous works, the main novelties are:

- *Full hybrid search support*: so far, the proposed native indexes focus on entity queries. Semplore is the only solution capable of answering relational queries. However, it does not support patterns where the predicate is a variable, and returns only entities as results. That is, it is not fully schema-agnostic and also does not support attribute queries.

- *Efficient hybrid search*: while the database extensions can support all the discussed types, they require a large number of joins due to the mixture of entity and tuple results. Our native solution supports all the query types without incurring this additional cost.

- *Top-k and no top-k*: our indexes are designed to include term score information. This is to support ranking schemes that conform with the term-based score assumption and top-*k* processing techniques that rely on these scores. As discussed, top-k rank join might be preferred over other join implementations, or vice versa, depending on the nature of the data and query. Our solution supports both top-k and non-top-k joins.

We first present a *general hybrid index scheme* based on which all the access patterns needed to support the proposed query model can be specified. Then, we present our solution *HybIdx* that instantiates this scheme.

6.3.1 Hybrid Index Schemes

An index is a data structure that enables lookups of values given a key. With respect to the data model, values that can be indexed correspond to elements in the RDF graph, i.e. RDF terms and triples (or even subgraphs). The keys are RDF or keyword terms. Conceptually, index solutions can be conceived as particular index schemes consisting of key-value lookup patterns:

Definition 6.1 (Key/Value Pattern). *Let atomic RDF key patterns be the sets* t_s^{RDF}, t_p^{RDF} *and* t_o^{RDF} *of all RDF terms that appear at the position s, p and o of the triples* $\langle s, p, o \rangle \in G$, *respectively. Likewise, let atomic keyword key patterns be the sets* t_s^k, t_p^k *and* t_o^k *of all keyword terms that appear in text(s), text(p) and text(o) of all triples* $\langle s, p, o \rangle \in G$, *respectively. Correspondingly, the combined sets of atomic RDF and keyword key patterns are denoted as* t_s, t_p *and* t_o. *A compound key pattern is the tuple* t_1, t_2, t_3, *where* $t_i, 1 \leq i \leq 3$, *might be* t_s, t_p *or* t_o, *or simply unspecified. A value pattern is the set of all RDF triples in G,* $\langle \mathbf{s}, \mathbf{p}, \mathbf{o} \rangle$, *or the set of all RDF terms* t_s^{RDF}, t_p^{RDF} *or* t_o^{RDF} *as defined before.*

Note that a compound key pattern is simply a generalization of an atomic key pattern, i.e. it is atomic when two elements are unspecified.

Definition 6.2 (Index Scheme). *An* index scheme *is a set of key-value patterns* **key** $\mapsto$ **value**, *where* **key** *denotes the set of all compound key patterns and* **value** *the set of all value patterns.*

With compound key patterns, RDF/keyword terms at position s, p or o or a combination of them can be used as keys. In fact, every key represents a query triple pattern: while atomic key pattern captures keys that correspond to triple patterns with exactly one RDF/keyword term, triple patterns with several RDF/keyword terms are supported by compound key patterns. Matches to these patterns are returned as the result of an index lookup. However, instead of the matching triples, any RDF term at position s, p or o of these triples can be specified as the value to be returned. For instance, the key-value pattern $\mathbf{t}_o \mapsto \mathbf{t}_s^{RDF}$ supports the retrieval of RDF terms $t \in \mathbf{t}_s^{RDF}$ that appear at the subject position of triples having an object matching the given key $t \in \mathbf{t}_o$. As opposed to that, the pattern $\mathbf{t}_o, \mathbf{t}_p \mapsto \langle \mathbf{s}, \mathbf{p}, \mathbf{o} \rangle$ enables the retrieval of RDF triples having an object matching $t_o \in \mathbf{t}_o$ and a predicate matching $t_p \in \mathbf{t}_p$.

Further, we leverage *prefix lookups* to reduce the number of key-value patterns needed to support the many kinds of hybrid search queries. This lookup capability is for instance, supported by standard implementations of the inverted index. With this, we can further distinguish between standard compound key patterns $\mathbf{t}_s, \mathbf{t}_p, \mathbf{t}_o$ and *prefix compound key patterns* $\mathbf{p}(\mathbf{t}_s, \mathbf{t}_p, \mathbf{t}_o)$. With the latter, lookups are possible even when only a prefix of the key is specified. For a compound key with n elements, the prefix of n with length i is simply n without the last $n - i$ elements. For instance, given $\mathbf{p}(\mathbf{t}_o, \mathbf{t}_p) \mapsto \langle \mathbf{s}, \mathbf{p}, \mathbf{o} \rangle$, the prefix key with length one is simply $t_o \in \mathbf{t}_o$, which yields all triples with an object matching t_o. Conceptually, a prefix pattern $\mathbf{p}(\mathbf{t})$ can be treated as a set of patterns, i.e. all patterns that correspond to $\mathbf{p}(\mathbf{t})$ or any prefix of $\mathbf{p}(\mathbf{t})$. For instance, the set of patterns represented by $\mathbf{p}(\mathbf{t}_o, \mathbf{t}_p)$ comprises $\mathbf{t}_o, \mathbf{t}_p$ and $\mathbf{t}_o$.

6.3.2 HybIdx: Hybrid Search Index

Our solution is a generalization of indexing approaches proposed for unstructured and structured data, i.e. those that map (1) keyword terms to documents [ZM06] or (2) compound RDF terms representing triple patterns to RDF triples [NW08]. We use the general key pattern $\mathbf{t}$, which can be either a keyword key pattern or an RDF key pattern. Accordingly, a compound key pattern $\mathbf{t}_s, \mathbf{t}_p, \mathbf{t}_o$ can be composed of RDF key patterns and/or keyword key patterns. In particular, the index scheme is defined as follows:

Definition 6.3 (Full Hybrid Index). *A full hybrid index is defined by the scheme:*

$$\mathbf{p}(\mathbf{t}_s, \mathbf{t}_p, \mathbf{t}_o) \;\mapsto\; \langle \mathbf{s}, \mathbf{p}, \mathbf{o} \rangle$$
$$\mathbf{p}(\mathbf{t}_p, \mathbf{t}_o, \mathbf{t}_s) \;\mapsto\; \langle \mathbf{s}, \mathbf{p}, \mathbf{o} \rangle$$
$$\mathbf{p}(\mathbf{t}_o, \mathbf{t}_s, \mathbf{t}_p) \;\mapsto\; \langle \mathbf{s}, \mathbf{p}, \mathbf{o} \rangle$$

Due to prefix lookup, this index scheme supports exactly seven hybrid triple patterns $\langle s, p, o \rangle$ on the graph where s, p and o are variables, RDF or keyword terms. These correspond to the key pattern where all three elements are RDF/keyword terms, i.e. (1) $\mathbf{t}_s, \mathbf{t}_p, \mathbf{t}_o$, the patterns where two elements are RDF/keyword terms, i.e. (2) $\mathbf{t}_s, \mathbf{t}_p$, (3) $\mathbf{t}_s, \mathbf{t}_o$ and (4) $\mathbf{t}_o, \mathbf{t}_p$, and the patterns where only one element is an RDF/keyword term, i.e. (5) $\mathbf{t}_s$, (6) $\mathbf{t}_p$ and (7) $\mathbf{t}_o$. Note that the order of elements in the compound key patterns does not matter when considering the entire pattern, e.g. $\mathbf{p}(\mathbf{t}_s, \mathbf{t}_p, \mathbf{t}_o)$ and $\mathbf{p}(\mathbf{t}_p, \mathbf{t}_s, \mathbf{t}_o)$ are the same, representing the same type of triple patterns where s, p and o are RDF/keyword terms. However, it does matter when considering its prefixes, e.g. $\mathbf{p}(\mathbf{t}_s, \mathbf{t}_p, \mathbf{t}_o)$ contains $\mathbf{t}_s, \mathbf{t}_p$ as one prefix but not $\mathbf{t}_p, \mathbf{t}_s$, which is only available with $\mathbf{p}(\mathbf{t}_p, \mathbf{t}_s, \mathbf{t}_o)$.

Clearly, this index supports all keys that can be constructed from the combinations of keyword/RDF terms at subject, predicate and object position. Thus, the upper bound of key-value pairs captured by the index is $|\mathbf{t}_s| \times |\mathbf{t}_p| \times |\mathbf{t}_o| \times |\langle s, p, o \rangle \in G|$. However, it might not be necessary to support all possible access patterns using such a full index. We observe that all triple patterns found in real-world structured SPARQL queries (e.g. queries against DBpedia [MLAN11] or queries in the USEWOD2012[4] query logs) contain at least one variable. Consequently, we create indexes that support access patterns with up to two RDF/keyword terms, i.e. the six patterns 2-7 mentioned above:

Definition 6.4 (Reduced Hybrid Index). *A reduced hybrid index is defined by the scheme:*

$$\mathbf{p}(\mathbf{t}_s, \mathbf{t}_p) \;\mapsto\; \langle \mathbf{s}, \mathbf{p}, \mathbf{o} \rangle$$
$$\mathbf{p}(\mathbf{t}_p, \mathbf{t}_o) \;\mapsto\; \langle \mathbf{s}, \mathbf{p}, \mathbf{o} \rangle$$
$$\mathbf{p}(\mathbf{t}_o, \mathbf{t}_s) \;\mapsto\; \langle \mathbf{s}, \mathbf{p}, \mathbf{o} \rangle$$

To support ranking, we further introduce a rank-aware index. Prefix key patterns actually capture several patterns. There is more than one score for each prefix key pattern, namely one for the entire pattern and one for each prefix. This

---

[4]http://data.semanticweb.org/usewod/2012/challenge.html, retrieved 2013-01-18

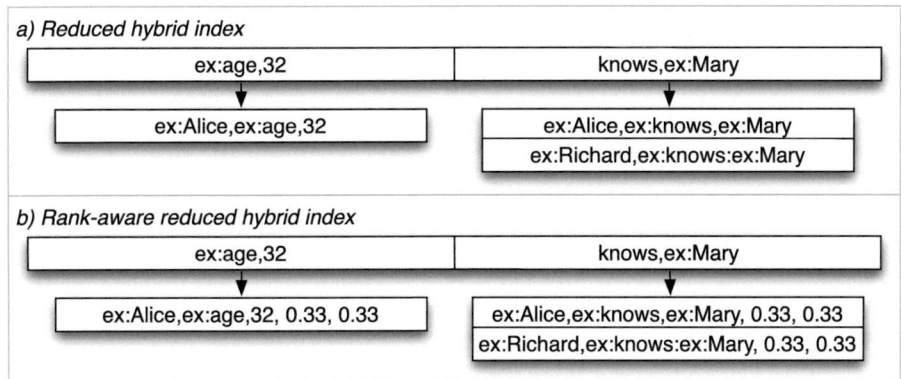

Figure 6.3: Examples of a) reduced hybrid index and b) rank-aware reduced hybrid index.

results in two scores for each prefix key pattern supported by the reduced hybrid index:

Definition 6.5 (Rank-Aware Reduced Hybrid Index). *Let* $r = \langle s, p, o \rangle$, *a rank-aware hybrid index* is defined by:

$$\mathbf{p}(\mathbf{t}_s, \mathbf{t}_p) \mapsto (r, score(t_s, r), score(\{t_s, t_p\}, r))$$
$$\mathbf{p}(\mathbf{t}_p, \mathbf{t}_o) \mapsto (r, score(t_p, r), score(\{t_p, t_o\}, r))$$
$$\mathbf{p}(\mathbf{t}_o, \mathbf{t}_s) \mapsto (r, score(t_o, r), score(\{t_o, t_s\}, r))$$

Example 6.1. *Fig. 6.3a shows two example entries for the* $\mathbf{p}(\mathbf{t}_p, \mathbf{t}_o) \mapsto \langle s, p, o \rangle$ *access patterns of the reduced hybrid index. Note that the index keys contain keyword terms, RDF terms as well as a combination of both (e.g.* knows, ex:Mary*). The same example is shown in Fig. 6.3b for a rank-aware reduced hybrid index where every matching triple is associated with two scores, one for the entire pattern with two elements, and one for the one-element prefix, e.g. the score for matching* age *and the score for matching both* age *and* 32.

The merits of this solution is that the same triple-based strategy is used to serve both structured and keyword parts of the hybrid queries. Given any hybrid triple pattern, only lookups have to be performed on these triple indexes, as opposed to costly joins as discussed for Semplore and the database extensions. This is especially beneficial when joining results from two or more hybrid triple patterns. Our solution requires only direct joins between triples while these previous works involve more complex joins between entities and triples. Based on the scores stored in the rank-aware index, rank join can be supported in addition to standard join operators. Now, we show that with the reduced hybrid index, all the discussed query types can be supported:

- *Unstructured vs. structured*: the fragment $t_o^k \mapsto \langle s, p, o \rangle$ captured by the pattern $p(t_o, t_s) \mapsto \langle s, p, o \rangle$ supports keyword queries where $t \in t_o^k$ is the keyword term and the returned entity result is $s \in s$. Structured query patterns are supported by the fragments $p(t_o^{RDF}, t_s^{RDF}) \mapsto \langle s, p, o \rangle$, $p(t_p^{RDF}, t_o^{RDF}) \mapsto \langle s, p, o \rangle$ and $p(t_s^{RDF}, t_p^{RDF}) \mapsto \langle s, p, o \rangle$, i.e. those key-value pairs where the keys are RDF terms.

- *Entity vs. attribute vs. relational*: entity queries require lookups for triple patterns where the subject is a variable and the predicate and object might be keyword or RDF terms. This is supported by $p(t_p, t_o) \mapsto \langle s, p, o \rangle$. Since relational queries also require access patterns where the subject is a variable (the difference to entity queries lies in the use of several distinguished variables), they do not require any additional support. For attribute queries, there is $p(t_s, t_p) \mapsto \langle s, p, o \rangle$, which enables the retrieval of attribute values given a subject, a predicate or both as RDF/keyword terms.

- *Schema-based and schema-agnostic*: The access patterns needed to support these types of queries are $p(t_s, t_p) \mapsto \langle s, p, o \rangle$ and $p(t_o, t_p) \mapsto \langle s, p, o \rangle$, where the attribute/relation names need to be specified, and $p(t_s, t_o) \mapsto \langle s, p, o \rangle$, where they occur as variables.

6.3.3 HybIdx Implementation

HybIdx as an index scheme, is independent from the concrete index implementation. It can be implemented on top of any data structure that supports the mapping of single items (keys) to lists of items (values).

6.3.3.1 Inverted Indexes for Compound Keys

We use inverted indexes, which originally map keyword terms to documents. We extend the inverted index implementation provided by Lucene, which comprise sparse indexes over sorted arrays, to map compound keyword/RDF terms to triples. We implement a compound term as a concatenated term, i.e. the compound key t_s, t_o, t_p is simply the term concatenation "$t_s//t_o//t_p$". For instance, the compound key *age, 32* in our example is stored in the index as the term *age//32*. We firstly construct the sets of all RDF terms, $\mathbf{t}_s^{RDF}$, $\mathbf{t}_p^{RDF}$ and $\mathbf{t}_o^{RDF}$, each comprising the elements s, p and o of all the triples $\langle s, p, o \rangle \in G$, respectively. By extracting the keywords from these elements, we obtain the set of all keyword terms, i.e. each $\mathbf{t}_s^k$, $\mathbf{t}_p^k$ and $\mathbf{t}_o^k$ contains all the elements $k_s \in text(s), k_p \in text(p)$ and $k_o \in text(o)$, respectively, for all $\langle s, p, o \rangle \in G$. Then depending on the indexes, different compound keys have to be constructed, e.g. with the reduced HybIdx index, we have three 2-elements compound key patterns. For instance for $\mathbf{p}(\mathbf{t}_s, \mathbf{t}_p)$, we construct all combinations of RDF terms from elements in $\mathbf{t}_s^{RDF}$ and $\mathbf{t}_p^{RDF}$, and all combinations of keyword terms from $\mathbf{t}_s^k$ and $\mathbf{t}_p^k$. Finally, we store the resulting compound keys as concatenated terms in the index, e.g. to obtain *age//32*.

6.3.3.2 Dictionary Encoding of Key Values

Common among inverted index implementations is the use of a dictionary, where terms and documents are assigned identifiers, which are then used for indexing [ZM06]. We use dictionary encoding also for RDF triples, i.e. for the values $\langle s, p, o \rangle$ or $(r, score(t_s, r), score(\{t_s, t_p\}, r))$ of the HybIdx indexes. Encoding triples requires dealing with three RDF terms. Often, triples returned from an index are further joined to compute the final query results. This involves accessing individual terms in the triples. Therefore, we apply dictionary encoding at the level of individual terms in the triples. Similarly to the document case, the dictionary is only accessed to return the final results while all intermediate processing is performed on the more compact encoded values.

6.3.3.3 Index Updates

Since HybIdx is implemented as an inverted index, i.e. consists of inverted lists representing (concatenated) term to triple mappings, the many existing techniques developed for updates can be directly applied. In particular, we do not update the indexes in real-time, but keep the changes in a temporary in-memory index first, making them immediately available for searches, and then periodically write them to disk as incremental updates [ZM06].

6.4 Related Work

Indexing Schemes. Related works in this direction have been discussed in detail in Section 6.2.2. Our solution provides a generalization of inverted indexes for keyword-based querying (see overview in [ZM06]) and triple indexes for BGP-based querying [HD05, NW08] to answer different access patterns possible with HGPs.

    SPARQL Full-Text Extension. HGPs extend both the syntax (RDF terms + keyword terms) and semantics (keyword terms are evaluated with IR-style relevance) of SPARQL BGPs. SPARQL full-text extensions are provided by a number of vendors (e.g. Virtuoso, OWLIM). The semantics supported by them also build upon the IR-style relevance employed by the underlying IR engine. Due to the absence of standardization, each vendor uses its own proprietary syntax. Common is the use of a predefined full-text predicate, e.g. *ex:contains*[5] such that Q_1 would be expressed as:

$$\langle ?s, ?p, ?k \rangle, \langle ?k, ex{:}contains, dbpedia\ experiments \rangle$$

Possibly influenced by this syntax, the full-text support implemented by vendors is as discussed: the k index is used to retrieve RDF terms matching *dbpedia experiments* as bindings for $?k$, and then joined with triple bindings for $\langle ?s, ?p, ?k \rangle$. We explicitly distinguish RDF terms from keyword terms, thus avoiding the use of such a predefined predicate. This is close in spirit to languages like XQuery Full-Text [AYL06], with the difference that it deals with RDF graphs not with XML trees. A proposal for SPARQL/RDF that is close to our solution is described in [ERSW10], where keyword terms can be associated with triple patterns. Our proposal enables more fine-grained full-text constraints in that every element in the triple pattern can be a keyword term. As a result, the various types of queries discussed in Section 6.2.1 can be expressed as HGPs.

    Hybrid Search. Besides the works on indexing already discussed in Section 6.2.2, there are other directions studied in the area of DB & IR integration [Wei07]. Chakrabarti et al. [CSS10] discuss how keyword-based search can be extended by adding structure to data and query answers. Recent work on QUICK by Pound et al. [PIW10] deals with document retrieval based on entity queries where keywords can also match structural elements of the data graph. However, relational queries are not supported. There are also works on auto-completion, which are based on indexing ranges of terms instead of single terms. ESTER

---

[5]http://www.w3.org/2009/sparql/wiki/Feature:FullText, retrieved 2013 01 18

[BCSW07] answers queries over structured ontologies based on the prefix search capability of this auto-completion index. Also, this index is entity-based. Relational queries are possible but require a large number of joins because ESTER employs a strategy similar to the one discussed for Semplore.

Query Processing. For inverted indexes, query processing is mainly concerned with the fast intersection of inverted lists to obtain matching documents [ZM06]. There is also work on the efficient processing of SPARQL queries over RDF data [NW08, NW09]. As discussed in Section 6.2.3, processing HGPs is more similar to processing BGPs on RDF data than to processing keyword queries on inverted indexes. Optimization techniques, such as join ordering and sideways information passing are therefore applicable. We also employ top-k processing techniques [IBS08] (rank join) to report the top-k results without having to process all input data.

6.5 Evaluation

We perform the evaluation on a total of six indexing schemes, representing HybIdx and existing approaches discussed in Section 6.2.2.

6.5.1 Systems

We use **OWLIM-SE**[6] as a representative for database extensions of Type 2 (see Section 6.2.2.2), i.e. it uses a separate Lucene index for indexing RDF terms. **ID** is the native index solution for indexing dataspaces. **VI** is the vertical index scheme where one index is created for every attribute. VI only indexes a maximum of 300 attributes because of the overhead associated with managing and accessing a large number of separate indexes [BMV11]. **SE** is the Semplore system. **HySort** is our system using the reduced hybrid index where values are sorted on the term identifiers and the top-k results are extracted after all results have been calculated. **HyTopK** uses the same reduced hybrid index but with top-k processing. For this, values are sorted on the term scores.

All systems take the parameter k to determine how many top results should be returned. However, only HyTopK employs top-k processing to terminate after computing these results whereas the other systems compute all results and then perform sorting to obtain the top-k ones.

---

[6]http://owlim.ontotext.com/display/OWLIMv50/OWLIM-SE, retrieved 2013-01-18

With the exception of OWLIM, all systems are based on the same Lucene index implementation and optimizations discussed in Section 6.3.3. For combining results, hash join, and when possible, merge and index-based joins are executed for all other systems, while HyTopK uses rank join. Query plans are left-deep and created by a heuristic optimizer.

The evaluation was performed on a server with two 2.3 GHz CPUs and 12GB RAM, of which 8 GB were assigned to the JVM. During the evaluation, we cleared all caches after each query evaluation, including the operating system disk caches. All queries were run a total of ten times and the reported times are the average of the last five runs to account for the warm-up of the Java JIT compiler.

6.5.2 Datasets and Queries

The evaluation was performed on datasets of varying sizes. Some include a large number of documents (WP, AQY, WDB), whereas others contain a large amount of structured data (IMDB, YAGO, WDB). Queries for each dataset are based on the ones used in previous works. Keyword queries are translated manually to hybrid queries, where all keywords are incorporated as keyword terms. Fig. 6.4 shows a sample of queries that we will discuss later. All queries used in the evaluation can be found in Appendix A.3.1.

WP. This export of Wikipedia used by a recently published keyword search benchmark [CW10] contains about 5k revisions of pages and information about the revision authors. Keyword queries available for this dataset [CW10] that were translated to hybrid queries include 35 schema-agnostic entity queries and one relational query. Queries that require OR semantics were not included as our implementation currently only supports AND semantics.

IMDB. This one contains information about movies and actors. For this, there are 20 schema-agnostic entity queries and 26 relational queries defined in the benchmark [CW10]. Four keyword queries from this benchmark were left out because they could not be translated to our query model as they ask for unspecified paths between two entities.

YAGO. This is one part of the knowledge base used in [KSI+08]. It contains cross-domain knowledge extracted from Wikipedia, such as people, organizations, locations, etc. and relationships between them. From the hybrid queries used in [KSI+08], we took 67 queries (4 entity and 63 relational queries) that are compatible with our query model (the *connected* constraint used by these queries is not supported by our implementation).

$$WDB_4 \quad \langle ?x, type, settlement \rangle \langle ?x, label, sydney \rangle$$
$$\langle ?x, city, ?y \rangle \langle ?y, type, airport \rangle$$
$$WDB_6 \quad \langle ?x, type, animal \rangle \langle ?x, label, ?y \rangle$$
$$AQY_{238} \langle ?x, label, damon \rangle \langle ?x, haswonprize, ?y \rangle$$
$$\langle ?y, label, 2004 \rangle \langle ?d, mentions, ?y \rangle$$

Figure 6.4: Selected evaluation queries.

AQY. This consists of YAGO and the AQUAINT-2 news document collection annotated with entities from YAGO, as used in [PIW10]. There are about 900k documents and 17M YAGO entity annotations. All queries retrieve documents based on the annotated entities. They all are relational queries as entities are connected to documents via a special mentions predicate.

WDB. We created this dataset by enriching entities in DBpedia with their corresponding Wikipedia page. In total, it includes about 73M triples and 6.5M documents. We add keyword terms to structured queries in the DBpedia SPARQL benchmark [MLAN11] to create hybrid queries (9 schema-agnostic entity queries and 10 relational queries). In addition, we use random sampling to create the **WDB-P** query set comprising 500 queries that consist of one single pattern (each with up to 5 keyword terms).

Tab. 6.2a shows the average number of keyword terms per RDF term at the subject, predicate, and object position. We see the datasets that include documents (WP, AQY and WDB) have a higher number of keyword terms at the object position. WP has a particularly high number of keyword terms as it does not contain as much structured data as AQY and WDB do. Also, subjects in YAGO, AQY, and WDB contain more keyword terms than the subjects in WP and IMDB, which is due to the fact that both WP and IMDB are exports of relational datasets whose entity URIs do not contain words but only numerical identifiers. YAGO, AQY and WDB on the other hand have URIs encoding the names of the resources that can be used in query patterns.

Tab. 6.2c shows how many keywords occur on average at the subject, predicate and object position as well as in the whole query (constants are not counted). For instance, we can see that the WP query set mainly contains keyword-based entity queries where keywords occur almost exclusively at the object position. In all query sets, keywords are also used at the predicate position to query the schema (for constructing schema-agnostic queries). YAGO queries also retrieve attribute values for some entities, given as keywords.

	WP	IMDB	YAGO	AQY	WDB
a) Keyword terms per RDF term					
Subj.	3.00	3.09	4.48	4.19	4.89
Pred.	3.02	3.68	3.02	3.06	2.38
Obj.	34.30	3.17	3.57	11.50	12.38
b) Dataset and index sizes (in GB)					
Dataset	0.22	0.42	1.78	6.6	19.36
VI	0.05	0.11	0.20	1.56	5.37
ID	0.13	0.26	0.77	7.01	16.43
SE	0.05	0.28	0.75	4.85	7.50
Hy*	0.44	1.12	5.01	28.11	86.71
OWLIM	0.27	0.68	1.55	13.03	34.18
c) Query keywords statistics					
Keywords	2.14	5.15	2.70	4.60	3.42
Subj-Kw.	0.00	0.00	0.76	0.00	0.00
Pred-Kw.	0.06	2.43	1.57	2.53	1.21
Obj-Kw.	2.08	2.72	0.37	2.07	2.21
d) Query compatibility					
#Queries	36	46	67	15	19
VI	35	20	0	0	9
ID	35	20	4	0	11
SE	0	26	67	13	7
Hy*	36	46	67	15	19
OWLIM	36	46	67	15	19

Table 6.2: Dataset and query statistics.

Tab. 6.2b presents the size of all datasets and indexes for each dataset (in GB). Hy* requires more storage space than other systems, but no more than 5 times the size of the datasets. This increased space requirement is expected, given Hy* targets many more access patterns and query types that are not possible with the other indexes. The experimental results discussed in the following suggest that this index scheme not only increases the expressiveness of supported queries, but also yields superior time performance.

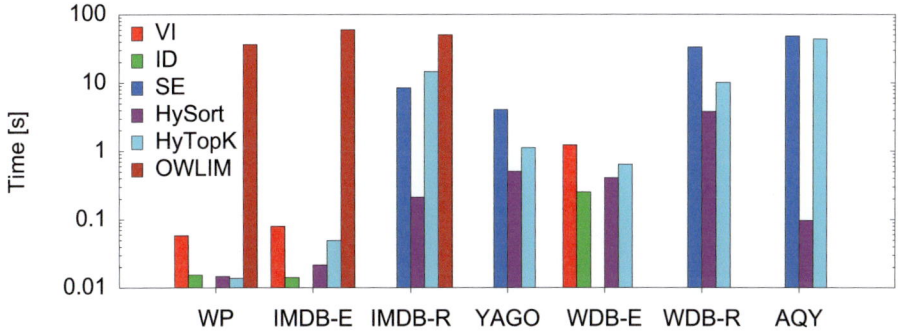

Figure 6.5: Average query times for all query sets (excluding WDB-P).

6.5.3 Results

For each query set, Tab. 6.2d shows the number of queries that can be executed using each system. For example, VI is able to execute only 20 of the 46 IMDB queries, which is due to its focus on schema-based entity queries. SE cannot evaluate any WP query because it requires a constant at the predicate position. VI and ID are able to execute all but the one relational query in WP. Whereas the other systems can only execute certain subsets, Hy* and OWLIM can execute all queries.

Overview. Fig. 6.5 gives an overview of the average query processing times for all systems and queries (excluding WDB-P). For each query set we include only systems that are able to execute at least some of the queries in the query set. Then, we compute the average only over queries that were executable on all such systems in order to make the results comparable. For example, SE cannot execute any query of the WP dataset and is therefore not included in the results. The results for WP only include the average of 35 queries that were executable on VI, ID, OWLIM and Hy* (from a total of 36 queries). We split the IMDB and WDB query sets into the two sets of entity and relational queries (IMDB-E,IMDB-R and WDB-E, WDB-R).

For OWLIM, we only include results for WP and IMDB, as queries for the other datasets timed out (after 60 seconds). As discussed, this is because even for a single hybrid triple pattern, OWLIM needs to join RDF terms obtained for the keyword with triples matching the pattern. Further, OWLIM cannot take advantage of the indexes to perform joins, while HySort can perform index-based joins, where results from one side of the join are used to perform lookups on the

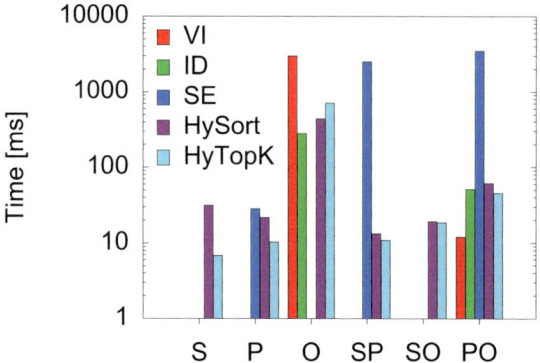

Figure 6.6: Average query times for single pattern queries WDB-P (at $k = 10$) for different pattern types. The name of the pattern type indicates where constants appear in the pattern, e.g. SP refers to patterns with constants at subject and predicate positions and a variable at object position.

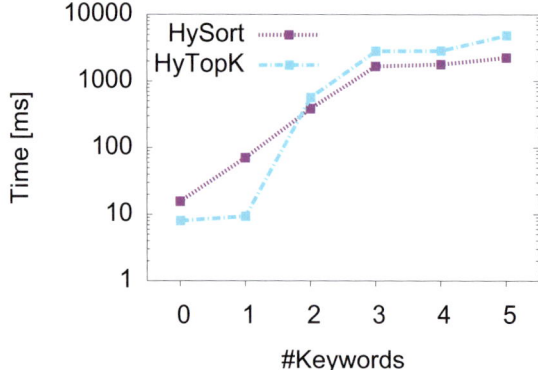

Figure 6.7: Average query times for O patterns (i.e. with constant objects) in WDB-P for different numbers of keywords.

other side. This considerably improves performance for queries with selective triple patterns.

We now begin with the analysis of the generated single pattern queries to obtain a basic understanding of the capabilities of different systems. Then, we turn attention to the main queries presented in Fig. 6.5, based on their decomposition into entity, document and relational queries.

Single Pattern Queries. Fig. 6.6 shows the average evaluation time for WDB-P queries, each consisting of a single pattern. We group patterns by the positions where constants appear, i.e. PO refers to patterns that have a variable as subject and constants at the predicate and object position. First, we see that ID and VI only answer O and PO patterns. SE only supports P, SP and SO patterns, whereas Hy* support all patterns.

The predicate is specified in PO patterns. Here, VI can perform a single lookup in the index built for a particular predicate, thereby outperform ID and Hy* that have larger indexes. With O patterns, VI has to perform lookups in all its predicate indexes, leading to much worse performance. ID outperforms Hy* for both, O and PO patterns as ID only stores entities instead of triples. SE requires joins to answer SP and PO, leading to worse performance compared to the Hy* approaches. For P patterns, SE does not require joins and therefore has performance comparable to HySort.

For most patterns, HyTopK outperforms HySort as it does not have to process all inputs to obtain the top-k results. The exception are O patterns, where HyTopK has an average query time of 711.3 ms compared to 439.4 ms for HySort. Fig. 6.7 shows the query times for O patterns on HySort and HyTopK for different numbers of keywords in the patterns. We see that for zero or one keyword, HyTopK performs better, whereas HySort performs better for two or more keywords. When a pattern contains more than one keyword, the query engine performs an intersection between the matches for each keyword (AND semantics). In this case, HySort uses efficient merge join as all triples are sorted on one of the variables in the pattern. Instead, HyTopK performs a rank join, which compared to merge join, requires overhead in maintaining hash tables.

Entity Queries. Fig. 6.8a shows average query times for all entity queries that were executable on VI, ID and Hy*, i.e. entity queries where the predicate is a variable or an RDF term. This includes queries from WP, IMDB-E and WDB-E. We can see here that VI is outperformed by all other systems because it has to access all its indexes when the predicates are not given. The average time of VI is 245.1 ms, compared to 45.9 ms for ID, 67.6 ms for HySort and 48.9 ms for HyTopK. While both HySort and HyTopK are faster than VI, HySort is still outperformed by ID because the latter only stores entities instead of triples. Through top-k processing, HyTopK's results are close to the ones achieved by ID.

Relational Queries. Fig. 6.8b shows the average times for all relational queries that were executable with SE, HySort and HyTopK. This includes queries from IMDB-R and WDB-R. With an average query time of 638.4 ms, HySort

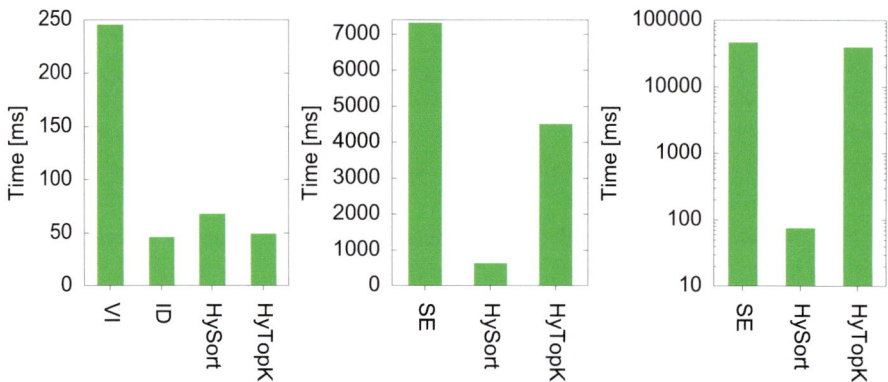

Figure 6.8: Average query times for a) entity queries, b) relational queries, c) document queries ($k = 1$). All results exclude WDB-P.

outperforms both HyTopK (4511.8 ms) and SE (7310.66 ms). While HySort has to produce all results in order to identify the top-k ones, it still outperforms HyTopK. It seems that the ability to take advantage of available indexes to perform index-based joins is more important w.r.t. relational queries that involve more complex joins, compared to entities queries (where HyTopK is better than HySort). SE has a larger overhead than both HySort and HyTopK as additional merge joins are necessary for patterns that have keywords. Hence, it exhibits the worse performance.

WDB_4 is an example of a relational query (see Fig. 6.4) where HySort (734.0 ms) outperforms HyTopK (2054.0 ms). The initial join between the first two pattern produces only few results, which HySort uses to perform an index-based join with the third pattern, for which only a few lookups are needed. HyTopK, on the other hand, accesses the matching triples for each pattern in the order of their scores. Depending on the score distribution it can happen that a large part of the input needs to be read until joining triples are found.

WDB_6 (Fig. 6.4) is a query with low selectivity where HyTopK outperforms HySort (7873.3 ms vs. 22669.6 ms). Here, both patterns match many triples. Thus, index-based joins do not perform better as they require many lookups.

In other words, whether top-k processing should be used or not depends on the complexity of the queries (the complexity of joins). Our index solution supports both these paradigms; one way to exploit this index is to apply optimization techniques [IBS08] that not only find the optimal join orders but also which type of joins to be performed.

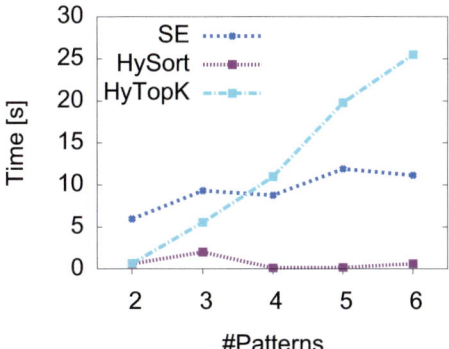

Figure 6.9: Average query times for relational queries in IMDB and YAGO for different numbers of query patterns.

Document Queries. Fig. 6.8c shows the average query times for SE, HySort and HyTopK for the 13 queries of the AQY query set. With an average time of 74.9 ms at $k = 1$ compared to 45977.7 ms and 39163.5 ms, HySort outperforms SE and HyTopk by several orders of magnitude. All queries contain the pattern $\langle x, mentions, y \rangle$. Using the $\mathbf{t}_p \rightarrow \langle \mathbf{s}, \mathbf{o} \rangle$ index, all annotation triples have to be retrieved for every execution. For HyTopK, the drawback is that all annotations are stored sorted on their score. Hence, a lot of them might have to be loaded to find one matching the join condition. HySort on the other hand takes advantage of the $\mathbf{t}_o, \mathbf{t}_s \rightarrow \langle \mathbf{s}, \mathbf{p}, \mathbf{o} \rangle$ index to retrieve only those triples matching the join condition.

For query AQY_{238} (Fig. 6.4), which finds all documents that mention an entity labeled *damon* that won a prize in 2004, HySort can first perform joins to find entities that match these conditions and then use an index-based join to find all documents mentioning that entity. HyTopK performs worse (25427.7 ms vs. 86.4 ms) because it may process all *mentions* triples in the worst case and cannot take advantage of the available indexes as HySort does.

Query Size. For different query sizes (measured in terms of the number of patterns), Fig. 6.9 presents average time for relational queries on IMDB-R and YAGO. We see that for HyTopK and SE, processing times increase with the number of patterns, by factors of 29.7 and 1.9, respectively, from 2 to 6 patterns. Processing times for HySort remain constant or even decrease. The reason for this is that due to index-based joins, HySort's performance is not solely dependent on query size. In the case of highly selective queries, HySort only

157

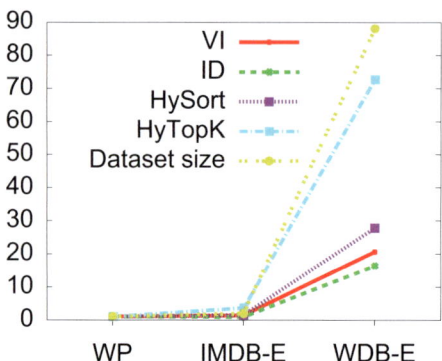

Figure 6.10: Average query times for entity queries in WP, IMDB and WDB
(excluding WDB-P), relative to query times for WP.

requires a few index lookups to compute the results whereas SE and HyTopK
have to process all the data for each query pattern (in the worst case).

Scalability. Fig. 6.10 shows processing times for entity queries on WP, IMDB-
E, and WDB-E relative to the processing times obtained for WP. Additionally,
the graph also shows the relative size of the datasets w.r.t. the WP dataset. The
IMDB (WDB) dataset is 2 times (88 times) larger than the WP dataset. We can
we see that the average query times for VI and ID increase less (e.g. by factors of
20.6 and 16.3, respectively, for WDB) than those for HySort and HyTopK (27.8
and 72.7). This is due to differences in index size as well as the return values
employed by the indexing schemes. Whereas both VI and ID have single entities
as values, Hy* stores triples. Processing and decoding triples require higher
costs because they contain 3 different terms, thus leading to worse performance
for large datasets. Triples however, are needed for relational queries. The results
however indicate that the time increase incurred by HyTopK and especially by
HySort, is less than the increase in dataset size. This is because the increase
in index size hence the performance, is largely determined by the number of
keyword terms, not the data size.

6.6 Conclusion

Building upon SPARQL and RDF, we propose a hybrid search approach that
supports different types of hybrid queries over text-rich data graphs. We provide an indexing solution, HybIdx, which supports the different access patterns

needed to support these queries. We collect data and queries from existing benchmarks and experimental studies to perform a systematic comparison of indexing schemes for hybrid search. The conclusions of this study are: (1) existing queries range from attribute to entity to complex schema-agnostic relational queries. (2) Database extensions capable of dealing with this variety of queries are not time efficient, requiring complex joins. (3) Existing native indexes are efficient but focus on a specific type of queries, i.e. entity queries. (4) HybIdx is the only solution that is both efficient and versatile in terms of query type support. For relational and document queries, it outperforms the second best approach by one and three orders of magnitude, respectively. For entity queries, the native solution is slightly (6%) faster, but is entirely optimized towards these queries such that other types of queries are not possible.

Chapter 7

Processing Flexible Hybrid Graph Patterns

7.1 Introduction

In the previous chapter, we tackled the problem of building efficient indexes for evaluting hybrid graph patterns. This hybrid query model captures the semantics of various proprietary SPARQL full-text extensions employed by RDF store venders and can also be uscd to specify a range of query types, from entity to full relational queries. However, as we already observed in Section 2.4, while HGPs make it easier for users to specify structured queries, knowledge of the structure in the data is still required. Users have to express their information needs in technical terms, i.e. in terms of triple patterns. For example, they need to know when and how to specify joins between two patterns (by using variables that have the same name). This structure information is useful, making up the difference between structured and keyword queries. However, users might be able to capture only some but not all the structure information of a query.

To this end, we proposed the use of *Flexible Hybrid Graph patterns* that add the capability of relaxing the structure of hybrid graph patterns. However, the additional flexibility also introduces ambiguities concerning the interpretations of fHTPs and fHGPs. In this chapter, we present the following contributions towards supporting flexible querying of hybrid data graphs:

- The flexibility introduced by fHGP results in ambiguity. We show how an *fHGP can be translated into a set of unambiguous HGPs*. Then, based on the introduced semantics of HGP, these HGP-interpretations of an fHGP can be processed using SPARQL full-text extensions provided by RDF vendors. Instead of producing all results, top-k processing [IAE04,

ISA⁺04, IAE⁺06] based on the pull/bound rank join (PBRJ) template for instance, can be used to restrict attention to the best results and to terminate early. Finally, results of all its interpretations can be combined to produce results for an fHGP.

- Hence, processing fHGP interpretations can be cast as a multi-query processing problem. We show that processing interpretations one-by-one is however inefficient, as results for several interpretations often overlap, meaning this multi-query processing can be optimized by sharing intermediate results. The main technical contribution of this work is the *Multi-Query PBRJ*. Compared to PBRJ, this extension processes several interpretations simultaneously to share their intermediate results. We introduce novel optimizations that are only possible with the Multi-Query PBRJ.

- With this, we show run-time join order optimization is actually orthogonal to the top-k mechanisms, and propose the use of probing sequence selectors to achieve that. We propose score bounds specific to the interpretations that are tighter than the PBRJ bound obtained for the whole query (all interpretations). They enable more aggressive pulling and bounding, hence earlier reporting of top-k results.

- We implement our approach and top-k baselines for processing HGP-interpretations of an fHGP. Experiments show that sharing results of queries processed simultaneously is several (3-5) times faster than processing the queries one-by-one (without sharing). Further, the join order optimization and more aggressive interpretation-specific pulling/bounding leads to consistent improvements, up to about 50% and 10%, respectively.

In this chapter, we use the definitions of HGPs and fHGPs first given in Section 2.4. For ease of reading, we repeat the important definitions here:

Definition 2.13 (Hybrid Graph Pattern). *Let $\mathcal{V}$ be the set of all variables. A hybrid triple pattern (HTP) $\langle s, p, o \rangle \in (\mathcal{V} \cup \mathcal{U} \cup \mathcal{K}) \times (\mathcal{V} \cup \mathcal{U} \cup \mathcal{K}) \times (\mathcal{V} \cup \mathcal{U} \cup \mathcal{L} \cup \mathcal{K})$ is a triple where the subject, predicate and object can either be a variable in $\mathcal{V}$ or a constant. The latter is either an RDF term in $\mathcal{U} \cup \mathcal{L}$ or a bag of keyword terms in $\mathcal{K}$. Two HTPs t_i and t_j that share a common variable v, establish the join condition (v^i, v^j), where v is called the join variable, and v^i and v^j denotes the variable v in t_i and v in t_j, respectively. A hybrid graph pattern (HGP) is a set of HTPs, $Q = \{t_1, \ldots, t_n\}$.*

Definition 2.14 (HGP Result). *Let $G = (G^R, text)$ be a hybrid data graph, Q be an HGP query, and $\mathcal{V}$ be the set of all variables and $\mathcal{K}$ the set of all bags of keyword terms. Let μ' be the function that maps elements in Q to elements G^R:*

$$\mu' : \mathcal{V} \cup \mathcal{U} \cup \mathcal{L} \cup \mathcal{K} \rightarrow \mathcal{U} \cup \mathcal{L} \begin{cases} (1)\ v \mapsto \mu(v) & \text{if } v \in \mathcal{V} \\ (2)\ K \mapsto t & \text{if } K \in \mathcal{K} \\ (3)\ t \mapsto t & \text{if } t \in \mathcal{U} \cup \mathcal{L} \end{cases}$$

where the mapping $\mu : \mathcal{V} \rightarrow \mathcal{U} \cup \mathcal{L}$ is employed to map variables in Q to RDF terms in G^R. A mapping μ is a result to Q if it satisfies $\langle \mu'(s), \mu'(p), \mu'(o) \rangle \in G^R$, $\forall \langle s, p, o \rangle \in Q$. We denote the set of all result bindings for HGP Q over G^R as $\Omega_{G^R}(Q)$ (we omit G^R if clear from context), i.e. $\mu \in \Omega_{G^R}(Q)$. The set of all bindings for a single hybrid triple pattern $t \in Q$ is $\Omega_{G^R}(t)$.

Definition 2.15 (fHGP). *A flexible hybrid triple pattern (fHTP) is a sequence $f = (e_1, \ldots, e_n)$ with no more than three elements, i.e. $|f| \leq 3$, where each $e_i \in f$ is either a constant (RDF term or bag of keywords) or a variable. A flexible hybrid graph pattern (fHGP) is a set of fHTP $Q = \{f_1, \ldots, f_n\}$.*

Fig. 7.1 shows an excerpt of the hybrid data example in 2.1 that is used in the examples throughout this chapter. We also repeat Fig. 2.5 that shows two example HGPs whose information need is captured by fHGP $Q = \{(type, city), (continent, europe), (capital)\}$.

7.2 Processing Flexible Hybrid Graph Patterns

We will firstly capture interpretations of an fHGP, then discuss how to compute them, and finally, define that a result to an fHGP is the union of the results of all its interpretations.

7.2.1 Interpretations of fHTP and fHGP

Interpretations of an fHTP can be constructed when we consider it as a triple pattern and "missing elements" as placeholders that have to be instantiated:

Definition 7.1 (fHTP Interpretation). *Given a function var that returns a new unique variable on each call, HTP-interpretations $I(f)$ of an fHTP f can be derived for three cases:*

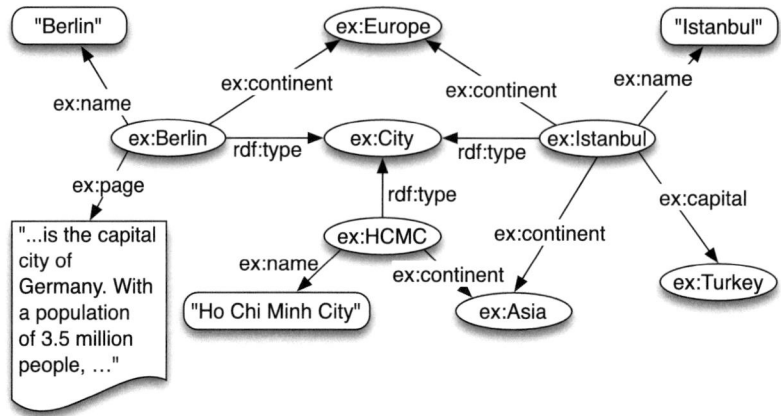

Figure 7.1: Excerpt of the example hybrid data from Fig. 2.1 used throughout this chapter.

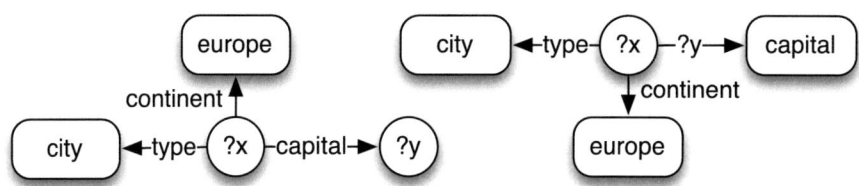

Figure 2.5: Two example hybrid graph patterns that aim at the same information need: "cities in Europe that are capitals". In the left query, the capital status of a city is expressed by a *capital* keyword at the predicate position, whereas in the other query, it is expressed by the *capital* keyword at the object position, i.e. *capital* should appear in the literal value.

- $|f| = 3, f = (e_1, e_2, e_3)$: *when f contains three elements, it has one single HTP-interpretation:*

$$I(f) = \{\langle e_1, e_2, e_3 \rangle\}$$

- $|f| = 2, f = (e_1, e_2)$: *when it contains two elements, it has three HTP-interpretations:*

$$I(f) = \{\langle e_1, e_2, \mathsf{var}\rangle, \langle e_1, \mathsf{var}, e_2\rangle, \langle \mathsf{var}, e_1, e_2\rangle\}$$

- $|f| = 1, f = (e_1)$: *it also has three HTP-interpretations when it contains one element:*

$$I(f) = \{\langle e_1, \mathsf{var}, \mathsf{var}\rangle, \langle \mathsf{var}, e_1, \mathsf{var}\rangle, \langle \mathsf{var}, \mathsf{var}, e_1\rangle\}$$

We denote a single HTP-interpretation of f as $f^* \in I(f)$.

In addition to the ambiguity at the level of the constituent fHTPs, fHGPs also capture "join interpretations", i.e. there are several ways to join HTP-interpretations of fHTPs to form a connected HGP. As discussed, two HTPs establish a join condition when they share the same variable. During the creation of HTPs from an fHTP presented above, only distinct variables are created. Thus, at the beginning, there are no such "implicit" join conditions captured by the use of same variables. Instead, join conditions have to be discovered, which connect two distinct variables instead of the same ones. We introduce the notion of explicit join conditions to distinguish them from implicit ones:

Definition 7.2 (Explicit, Valid Join Condition). *Let t_i and t_j be two HTP-interpretations and v^i and v^j two distinct variables in t_i and t_j, respectively. An explicit join condition $C(t_i, t_j) = (v^i, v^j)$ indicates that t_i and t_j should be joined on the bindings obtained for v_i and v_j (note the order does not matter, i.e. $(v^i, v^j) = (v^j, v^i)$). Let V^i, V^j denote the sets of variables in t_i, t_j, respectively. Then, the set of all valid explicit join conditions established by them are $C(t_i, t_j) = \{(v^i, v^j) | v^i \in V^i, v^j \in V^j\}$.*

With these concepts, we now define an interpretation of an fHGP as being composed of two components, one capturing HTP-interpretations of each fHTP in the fHGP, and the other represents all explicit join conditions necessary to connect these HTPs to form a connected graph:

Definition 7.3 (fHGP Interpretation). *Given an fHGP $Q = \{f_1, \ldots, f_n\}$, the set of all valid interpretations of Q is $I(Q)$, where each $(Q^*, C) \in I(Q)$ is a tuple consisting of (1) a pattern-interpretation, which is a set of HTP-interpretations $Q^* = \{f_1^*, \ldots, f_n^*\}$ that satisfies the following conditions:*

- $|Q^*| = |Q|,$

- *Each $f_i^* \in Q^*$ is an interpretation of the corresponding fHTP $f_i \in Q$, i.e.*
  $f_i^* \in I(f_i),$

and (2) a join-interpretation C, that satisfies:

- *all join conditions $c \in C$ are valid as per Def. 7.2,*

- *the HGP captured by Q^* and C is connected, i.e. there is path of join
  conditions and patterns from any $f_i^* \in Q^*$ to any other $f_j^* \in Q^*$ with $i \neq j$.*

Example 7.1. *Fig. 7.2 shows interpretations of Q, our example fHGP. A pattern-interpretation of Q is $Q_A^* = \{\langle ?r_1,$
continent, europe$\rangle, \langle ?r_2, type, city\rangle, \langle ?r_5, capital, ?r_6\rangle\}$. Together with the
join-interpretation $C_A = \{(?r_1, ?r_2), (?r_1, ?r_5)\}$, we have the first interpretation
(Q_A^*, C_A).*

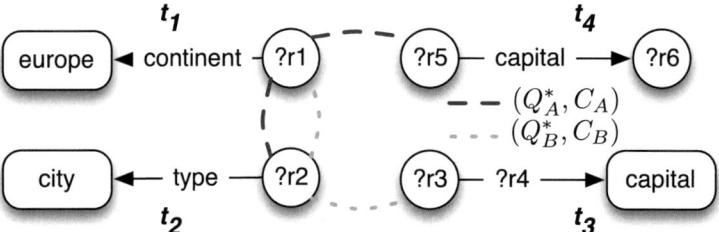

Figure 7.2: Two interpretations $(Q_A^*, C_A) = (\{t_1, t_2, t_4\}, \{(?r_1, ?r_2), (?r_1, ?r_5)\})$
and $(Q_B^*, C_B) = (\{t_1, t_2, t_3\}, \{(?r_1, ?r_2), (?r_2, ?r_3)\})$ of our example
fHGP (*type:city, continent:europe, capital*). The join conditions
are indicated by the dashed lines.

7.2.2 Computing Interpretations and Answers

Given the above specifications, it is now straightforward to derive *all and only
valid* interpretations. All pattern interpretations can be generated by creating all

interpretations $I(f_i)$ for every $f_i \in Q$. All valid join conditions, $C(f_i^*, f_j^*)$, can be captured when considering all possible pair of these interpretations (f_i^*, f_j^*). Together, these two components capture the space of all results. As we construct this search space, we can construct the graph representing interpretations. In every iteration, we construct the search space for one interpretation of Q, i.e. for a subset of HTP-interpretations and join conditions. We terminate one iteration early and move on to the next when we observe there are no join conditions that can be used to connect two given HTP interpretations. To ensure the constructed graph is sound, we verify all conditions specified in Def. 7.3 in every iteration: every result is constructed only from valid join conditions $C(f_i^*, f_j^*)$ and HTP interpretations $I(f_i)$; this is accounted for while we construct the search space. Further, during graph construction, we ensure that every constructed graph is connected and contains one interpretation for every fHTP in Q.

An fHGP can be seen as a set of HGPs. Thus, answers for an fHGP can finally be computed as the union of answers for all HGPs that are interpretations of that fHGP:

Definition 7.4. *Let Q be an fHGP and $I(Q)$ be the set of all valid interpretations of Q. The set of all answers $\Omega(Q)$ to Q is $\bigcup_{Q^* \in I(Q)} \Omega(Q^*)$, where $\Omega(Q^*)$ is set of all result bindings for HGP query Q^* (see Def. 2.14).*

7.3 Multi-HGP Query Processing

In this section we propose a top-k procedure for processing multiple HGP queries at once. That is, it simultaneously processes all interpretations to output the k best results for a given fHGP. For top-k, a generic ranking solution is typically assumed to decide which results are best [IAE04, SP10]. We use the following ranking:

Definition 7.5 (Monotonic Scoring Function). *Given a HGP-interpretation $Q^* = \{f_1^*, \ldots, f_n^*\}$, a binding $\mu_i \in \Omega(f_i^*)$ for a triple pattern f_i^* (we write $\mu_i \in f_i^*$ as shorthand), called a* base binding, *is associated with a score, $score(\mu_i) \in [0,1]$. A monotonic scoring function $\mathcal{S}(score(\mu_1), \ldots, score(\mu_n))$ is used to aggregate scores of base bindings μ_i obtained for triple patterns to obtain the scores of joined results.*

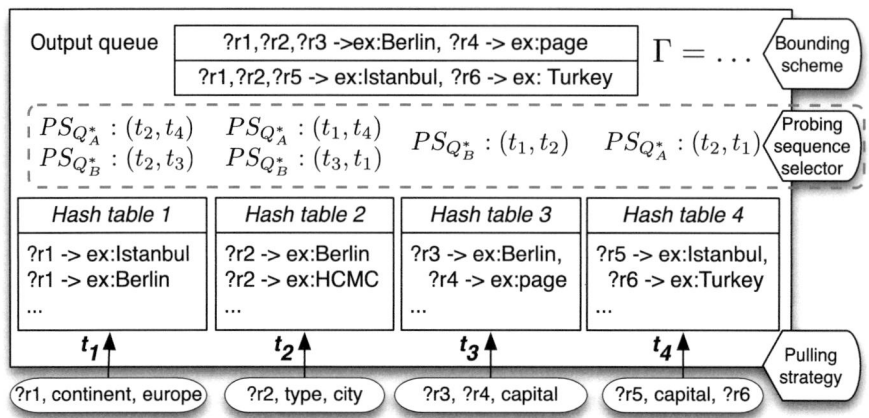

Figure 7.3: Multi-Query PBRJ instance for the example interpretations from Fig. 7.2. The dashed rectangle captures our extensions that distinguish the Multi-Query PBRJ from the PBRJ template.

7.3.1 Single-Query PBRJ

Evaluating an HGP is a graph pattern matching task, which is typically performed by a series of access operations to obtain base bindings for the constituent HTPs, and join operations to combine these bindings. For computing only top-*k* results, *rank joins* have been proposed. Relying on an ordered access to their inputs, these are join operators that report results ordered on their score. By maintaining bounds on the scores of future results, it can guarantee at some point that no better results can be produced, hence safe termination without loosing any of the top-*k* results.

The pull/bound rank join (PBRJ) template represents a general approach that conceptually, covers all previously proposed rank join implementations [SP10]. It employs a multi-way join operator that uses a global threshold to bound the scores of future results. It is parameterized by a *pulling strategy* and a *bounding scheme* that selects the next input to read and computes the upper bound on scores of future results, respectively.

Example 7.2. *Fig. 7.3 illustrates the operation of the PBRJ template as well as our Multi-Query PBRJ extension. For now, let us exclude Multi-Query PBRJ specific parts, namely the dashed rectangle and HTP t_4 with hash table 4. The remaining 3 HTPs represent the Q_B^* part of the interpretation (Q_B^*, C_D)*

from Fig. 7.2 (join conditions C_B are not shown in Fig. 7.3 for the sake of presentation). The PBRJ template has an input for each of the 3 HTPs in Q_B^* and a corresponding hash table. Central to PBRJ is the pulling strategy, which is used to choose from which input to pull the next binding from. For instance, PBRJ may start with pulling from t_1, producing the binding $\rho_1 = ?r_1 \rightarrow ex:Istanbul,$ which is created from $\langle ex:Istanbul, ex:continent, ex:Europe \rangle$ that matches t_1 in the data graph. After a binding ρ_i was pulled from the input for t_i, it is first stored in its corresponding hash table (table 1 in this case) and then used to generate join results by probing all other hash tables. A join result is given when all other hash tables have bindings that w.r.t. the join conditions in C_B, can be joined with our binding ρ_1. This is not the case in the beginning, hence, PBRJ continues with pulling other bindings. When a result can be generated, it is stored in the output queue. For instance the bindings $?r_1 \rightarrow ex:Berlin$ (from t_1), $?r_2 \rightarrow ex:City$ (from t_2), and $?r_3 \rightarrow ex:Berlin, ?r_4 \rightarrow ex:page$ (from t_3) can be joined according to the join conditions $C_B = \{(?r_1, ?r_2), (?r_2, ?r_3)\}$ on ex:Berlin. Note that PBRJ is a multi-way join, which in this case, only yields a result when triples to all three patterns can be joined. The bounding scheme is used to calculate an upper bound Γ on the scores of future join results. If that result in the output queue exceeds Γ, it can be reported as a final result. The algorithm terminates after k final results in the output queue can be reported as the best ones.

Clearly, the pulling strategy and bounding scheme capture the variability with regard to input selection and bound calculation, and ultimately, determine the efficiency of the top-k procedure. We will now extend PBRJ to the multi-query case and propose specific pulling and bounding scheme.

7.3.2 Multi-Query PBRJ with Join Ordering

The PBRJ template is the top-k variant of the join processing commonly employed by RDF stores. For processing HTPs, stores make use of an inverted index to deal with keyword matching, i.e. to return base bindings that are associated with a score, indicating its degree of matching w.r.t. the HTP. Instead of rank joins, standard join implementations that simply process all inputs are used.

Multi-Query. We build upon PBRJ and inverted indexes for processing HGPs and HTPs, respectively. However, while PBRJ is only applicable to one single query, we propose a multi-query extension to process all interpretations of an fHGP. This is because the simple solution of processing the interpretations *sequentially*, e.g. using one multi-way rank join operator for each HGP, is clearly inefficient as interpretations overlaps on the HTPs they are composed of, hence their inputs as well as intermediate joins can be shared. For instance, the two interpretations in Fig. 7.2 share two HTPs and also the join between them. In order to take advantage of these "overlaps" we extend the PBRJ template for processing multiple HGPs *simultaneously* in one single multi-way join operator.

Algorithm 7.1: Multi-Query PBRJ($I(Q), \mathcal{S}, k$)

Input: Interpretations $I(Q) = \{(Q_1^*, C_1), \ldots, (Q_n^*, C_n)\}$, union
$\quad\quad U = \bigcup_{(Q^*, C) \in I(Q)} Q^*$, scoring function $\mathcal{S}$

Data: pulling strategy P, bounding scheme B, probing sequence selector L,
$\quad\quad$ hash tables $T_1, \ldots, T_m$ for each $f_i^* \in U$, output queue O, intermediate
$\quad\quad$ result cache V, threshold Γ

Output: set of k join results O

1 **while** $|O| < k \vee min_{o \in O} S(o) < \Gamma$ **do**
2 $\quad$ $i \leftarrow P.chooseInput(U)$
3 $\quad$ $\rho_i \leftarrow$ next unseen binding of f_i^*
4 $\quad$ $T_i \leftarrow T_i \cup \{\rho_i\}$
5 $\quad$ $V \leftarrow \emptyset$
6 $\quad$ $\mathbf{PS} \leftarrow L.selectSequences(I(Q), f_i^*)$
7 $\quad$ **foreach** $(Q^*, C) \in I(Q)$ *with* $f_i^* \in Q^*$ **do**
8 $\quad\quad$ $R \leftarrow \{\rho_i\}$
9 $\quad\quad$ $PS_{Q*}^{prefix} \leftarrow \emptyset$
10 $\quad\quad$ **foreach** $f_j^* \in PS_{Q^*} \in \mathbf{PS}$ **do**
11 $\quad\quad\quad$ $PS_{Q*}^{prefix} \leftarrow PS_{Q*}^{prefix} + f_j^*$
12 $\quad\quad\quad$ **if** $PS_{Q*}^{prefix} \in V$ **then** $R \leftarrow V[PS_{Q*}^{prefix}]$
13 $\quad\quad\quad$ **else**
14 $\quad\quad\quad\quad$ $R \leftarrow R \bowtie T_j$
15 $\quad\quad\quad\quad$ **if** $\exists PS \in \mathbf{PS} : isPrefix(PS_{Q*}^{prefix}, PS)$ **then**
16 $\quad\quad\quad\quad\quad$ $V[PS_{Q*}^{prefix}] \leftarrow R$

17 $\quad\quad$ Add results in R to O, retain only top-k in O
18 $\quad$ $\Gamma \leftarrow B.updateBound(\rho_i)$
19 **return** O

Join Ordering. Further, works on PBRJ so far focused on reducing the *input depths*, i.e. the number of inputs to be read, using different strategies for pulling, and reporting results as early as possible through aggressive bounding. However, as illustrated by the example, the PBRJ simply probes all hash tables for the other inputs to produce join results for a binding to one input. There is no strategy as to which tables shall be preferred, i.e. there is no order for probing the hash tables, hence no order for executing joins. To address this, we propose the use of a *probing sequence selector* as an additional parameter to the PBRJ template. Intuitively, a probing sequence is a list of HTPs, specifying the order in which their corresponding hash tables should be probed to obtain join results [VNB03]:

Definition 7.6 (Probing Sequence). *Let (Q^*, C) be an interpretation of an fHGP and $f_i^* \in Q^*$ an HTP, then a probing sequence for f_i^* is a list $PS_{Q^*}(f_i^*) = (f_{\pi_1}^*, \ldots, f_{\pi_{|Q^*|}}^*)$ where $\pi_1, \ldots, \pi_{|Q^*|}$ denotes a permutation $1, \ldots, i-1, i+1, \ldots, |Q^*|$ (a permutation without i). Let V^n denote the set of variables in the HTP f_n^*. A probing sequence for f_i^* is valid if for any $f_{\pi_k}^* \in PS_{Q^*}$ there is a join condition (v', v^{π_k}) with $v^{\pi_k} \in V^{\pi_k}$ and $v' \in \{V^i\} \cup \bigcup_{j \in 1, \ldots, k-1} V^{\pi_j}$, i.e. there is a join condition between $f_{\pi_k}^*$ and any preceding HTP in the sequence or the input f_i^* itself.*

Intuitively, the condition ensures that each pattern in the sequence can be joined to at least one preceding pattern.

Example 7.3. *Given interpretation (Q_A^*, C_A) from Fig. 7.2 and its three HTPs t_1, t_2, t_4, a probing sequence for t_1 and Q_A^* is $PS_{Q_A^*}(t_1) = (t_2, t_4)$. It is valid because there is the join condition $(?r_1, ?r_2)$ for variables $?r_1, ?r_2$ in t_1, t_2, respectively, and $(?r_1, ?r_5)$ for $?r_1, ?r_5$ in t_1, t_4, respectively. Using these join conditions, bindings for t_1 are first joined with bindings for t_2 to obtain intermediate results $t_1 \bowtie t_2$, which are then joined with t_4 bindings to obtain final results $t_1 \bowtie t_2 \bowtie t_4$. To be precise, because the union set of join variables $\{V^i\} \cup \bigcup_{j \in 1, \ldots, k-1} V^{\pi_j}$ is considered, t_4 might be joined with t_1 using $(?r_1, ?r_5)$ or other conditions involving variables of HTPs that precede t_4 in the sequence (e.g. it might be joined with bindings to t_2 using the condition $(?r_2, ?r_5)$). Note that the join order only affects intermediate results but not the final results. For instance, another valid sequence is $PS_{Q_A^*}(t_1) = (t_4, t_2)$, producing different intermediate results $(t_1 \bowtie t_4)$, but the same final results (join is commutative). Fig. 7.3 shows only the sequence for t_1 and Q_A^* that has been chosen by the selector (discussed later).*

Using this notion of probing sequence, we propose to optimize the join order as well as avoiding the redundant processing of HTP inputs as well as intermediate results that can be shared across several HGPs. A probing sequence captures the sequence of inputs as well as the order in which they are joined. Probing sequences are constructed separately for different HGPs of an fHGP. However, when HGPs overlap on inputs or intermediate results, these overlaps can be detected by comparing their sequences. Even when entire sequences produce different results (for different interpretations), their overlapping parts represented by *common sequence prefixes* capture the same results that can be shared, i.e. intermediate results for the same prefix have to be calculated only once.

Algorithm. Putting all this together, Alg. 7.1 shows our Multi-Query PBRJ algorithm. It takes a set of interpretations $I(Q) = \{(Q_1^*, C_1), \ldots, (Q_n^*, C_n)\}$ as input and produces top-k results. We obtain the union set U of all HTPs in interpretations $I(Q)$, and create an input hash table T_i for each $f_i^* \in U$. In this way, all inputs are only read once, but may be used for several interpretations. In addition to the pulling strategy P and bounding scheme B, the Multi-Query PBRJ is parameterized by a probing sequence selector L.

During each iteration, the pulling strategy chooses an HTP (among all patterns in U) to read the next binding ρ_i from (line 2), which is then stored in hash table T_i (line 4). First, the intermediate result cache V is reset and L is called to select probing sequences **PS** for all interpretations $(Q^*, C) \in I(Q)$ that f_i^* appears in. Using the input binding ρ_i the algorithm creates final join results for each interpretation (Q^*, C) as follows:

Set R keeps track of intermediate results and is first initialized to contain only ρ_i. We then iterate over all f_j^* in the probing sequence $PS_{Q^*} \in \mathbf{PS}$ for the current interpretation (Q^*, C). First, the current prefix in $PS_{Q^*}^{prefix}$ is updated (line 11). If the intermediate result cache V contains the prefix, no join operation is performed and R is directly retrieved from the cache (line 12). Otherwise, table T_j is probed and joined with R to obtain new intermediate results (line 14). If there is a sequence $PS \in \mathbf{PS}$ such that PS has $PS_{Q^*}^{prefix}$ as a prefix, we store R in cache V for later reuse by another probing sequence (line 16). Final results in R containing one binding for each pattern in Q^* are added to output O that holds the current top-k results (line 17).

After all interpretations have been processed, the bounding scheme is called to update the threshold Γ, which is an upper bound on scores of future join results (line 18). Note that only a maximum of k results are kept in the output O. These are the best ones produced so far, but not necessarily the k ones that can be reported. The algorithm terminates when O indeed contains k best results, i.e.

when the one with the lowest score (the k-th element) exceeds the threshold Γ (line 1).

Example 7.4. *Fig. 7.3 illustrates the Multi-Query PBRJ, which takes all four HTPs of the 2 interpretations (Q_A^*, C_A) and (Q_B^*, C_B) as inputs. Furthermore, each input is now also associated with a list of probing sequences, one for each interpretation it participates in (i.e. the one chosen by the selector, discussed later): inputs 1 and 2 have two probing sequences each, because they appear in both interpretations, while inputs 3 and 4 have only one sequence since they appear only in one interpretation. Now, given the t_1 binding $?r_1 \rightarrow ex{:}Istanbul$ and the interpretation Q_A^* to be processed, the corresponding probing sequence $PS_{Q_A^*}(t_1) = (t_2, t_4)$ is used to determine the order of joining it with bindings to t_2 and t_4. The two probing sequences for t_1 share the prefix t_2, thus the previously produced join results $t_1 \bowtie t_2$ for Q_A^* can also be used for Q_B^* when it is processed according to the sequence $PS_{Q_B^*}(t_1) = (t_2, t_3)$.*

The proof showing that the proposed algorithm yields *all and only valid* top-k results follows from results already established for PBRJ template: given the pulling strategy P considers all requires inputs and the bounding scheme B yields the correct upper bound on the scores of future join results, the results reported by PBRJ are indeed the top-k ones. When there is only one HGP to be processed, our extension differs to that only in the use of the selector L. The selector however, does not have an effect on the final results produced in O (discussed in detail in Section 7.3.3), i.e. the O produced by PBRJ and our approach is the same, hence, the reported top-k results from O depend only on P and B. If several HGPs have to be processed, O contains the union of results produced for each HGPs. If P is now adapted to consider inputs from all HGPs, and B yields the correct upper bound on the scores of future join results over all HGPs, then we can provide the same top-k guarantee. We will discuss our specific proposals for B and P in Section 7.3.4.

7.3.3 Probing Sequence Selection

Join ordering has been shown to be difficult in the top-k setting where tree-structured query plans of binary join operators with local thresholds are employed to process data [IAE04, ISA+04, IAE+06]. This is because here the join order, due to the use of local thresholds, also has an effect on the inputs read, hence also the reduction on the threshold. Changing the join order may lead to different input depths and threshold [IAE04]. Hence, join order cannot be seen and optimized independently from the pulling and bounding strategy that targets at reducing the input depth [ISA+04] and threshold, respectively.

We now show this problem does not occur with the proposed Multi-Query PBRJ, because it uses a multi-way join to combine results from all inputs and a global threshold to bound their scores. Note that because of the multi-way join, results in R added to O in Alg. 7.1 line 17 must contain one binding for every pattern in the HGP. Thus, while different probing sequences yield different intermediate results in R, the final results in R are only dependent on the inputs released by pulling strategy P, but are the same for all probing sequences, i.e. are dependent on P but not L. The bound determined by B is a global threshold calculated from these final results, hence is also not dependent on L. As a result, *join order is orthogonal to the pulling P and bounding B*, which we propose to optimize separately through the choice of probing sequence L.

Adaptive Optimization. Compile-time optimization of the probing sequences is possible when there are sufficient statistics available. In this work, we focus on adaptive optimization using statistics acquired at run-time. We collect lightweight statistics to reduce overhead. For each probing sequence, we store the number of *hits h*, i.e. how often it was executed, and how many *intermediate results i* were produced during the execution of the sequence. As discussed, all probing sequences for a particular input and HGP are equivalent in the number of final results they produce. Hence, a sequence with fewer intermediate results shall be preferred such that the latter measure can be employed to denote cost.

Selectors. We propose two selectors that use the cost per hit ratio $r = i/h$ (if $h = 0$ we set $r = 0$):

- The *direct selector* selects the probing sequence with the lowest cost per hit ratio r.

- The *lottery selector* is based on lottery scheduling [AH00]. For each probing sequence, we calculate its score as $s = 1/r$ (if $r = 0$ we set $s = 1$). Then, we select between probing sequences using their scores as probabilities.

To reduce the overhead, the probing sequence selector is only called in intervals, i.e. instead of using one sequence for every input binding (line 6 in Alg. 7.1), it is used for a batch of input bindings.

Example 7.5. *Suppose that the t_1 binding $?r_1 \rightarrow$ ex:Berlin was just pulled by the join operator and that all other inputs have been completely read. With* *sequence (t_2, t_4) for t_1 and (Q_A^*, C_A) we first obtain intermediate results $t_1 \bowtie t_2$ (because there is a t_2 binding, $?r_2 \rightarrow$ ex:Berlin), but no final results (no match in t_4). Using sequence (t_4, t_2) we could have stopped processing of (Q_A^*, C_A) for the binding after probing the t_4 hash table (because $t_1 \bowtie t_4$ is empty), thereby reducing costs.*

7.3.4 Interpretation-specific Bounding & Pulling

Pulling and bounding strategies rely on the notion of *score bounds*: given an input binding ρ_i for input f_i^*, the maximum score $\overline{S}(\rho_i)$ a final join result based on ρ_i can achieve is the score of ρ_i combined with the maximum scores of input bindings for all other inputs, i.e.

$$\overline{S}(\rho_i) = S(\bar{s}_1, \ldots, \bar{s}_{i-1}, score(\rho_i), \bar{s}_{i+1} \ldots, \bar{s}_n)$$

where $\bar{s}_j$ is the maximum score of input j. For example, let 1 be the maximum score of bindings from $t_1, t_3,$ and t_4, and ρ_2 be an input binding pulled from t_2, then its bound $\overline{S}(\rho_2)$ is the aggregated score $S(1, score(\rho_2), 1, 1)$.

To determine whether a result can be reported, i.e. exceeds the threshold Γ, the *corner bound* is commonly used as Γ [IAE04, SP10]: it maintains bounds $\overline{S}(\rho_i)$ for each input, where ρ_i is the last seen binding for the pattern $f_i^* \in Q^*$, and calculates Γ as the maximum of all inputs, i.e. $\Gamma = \max_{f_i^* \in Q^*} \overline{S}(\rho_i)$.

Interpretation-specific Bounding. The Multi-Query PBRJ has (1) inputs for several interpretations; and (2) one input might be used by different interpretations. To tackle the difference (1), we propose an interpretation-specific score bound. Intuitively, this bound for an input f_i^* does not aggregate over the scores of all other inputs of all HTPs, but only over those for a specific interpretation Q^*. For example, given the interpretation (Q_B^*, C_B) consisting of three HTPs, the input binding ρ_1 for t_1, the maximum score for t_2 and t_3 is 1, then the interpretation-specific score bound is calculated as $\overline{S}_{Q_B^*}(\rho_1) = S(score(\rho_1), 1, 1)$, i.e. S aggregates only over 3 HTPs in Q_B^* instead of using all 4 HTPs. To tackle difference (2), we note that the top-k results are determined from the union of candidate results obtained from all interpretations. That is, in order to provide the top-k guarantee, all interpretations in which the input appears are important for computing the bound based on that input. That is, this interpretation-specific bound has to be extended to cover all interpretations. Clearly, the bound should be maximized over all these interpretations to provide the top-k guarantee over their union. In this example, ρ_1 for t_1 appears in both interpretations. Thus, let the maximum score for

t_4 be 0.9, then we have $\overline{\mathcal{S}}_{t_1}(\rho_1) = \max\{\mathcal{S}(score(\rho_1), 1, 1), \mathcal{S}(score(\rho_1), 1, 0.9)\}$. Putting these together, we define the following bounds:

Definition 7.7 (Score Bounds). *Let f_i^* be an HTP and Q_j^* be a subquery that can be joined to form Q^* such that the join result for Q^* is $\Omega(Q^*) = \Omega(Q_j^*) \bowtie \Omega(f_i)$, and let $\rho_i \in \Omega(f_i^*)$ be the last seen base input binding to f_i^*. The* interpretation-specific score bound *is*

$$\overline{\mathcal{S}}_{Q^*}(\rho_i) = \mathcal{S}(\overline{s}_{f_1^*}, \ldots, \overline{s}_{f_{i-1}^*}, score(\rho_i), \overline{s}_{f_{i+1}^*}, \ldots, \overline{s}_{f_n^*})$$

for $f_1^*, \ldots, f_n^* \in Q^*$. Let $I(Q)$ be the set of all interpretations, the interpretation-specific corner bound *is*

$$\Gamma = \max_{Q^* \in I(Q), f_i^* \in Q^*} \overline{\mathcal{S}}_{Q^*}(\rho_i)$$

The multi-query corner bound Γ is updated when a new unseen binding is processed to reflect that the score of the last seen binding ρ_i shall be updated with the score of the new binding (see line 18 in Alg. 7.1). Note Γ is calculated only from interpretation-specific bound scores. Compared to the corner bound [IAE04, SP10] that uses the scores of all inputs that would overestimate the score of final join results, this one only uses those inputs that are actually used by the fHGP and thus, can provide a tighter bound.

$$\Gamma_{I-CBA} = max\{\overline{\mathcal{S}}_{Q^*}(\rho_1), \overline{\mathcal{S}}_{Q^*}(\rho_2), \overline{\mathcal{S}}_{Q^*}(\rho_3), \overline{\mathcal{S}}_{Q^*}(\rho_4)\} = 2.8$$

$\overline{\mathcal{S}}_{Q_A^*}(\rho_1) = 2.7$
$\overline{\mathcal{S}}_{Q_B^*}(\rho_1) = 2.8$

t_1	$\overline{s}_{t_1} = 0.9$	t_2	$\overline{s}_{t_2} = 1.0$	t_3	$\overline{s}_{t_3} = 1.0$	t_4	$\overline{s}_{t_4} = 0.9$
$score(\rho_1) = 0.8$		$score(\rho_2) = 0.6$		$score(\rho_3) = 0.7$		$score(\rho_4) = 0.3$	

$\mathcal{S}(\rho_1) = 3.7$

$$\Gamma_{CBA} = max\{\overline{\mathcal{S}}(\rho_1), \overline{\mathcal{S}}(\rho_2), \overline{\mathcal{S}}(\rho_3), \overline{\mathcal{S}}(\rho_4)\} = 3.7$$

Figure 7.4: Score bound calculation for input t_1 with corner bound (CB) and interpretation-specific corner bound (I-CB) (with sum as scoring function $\mathcal{S}$).

Example 7.6. *Fig. 7.4 shows the score bound calculation for input t_1 with the corner bound (CB) and the interpretation-specific corner bound (I-CB) for the running example using sum as the scoring function. For each input, maximum and last seen scores, $\bar{s}_{t_i}$ and $score(\rho_i)$, respectively, are shown. We can see that the score bound $\overline{S}$ aggregates all four inputs, whereas the interpretation-specific score bounds $\overline{S}_{Q_A^*}$ and $\overline{S}_{Q_B^*}$ aggregate just three inputs (t_1, t_2, t_4 and t_1, t_2, t_3, respectively). The resulting bound Γ_{I-CB} is lower than the corner bound Γ_{CB} and results can be reported earlier.*

Interpretation-specific Pulling. The main pulling strategies used in top-k processing are *round-robin* and *corner-bound-adaptive* [IAE04, SP10]. The former simply accesses all inputs in a round-robin fashion and can be directly applied in the multi-query case. The latter is based on the corner bound. It selects the input t_i that has the highest score bound $\overline{S}$. Instead, we use the interpretation-specific bound for our *interpretation-specific corner-bound-adaptive* strategy. We select $f_i^* \in U$ such that

$$\overline{S}_{f_i^*}(\rho_i) = \max_{Q^* \in I(Q), f_i^* \in Q^*} \overline{S}_{Q^*}(\rho_i)$$

is maximized, i.e. we select the input that has the highest interpretation-specific score bound for all interpretations it appears in.

7.4 Related Work

Hybrid Query Languages. It has been recognized that while keywords are necessary for querying textual data and also, can be used as an intuitive means to query structured data [HP02, LOF+08, TWRC09], exploiting the full richness of structure information in hybrid data requires query expressivity that goes beyond keywords. We propose HGP to capture the SPARQL full-text extensions provided by RDF stores. This is close in spirit to languages like XQuery Full-Text [AYL06], with the difference that it deals with RDF graphs not with XML trees. A proposal close to HGP is described in [ERSW10], where keyword terms are associated with RDF triple patterns. HGPs enable more fine-grained full-text constraints in that every element in a pattern can be a keyword term. Most notably, there exists no extension to SPARQL that in addition to the use of keywords, also enables querying with relaxed structure constraints. We account for this in proposing fHGPs.

Hybrid Query Processing. Chakrabarti et al. [CSS10] discuss how keyword-based search can be extended by adding structure to data and query answers. The QUICK system presented by Pound et al. [PIW10] deals with document retrieval based on entity queries where keywords can also match structure elements of the data. The work on indexing dataspaces [DH07] and the NAGA search engine [KSI+08] also support hybrid queries with keywords matching structure elements. While our solution targets general graph patterns, these works however focus on limited types of queries representing specific patterns, e.g. entity queries [PIW10, DH07]. Further, they tackle aspects that are orthogonal to the scope of this work, i.e. indexing [DH07] hybrid data and ranking hybrid results [PIW10, KSI+08], as opposed to top-k join processing.

Top-k Join Processing. Earlier works build upon tree-structured query plans of binary rank join operators with local thresholds [IAE04, ISA+04, IAE+06]. Recently, the PBRJ template was proposed [SP10] and used to examine rank join bounding schemes and pulling strategies from a conceptual point of view. Based on this template, we propose the Multi-Query PBRJ, which extends PBRJ's capabilities to process several queries simultaneously. We show that as opposed to earlier works [IAE04, ISA+04, IAE+06], join-order optimization can be done when separated from the pulling and bounding strategies using our probing sequence selector.

Multi-Query Optimization. Works in this direction focus on compile-time optimization. Because many queries have to be considered, the search space for the query optimizer becomes very large. Thus, different strategies have been proposed to reduce the search space [RSSB00]. Similar to these approaches, our work also builds upon the idea of sharing results between queries. However, the processing is performed in a top-k fashion and the optimization is done adaptively at query-time using simple, low-overhead statistics.

7.5 Evaluation

7.5.1 Datasets & Queries

The evaluation was performed on datasets of varying sizes. Some include a large number of documents (WDB), whereas others contain a large amount of structured data (IMDB, YAGO, WDB). Queries for each dataset are based on the ones used in previous works. Fig. 7.5 shows a sample of queries for all datasets. All queries used in this evaluation are listed in Appendix A.3.2.

IMDB. This dataset contains information about movies and actors. For this, we took 46 keyword queries from the benchmark [CW10]. Four queries were left out because they could not be translated to our query model (they ask for unspecified paths between two entities). The example query $IMDB_{41}$ asks for films with Audrey Hepburn from year 1951.

YAGO. We use the part of the YAGO knowledge base used in [KSI$^+$08]. It contains cross-domain knowledge extracted from Wikipedia, such as people, organizations, locations, etc. and relationships between them. From the hybrid queries used in [KSI$^+$08], we took 67 queries that are compatible with our query model (the *connected* constraint used by these queries is not supported by our implementation). We also created additional 9 queries with 2-4 joins as the previous queries have none or only one join. Example query $YAGO_3$ asks for the family name of writers influenced by the creator of "War of the Worlds".

WDB. We created this dataset by enriching entities in DBpedia 3.5.1 with their corresponding Wikipedia page. In total, it includes DBpedia plus 6.5M documents (79.5M triples total). For this dataset we created a total of 20 queries with 2-4 joins. For example, query WDB_8 asks for the notable works of best-selling, british authors. Query WDB_{13} asks for the alma mater and the doctoral advisor of the person that is know for the smallpox vaccine.

7.5.2 Systems

We aim to evaluate our approach and compare it with baseline solutions to the fHGP processing problem by adapting existing solutions for full-text SPARQL extension. In particular, we aim to assess the merits of the proposed top-k processing techniques. Thus, we obtain a top-k baseline by using an RDF store implementation that can process BGPs as well as HGPs using additional inverted indexes. Then, an fHGP is processed by computing its interpretations as proposed, and evaluating the resulting HGPs via top-k join processing. For the latter, we use a PBRJ implementation that does not share results (*Sharing Off*), i.e. process queries one-by-one, and select hash tables at random (*RND*), i.e. no join order optimization. We study two version of this baseline, one using corner-bound-adaptive (*CBA*) and the other employs round-robin (*RR*) as the pulling strategy. The corner bound is used by both.

The implementation of our approach is based on the same infrastructure, but employs Multi-Query PBRJ to enable sharing (*Sharing On*). To compare with RND, we examine the effects of different join orderings using the direct (*DIR*) and lottery (*LOT*) selector. We use our interpretation-specific corner-

WDB_8 (bestselling author, british, notablework)
WDB_{13} (knownfor:smallpox vaccine, doctoral advisor, alma mater)
WDB_{11} (type:populatedplace, country:germany, postal code, area code)
$IMDB_1$ (denzel washington)
$IMDB_{41}$ (person, name:audrey hepburn, cast, year:1951)
$YAGO_4$ (created:war of the worlds, influences, type:writer, familyname)

Figure 7.5: Selected evaluation queries.

bound-adaptive (I-CBA) pulling and bounding and compare it with CBA and RR.

Setting. All implementations were done in Java 6. The evaluation was run on a server with 2 Intel Xeon E5-2670 CPUs with 128GB RAM, of which 4GB were assigned to the Java VM. The indexes were stored on a RAID10 array of six 15k SAS disks. Before each query run, the disk caches of the operating systems were cleared as well as all internal caches of the query engine. All query times in the results are averages of five runs, of which the first was discarded to account for the warm-up of the Java JIT compiler.

7.5.3 Results

We observe that the main performance difference between our approach and the baseline lies in the sharing of results. Overall, sharing helps to improve the results by several factors (3-5). The join order optimization using DIR improves performance by up to 47% compared to LOT and RND. Further, using I-CBA for pulling and bounding leads to consistent improvements of up to 10%. We now discuss the effects of different factors.

Sharing. Fig. 7.6a shows the performance of different selectors for WDB queries with sharing enabled or disabled. Note the baseline is represented by the combination Sharing Off and RND. Only the number for the baseline is obtained using CBA, while other numbers in Fig. 7.6a are for I-CBA. We can clearly see that sharing intermediate results between probing sequences for an input is always beneficial. Query times for the DIR, LOT and RND selectors improve from 18.7s, 23.1s and 22.0s to 4.8s, 5.5s and 6.4s, respectively. The relative gain for RND with a factor of 3.4 is less than for DIR and LOT, where query times are 3.8 and 4.4 times lower with sharing. This suggests that using the cost estimates obtained at query-time is effective, and the DIR method that most aggressively orders the joins according to these costs is most efficient.

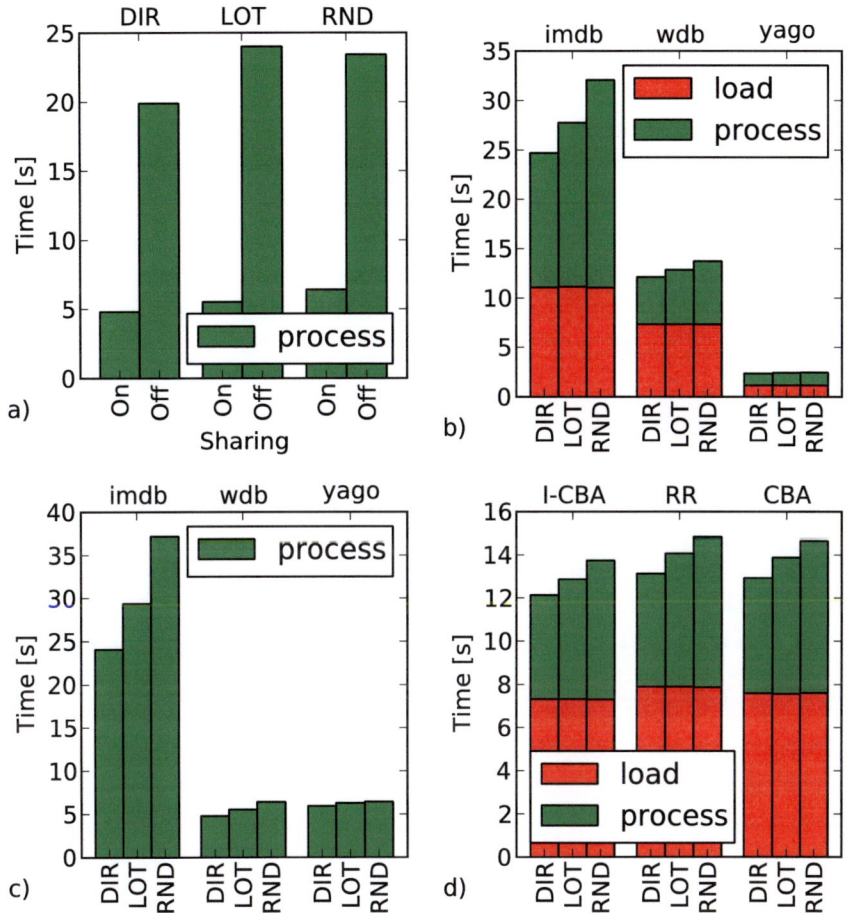

Figure 7.6: a) Performance of different selectors with sharing on/off and $k =$ 10, b) Performance for different datasets with I-CBA, sharing on, $k = 10$, c) Performance for queries with more than one join with I-CBA, sharing on, $k = 10$, d) Performance for different selectors with different pulling strategies, sharing on, $k = 10$.

Join Order. This effect of join ordering is further illustrated in Fig. 7.6b. Query processing time is split into loading data and (join) processing. Over all datasets, the query times of RND and LOT are on average 25% and 10% higher than the times of DIR (14.2s and 12.6s vs. 11.4s, respectively). We can clearly see that the difference in query times is due only to processing times as load times are the same for all selectors. This confirms our results established for join order optimization: the selector does not affect the input depths (pulling and bounding); thus, because the same strategy was used for pulling and bounding, input depths as reflected by load times do not change.

Further, Fig. 7.6c shows the processing times for queries with at least two joins, i.e. those for which join ordering is relevant. Here, the difference between the selectors becomes more pronounced: RND and LOT perform 47% and 20% worse than DIR, respectively (20.0s and 16.2s vs. 13.5s).

Query Size. We also study the aspect of query size. Fig. 7.7a shows the average query times over all datasets by the number of joins (0-5) for all selectors. We can see that for 0 and 1 joins there is no difference between the selectors as join ordering does not play a role here. For more than one join, however, the differences between the selectors clearly increase, indicating that join order optimization is more crucial with queries with more joins.

Pulling Strategies. Fig. 7.6d shows the times for WDB queries for all selectors and different pulling strategies. Overall, I-CBA outperforms both CBA and RR. For DIR, the query times of RR and CBA are 8% and 6% higher than the I-CBA query times (13.1s and 12.9s vs. 12.1s, respectively).

Dataset Size. While the IMDB dataset is much smaller than the YAGO and WDB datasets (5.6M, 13M, and 75M triples, respectively), its query times are the highest on average. This is due to the fact that the patterns in IMDB queries are less selective and contain long paths (e.g. $IMDB_{41}$). For $k = 10$ and the I-CBA strategy, 643.231 input bindings are read on average for each input, whereas the queries for WDB and YAGO only read 298.881 and 162.197 input bindings, respectively. Clearly, the larger amount of data that is processed leads to higher load and processing times.

Number of Results. Fig. 7.8a shows the load times of all queries with $k \in \{1, 10, 100\}$. As expected load times increase with higher values of k as more input data has to be loaded to compute a larger number of final join results. While the I-CBA strategy outperforms the CBA and RR strategies for all values of k, there is a difference in relative performance. For $k = 1$, I-CBA is 14% and 8% faster than RR and CBA, respectively, but for $k = 100$ it is only 3.3% and

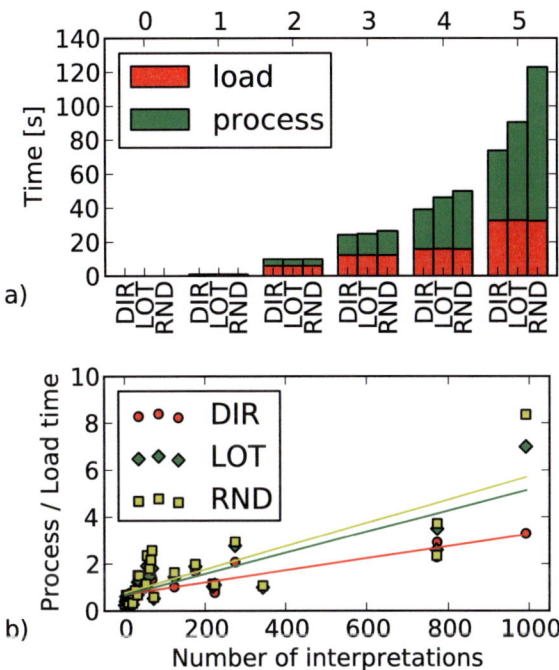

Figure 7.7: a) Query times over all datasets for queries with 0 to 5 joins, b) Ratio of process vs. load time by number of interpretations (both I-CBA strategy, $k = 10$).

2.5% faster. Hence, we conclude that the I-CBA strategy works especially well for producing the first results.

Fig 7.8b shows the number of intermediate results created during query processing for the three selectors and $k \in \{0, 10, 100\}$. Overall, DIR generates fewer intermediate results for all values of k than both LOT and RND. For $k = 1$, LOT and RND create 39% and 140% more intermediate results than DIR. For $k = 100$, the relative amount decreases for LOT (to 29%) and increases for RND (to 159%). First, this suggests that more aggressively optimizing for cost as done by DIR is better, especially when producing few results. Also, the join order becomes more important as more results and data are involved, as indicated by the large performance decrease of RND for large k.

Number of Interpretations. Generally, we expect both load and processing times to increase for queries with higher number of interpretations. However,

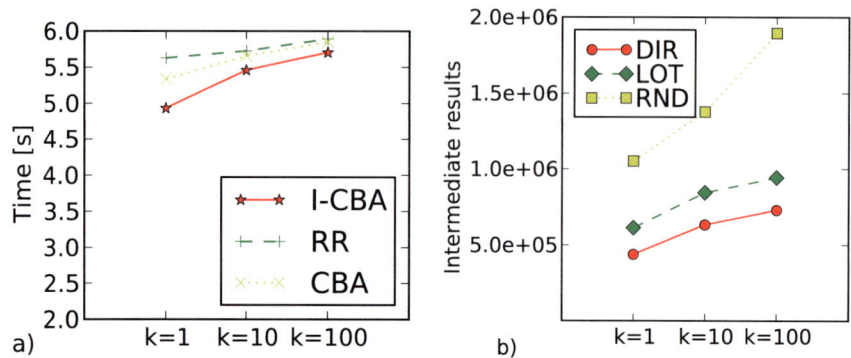

Figure 7.8: a) WDB load times for $k \in \{1, 10, 100\}$ (DIR selector), b) Number of intermediate results with $k \in \{1, 10, 100\}$ (I-CBA strategy).

given that a single pattern-interpretation can generate multiple join-interpretations we expect processing time to increase more than load time. Fig. 7.7b shows a plot of the ratio between processing and load time vs. the number of interpretations. We see that with a larger number of interpretations the ratio between processing and load time increases from below 1 for queries with only few interpretations up to 8 (RND) for queries with a high number of interpretations. From the linear fits, we can see this ratio increases more slowly for DIR compared to LOT and RND. It more effectively reduces the number of intermediate results than the LOT and RND selectors. This translates to a reduction of processing time especially for queries with many interpretations.

7.6 Conclusion

We have presented Flexible Hybrid Graph Pattern as an extension to SPARQL Basic Graph Pattern that enables users to query hybrid data graphs using keywords and relaxed-structured constraints. For processing such a query, we present a framework based on its translation to unambiguous graph queries, which is followed by multi-query processing. We propose a multi-query top-k processing technique that compare to top-k baselines that can be adapted for this problem, provides several times faster performance.

We focus on the framework and limit the technical scope to multi-query processing. Clearly, much future work is needed towards the effective and efficient processing of the proposed flexible patterns. Most important directions are ranking – not only results but also interpretations – as well indexing to provide faster access to patterns that involve keywords as well as those, they may involve several keywords and joins (materialized join indexes).

Chapter 8

Conclusion

8.1 Summary

In this thesis we presented our contributions concerning the efficient evaluation of queries over hybrid data. We motivated this work with the observation that in recent years the amount of publicly available structured data has been increasing, which, combined with the already large volume of unstructured data, gives rise to hybrid data. Accessing both, unstructured and structured data, in an integrated fashion, also known as DB & IR integration, has become an important research topic that has also gained commercial interest. Of particular importance are efficient processing techniques for queries over hybrid data. Here, we distinguish between three types of queries, namely unstructured keyword queries, structured queries, and hybrid queries. Each of these query types has advantages and disadvantages, motivating the research into efficient processing techniques for each type. We used the RDF data model as a formal model for representing hybrid data as a text-rich data graph. Based on this model, we gave formal definitions for unstructured keyword queries and structured SPARQL queries, and also introduced hybrid graph pattern queries as a representative for hybrid query languages.

We described the main challenge of query processing, regardless of query type, namely that the search space for finding valid answers is very large. In terms of query processing, this challenge can be tackled in two main ways: first, the amount of data to be processed may be reduced, e.g. by using specialized index structures, and, second, the data may be processed more efficiently, e.g. by employing intelligent algorithms that require less resources to obtain query answers. The approaches presented in Chapters 3 - 7 of the thesis used both of these options to increase the performance of query processing for all three query types. Concerning this we gave a number of hypotheses, which we will now examine to show that they have been validated by the work presented in the main part of the thesis.

Unstructured Queries. Evaluating keyword queries over hybrid data graphs entails finding elements in the data graph relevant for query keywords and then finding structures connecting them. For this, Steiner trees and graphs have been established as the general model for keyword query answers. As processing such queries relying on graph traversal only has been shown to be inefficient, previous approaches rely on materialized indexes of the neighborhoods of data elements. Concerning this, we gave the following hypothesis:

Hypothesis 1. *Given a set of data elements and their neighborhoods in a data graph, determining coverage at the level of paths, instead of graphs, allows for more fine-grained pruning and thereby reduces the size of the materialized index.*

In this thesis we presented our approach for evaluating keyword queries that uses an extension of the 2-hop cover concept to pre-compute and materialize the neighborhoods of data elements while determining coverage at the level of paths. In the experiments, we show that this reduces storage requirement by up to 86%. Further, storing neighborhoods as paths enables the use of the common database operations data access and join to deal with the keyword query problem on structured data graphs. We make use of top-k processing techniques and propose an extension of the hash rank join to not only terminate early after the k best results have been found, but also to select plans in a top-k fashion during query processing. In experiments we show that this approach improves scalability and performance compared to previous approaches (over 50% on average).

Structured Queries. In this thesis, we examined the processing of structured SPARQL queries in the context of Linked Data query processing, a novel paradigm for processing SPARQL queries directly over Linked Data by retrieving Linked Data sources at run-time via HTTP dereferencing and following links to discover new sources. This new mode of query processing presents novel challenges, which we detailed in this thesis, also showing how previous works tackled these challenges with bottom-up and top-down evaluation strategies. Based on this, we state the following hypothesis:

Hypothesis 2. *The combination of compile-time knowledge about sources with knowledge gained at run-time can be used to perform run-time refinements and thereby improve early result reporting, i.e. first query results are reported earlier.*

In this thesis, we proposed the mixed query evaluation strategy that combines knowledge available about previously indexed sources with knowledge gained at run-time through online discovery of new sources. This knowledge is used to first create a best-effort query plan at compile-time, which is then refined at run-time. Data sources are ranked according to their importance, for which we provide several metrics. In the experiments we show, that this mixed strategy outperform the previously proposed approaches in terms of early result reporting by up to 42%. Further, we proposed a novel operator, the symmetric index hash join, that combines stream-based query processing of data retrieved from remote Linked Data sources with data retrieved from local indexes in RDF stores. By employing separate access modules for index access, we ensure that query execution does not block and can proceed even when blocking I/O is performed in one part of the query plan.

Further, existing works focus on the ranking and pruning of sources, or on the efficient processing of data while it is retrieved from sources, i.e. joins and traversal algorithms for retrieving and processing data from sources. However, there exists no *systematic approach for query plan optimization*, especially the kind that considers both the problems of source selection and data processing in a holistic way. We therefore cast the query optimization problem in this setting as a multi-objective optimization problem that takes into account multiple optimization objectives, such as cost and output cardinality, such that the query optimizer is not only responsible for deciding how data is processed, but also which data is processed. In our proposed approach, we applied the classic dynamic programming algorithm to solve the multi-objective query optimization problem and stated the following hypothesis:

Hypothesis 3. *By introducing tight bounds that maintain the monotonicity with regard to the combination of subplans, the optimal substructure of the multi-objective query optimization problem is preserved when employing operator sharing, such that the classic dynamic programming algorithm for query optimization can be applied. Further, relaxing the comparability constraint enables the optimizer to prune suboptimal plans more aggressively. The generated query plans then represent the trade-off between the optimization objectives.*

In this thesis, we provide a tight bound based on the maximal benefit that can be achieved by sharing operators between two subplans. We prove that with this bound the monotonicity of the cost and cardinality functions are not violated with regard to the combination of subplans. With this result, the problem retains its optimal substructure even when employing operator sharing, i.e. the dynamic programming algorithm for query optimization can be applied. Further, we relax the comparability constraint such that plans are comparable when they produce results for the same (sub-)expression. Otherwise, each unique combination of input sources would lead to non-comparable plans, severely reducing the amount of plans pruneable by the optimizer. In the experiments, we show that baseline approaches seldom generate Pareto-optimal plans, while our approach generates Pareto-optimal plans that better represent the trade-off between the multiple objectives.

Hybrid Queries. We first introduced hybrid graph patterns (HGP) as a formalization of hybrid queries expressible in various proprietary full-text search extensions from various RDF store vendors. In hybrid graph patterns, keywords can be used instead of RDF terms at any possible in a basic graph pattern. Hybrid graph patterns can therefore be used to formulate a variety of hybrid queries that have been examined in previous works, such as entity, document, but also full relational queries. In the first part of our work on processing hybrid queries in this thesis, we examine the problem of creating indexes based on which hybrid queries can be efficiently processed. Here, we make the following hypothesis:

Hypothesis 4. *Hybrid queries combine structural constraints with keyword matching and can largely be categorized by the types of required access patterns as entity, attribute or relation queries. Hybrid indexes that combine RDF terms and keyword terms in their index keys and cover all possible access patterns improve query performance by reducing the number of joins necessary for answering hybrid queries.*

In this thesis, we first study previously proposed indexing schemes and show they do not support all access patterns, or only through the use of expensive joins. We then proposed HybIdx, which supports the different access patterns to support all types of queries. By explicitly indexing multiple access pattern we also reduce the need for joins when evaluating queries. We collect data and queries from existing benchmarks and experimental studies to perform a systematic comparison of indexing schemes for hybrid search. The conclusions of this study are: (1) existing queries range from attribute to entity to complex schema-agnostic relational queries. (2) Database extensions capable of dealing with this variety of queries are not time efficient, requiring complex joins. (3) Existing native indexes are efficient but focus on specific type of queries, i.e. entity queries. (4) HybIdx is the only solution that is both efficient and versatile in terms of query type support. For relational and document queries, it outperforms the second best approach by one and three orders of magnitude, respectively. For entity queries, the native solution is slightly (6%) faster but is entirely optimized towards these queries such that other types are not possible.

We further proposed to add to BGPs not only the use of keywords, but also the capability to relax its structure, resulting in flexible hybrid graph patterns (fHGP). Here, users can specify structural constraints where they are able to and to use keywords otherwise. We then show how the ambiguity introduced by the additional flexibility is resolved by interpreting flexible hybrid graph patterns as unambiguous hybrid graph patterns. For each fHGP there are multiple HGP-interpretations where the union of their results forms the result of the original fHGP. Further, we propose the use of top-k processing techniques based on the PBRJ template to efficiently process HGP-interpretations. To this end, we stated the following hypothesis:

Hypothesis 5. *The execution of multiple queries (interpretations) can be made more efficient by introducing interpretation-specific score bounds that are tighter than previous bounds and applying run-time join order optimization in addition to sharing intermediate results between the different interpretations.*

To validate this hypothesis, we proposed the Multi-Query PBRJ template, an extension of the PBRJ template that is able to process multiple HGP queries simultaneously. We propose an interpretation-specific score bound and implement it as a new bounding scheme and a new pulling strategy. We show in experiments that the new bound outperforms previous score bounds. Further, we show that, in the PBRJ template, the join order can be optimized independently from the top-k mechanisms. We capture the join order as probing sequences and adapt these at run-time using lightweight statistics. We use probing sequences to determine when intermediate results between the different interpretations can be shared. In the experiments we show that sharing intermediate results leads to large performance improvements (up to a factor of 4.4) and that join order optimization with lightweight statistics also increases performance (up to 47%), especially for queries with a large number of interpretations.

Conclusion. In all, we have validated the hypotheses stated at the beginning of this work, thereby advancing the state of the art in terms of processing queries over hybrid data. Even though our proposed approaches for the various types of queries are necessarily different in nature in order to tackle the specific challenges of each query type, they all have in common the general way in which the main challenge of query processing is approached. For each query type, we proposed ways reduced the amount of data that needs to be processed, but also ways to process this data more efficiently. Further, the proposed approaches are all validated through extensive experiments that show they improve upon the state of the art.

8.2 Future Work and Outlook

In this section, we discuss a number of open problems raised by the work presented in this thesis and also give an outlook on the future development of the area of hybrid data management.

Publishing Linked Data Statistics. The link-traversal approach is effective in discovering new sources at run-time and as such can take direct advantage of Linked Data sources, which require much less effort to maintain on the part of the data publisher than, for example, SPARQL endpoints. However, because there is little to no knowledge available about sources that are discovered at run-time, many sources are retrieved that do no contribute to the results of the query. The development of approaches and guidelines for publishing lightweight statistics about the content of Linked Data sources (for example on the level of domains) could help Linked Data query engines determine which sources are irrelevant and thereby increase query performance. A requirement would be that the overhead for computing and publishing these statistics is very low compared to SPARQL endpoints, such that data publishers may readily adopt these statistics.

Approximate Query Optimization. While the proposed approach for multi-objective query optimization using a dynamic programming algorithm was shown to be effective, it is still of high complexity. In the evaluation we showed that simple approximations can already decrease the query planning time dramatically while still being able to compute a large fraction of the Pareto-optimal plans. Here, the development of approximation approaches that have strict guarantees on the quality of the generated plans is necessary.

Workload-specific Hybrid Indexing. One main conclusion of the evaluation of hybrid indexes is that solutions that focus on a specific query type (e.g. entity queries) are able to outperform solutions that are more general and support more types of queries. As such, approaches that automatically determine the best indexing strategy given a particular workload would be beneficial or the development of ad-hoc indexing approaches that create new indexes as necessary.

SPARQL Keyword Extensions. In our work we provided a straightforward formalization of vendor-specific SPARQL extensions for full-text search. However, this formalization is restricted to basic graph patterns and would benefit from being extended to cover the complete SPARQL semantics. Further, adopting a common standard for full-text search in SPARQL would increase the adoption of full-text search in SPARQL and of SPARQL as a whole.

Outlook. In the recent past, industry leaders have announced or made available features that take advantage of hybrid data. The web search engine by Google started out with keyword search over unstructured Web pages, but today also combines this with the search over structured data (Knowledge Graph) to provide additional benefit to its users. Facebook also recently announced the upcoming availability of Graph Search[1], an approach for performing hybrid searches over social graph data. These developments show that the management of hybrid data will be of critical importance in the future. With the increasing availability of hybrid data it is necessary for researchers and companies to develop methods to help make sense of the data and discover uses that were not possible before. The efficient processing of queries over hybrid data is a basic building block in this effort.

---

[1]https://www.facebook.com/about/graphsearch, retrieved 2013-01-18

List of Abbreviations

List of Figures

List of Tables

Bibliography

[AH00]   Ron Avnur and Joseph M. Hellerstein. Eddies: Continuously
            Adaptive Query Processing. In *Proceedings of the 2000 ACM SIG-
            MOD International Conference on Management of Data*, pages
            261–272, 2000.

[AVL+11]   Maribel Acosta, Maria-Esther Vidal, Tomas Lampo, Julio Castillo,
            and Edna Ruckhaus. ANAPSID: An Adaptive Query Process-
            ing Engine for SPARQL Endpoints. In *Proceedings of the 10th
            International Semantic Web Conference (ISWC)*, pages 18–34,
            2011.

[AYL06]   Sihem Amer-Yahia and Mounia Lalmas. XML search: languages,
            INEX and scoring. *SIGMOD Record*, 35(4):16–23, 2006.

[AYLP04]   Sihem Amer-Yahia, Laks V. S. Lakshmanan, and Shashank Pandit.
            FleXPath: Flexible Structure and Full-Text Querying for XML. In
            *Proceedings of the 2004 ACM SIGMOD International Conference
            on Management of Data*, pages 83–94, 2004.

[BCSW07]   Holger Bast, Alexandru Chitea, Fabian M. Suchanek, and Ingmar
            Weber. ESTER: efficient search on text, entities, and relations. In
            *Proceedings of the 30th Annual International ACM SIGIR Con-
            ference on Research and Development in Information Retrieval*,
            pages 671–678, 2007.

[BHBL09]   Christian Bizer, Tom Heath, and Tim Berners-Lee. Linked Data
            - The Story So Far. *International Journal on Semantic Web and
            Information Systems*, 5(3):1–22, 2009.

[BKO+11]   Barry Bishop, Atanas Kiryakov, Damyan Ognyanoff, Ivan Peikov,
            Zdravko Tashev, and Ruslan Velkov. Owlim: A family of scalable
            semantic repositories. *Semantic Web*, 2(1):33–42, 2011.

[BKS01]   Stephan Börzsönyi, Donald Kossmann, and Konrad Stocker. The skyline operator. In *Proceedings of the 17th International Conference on Data Engineering (ICDE)*, pages 421–430, 2001.

[BMV11]   Roi Blanco, Peter Mika, and Sebastiano Vigna. Effective and Efficient Entity Search in RDF Data. In *Proceedings of the 10th International Semantic Web Conference (ISWC)*, pages 83–97, 2011.

[BVKD09]   Mihaela A. Bornea, Vasilis Vassalos, Yannis Kotidis, and Antonios Deligiannakis. Double index nested-loop reactive join for result rate optimization. In *Proceedings of the 25th International Conference on Data Engineering (ICDE)*, pages 481–492, 2009.

[BYRN99]   Ricardo A. Baeza-Yates and Berthier Ribeiro-Neto. *Modern Information Retrieval*. Addison-Wesley Longman Publishing Co., Inc., Boston, MA, USA, 1999.

[CGQ08]   Gong Cheng, Weiyi Ge, and Yuzhong Qu. Falcons: searching and browsing entities on the semantic web. In *Proceedings of the 17th World Wide Web Conference (WWW)*, pages 1101–1102, 2008.

[CHKZ03]   Edith Cohen, Eran Halperin, Haim Kaplan, and Uri Zwick. Reachability and distance queries via 2-hop labels. *SIAM J. Comput.*, 32(5):1338–1355, 2003.

[CSS10]   Soumen Chakrabarti, Sunita Sarawagi, and S. Sudarshan. Enhancing Search with Structure. *IEEE Data Eng. Bull.*, 33(1):3–24, 2010.

[CW10]   Joel Coffman and Alfred C. Weaver. A framework for evaluating database keyword search strategies. In *Proceedings of the 19th International Conference on Information and Knowledge Management (CIKM)*, pages 729–738, 2010.

[CY09]   Jiefeng Cheng and Jeffrey Xu Yu. On-line exact shortest distance query processing. In *12th International Conference on Extending Database Technology (EDBT)*, pages 481–492, 2009.

[DH04]   Amol Deshpande and Joseph M. Hellerstein. Lifting the burden of history from adaptive query processing. In *Proceedings of the*

30th International Conference on Very Large Data Bases (VLDB), pages 948–959, 2004.

[DH07]   Xin Dong and Alon Y. Halevy. Indexing dataspaces. In *Proceedings of the 2007 ACM SIGMOD International Conference on Management of Data*, pages 43–54, 2007.

[DIR07]   Amol Deshpande, Zachary G. Ives, and Vijayshankar Raman. Adaptive Query Processing. *Foundations and Trends in Databases*, 1(1):1–140, 2007.

[DYW$^+$07] Bolin Ding, Jeffrey Xu Yu, Shan Wang, Lu Qin, Xiao Zhang, and Xuemin Lin. Finding top-k min-cost connected trees in databases. In *Proceedings of the 23rd International Conference on Data Engineering (ICDE)*, pages 836–845, 2007.

[EN00]   Ramez Elmasri and Shamkant B. Navathe. *Fundamentals of Database Systems, 3rd Edition*. Addison-Wesley-Longman, 2000.

[ERSW10]   Shady Elbassuoni, Maya Ramanath, Ralf Schenkel, and Gerhard Weikum. Searching RDF Graphs with SPARQL and Keywords. *IEEE Data Eng. Bull.*, 33(1):16–24, 2010.

[GCHQ10]   Weiyi Ge, Jianfeng Chen, Wei Hu, and Yuzhong Qu. Object Link Structure in the Semantic Web. In *Proceedings of the 7th Extended Semantic Web Conference (ESWC)*, pages 257–271, 2010.

[GMUW00]   Hector Garcia-Molina, Jeffrey D. Ullman, and Jennifer Widom. *Database System Implementation*. Prentice-Hall, 2000.

[GS11]   Olaf Görlitz and Steffen Staab. SPLENDID: SPARQL Endpoint Federation Exploiting VOID Descriptions. In Olaf Hartig, Andreas Harth, and Juan Sequeda, editors, *COLD*, volume 782 of *CEUR Workshop Proceedings*. CEUR-WS.org, 2011.

[Har11]   Olaf Hartig. Zero-Knowledge Query Planning for an Iterator Implementation of Link Traversal Based Query Execution. In *Proceedings of the 8th Extended Semantic Web Conference (ESWC)*, pages 154–169, 2011.

[Har12]   Olaf Hartig. SPARQL for a Web of Linked Data: Semantics and Computability. In *Proceedings of the 9th Extended Semantic Web Conference (ESWC)*, pages 8–23, 2012.

[HBF09]   Olaf Hartig, Christian Bizer, and Johann Christoph Freytag. Executing SPARQL Queries over the Web of Linked Data. In *Proceedings of the 8th International Semantic Web Conference (ISWC)*, pages 293–309, 2009.

[HD05]   Andreas Harth and Stefan Decker. Optimized Index Structures for Querying RDF from the Web. In *Proceedings of the 3rd Latin American Web Congress (LA-Web)*, pages 71–80, 2005.

[HGP03]   Vagelis Hristidis, Luis Gravano, and Yannis Papakonstantinou. Efficient IR-Style Keyword Search over Relational Databases. In *Proceedings of the 29th International Conference on Very Large Data Bases (VLDB)*, pages 850–861, 2003.

[HHK+10] Andreas Harth, Katja Hose, Marcel Karnstedt, Axel Polleres, Kai-Uwe Sattler, and Jürgen Umbrich. Data summaries for on-demand queries over Linked Data. In *Proceedings of the 19th World Wide Web Conference (WWW)*, pages 411–420, 2010.

[HHP06]   Heasoo Hwang, Vagelis Hristidis, and Yannis Papakonstantinou. Objectrank: a system for authority-based search on databases. In *Proceedings of the 2006 ACM SIGMOD International Conference on Management of Data*, pages 796–798, 2006.

[HL11]   Hai Huang and Chengfei Liu. Estimating selectivity for joined RDF triple patterns. In *Proceedings of the 10th International Conference on Information and Knowledge Management (CIKM)*, pages 1435–1444, 2011.

[HP02]   Vagelis Hristidis and Yannis Papakonstantinou. DISCOVER: Keyword Search in Relational Databases. In *Proceedings of the 28th International Conference on Very Large Data Bases (VLDB)*, pages 670–681, 2002.

[HS12]   Andreas Harth and Sebastian Speiser. On completeness classes for query evaluation on linked data. In *Proceedings of the 26th*

AAAI Conference on Artificial Intelligence (AAAI), pages 613–619, 2012.

[HWYY07]   Hao He, Haixun Wang, Jun Yang, and Philip S. Yu. Blinks: ranked keyword searches on graphs. In *Proceedings of the 2007 ACM SIGMOD International Conference on Management of Data*, pages 305–316, 2007.

[IAE02]   Ihab F. Ilyas, Walid G. Aref, and Ahmed K. Elmagarmid. Joining ranked inputs in practice. In *Proceedings of the 28th International Conference on Very Large Data Bases (VLDB)*, pages 950–961, 2002.

[IAE04]   Ihab F. Ilyas, Walid G. Aref, and Ahmed K. Elmagarmid. Supporting top-k join queries in relational databases. *The VLDB Journal*, 13(3):207–221, 2004.

[IAE$^+$06] Ihab F. Ilyas, Walid G. Aref, Ahmed K. Elmagarmid, Hicham G. Elmongui, Rahul Shah, and Jeffrey Scott Vitter. Adaptive rank-aware query optimization in relational databases. *ACM Trans. Database Syst.*, 31(4):1257–1304, 2006.

[IBS08]   Ihab F. Ilyas, George Beskales, and Mohamed A. Soliman. A survey of top-*k* query processing techniques in relational database systems. *ACM Computing Surveys*, 40(4), 2008.

[IHW04]   Zachary G. Ives, Alon Y. Halevy, and Daniel S. Weld. Adapting to source properties in processing data integration queries. In *Proceedings of the 2004 ACM SIGMOD International Conference on Management of Data*, pages 395–406, 2004.

[ISA$^+$04] Ihab F. Ilyas, Rahul Shah, Walid G. Aref, Jeffrey Scott Vitter, and Ahmed K. Elmagarmid. Rank-aware query optimization. In *Proceedings of the 2004 ACM SIGMOD International Conference on Management of Data*, pages 203–214, 2004.

[IT08]   Zachary G. Ives and Nicholas E. Taylor. Sideways information passing for push-style query processing. In *Proceedings of the 24th International Conference on Data Engineering (ICDE)*, pages 774–783, 2008.

[KBMvK10] Riham Abdel Kader, Peter A. Boncz, Stefan Manegold, and Maurice van Keulen. ROX: The robustness of a run-time XQuery optimizer against correlated data. In *Proceedings of the 26th International Conference on Data Engineering (ICDE)*, pages 1185–1188, 2010.

[KNV03] Jaewoo Kang, Jeffrey F. Naughton, and Stratis Viglas. Evaluating window joins over unbounded streams. In *Proceedings of the 19th International Conference on Data Engineering (ICDE)*, pages 341–352, 2003.

[KPC+05] Varun Kacholia, Shashank Pandit, Soumen Chakrabarti, S. Sudarshan, Rushi Desai, and Hrishikesh Karambelkar. Bidirectional expansion for keyword search on graph databases. In *Proceedings of the 31st International Conference on Very Large Data Bases (VLDB)*, pages 505–516, 2005.

[KS00] Donald Kossmann and Konrad Stocker. Iterative dynamic programming: a new class of query optimization algorithms. *ACM Trans. Database Syst.*, 25(1):43–82, 2000.

[KSI+08] Gjergji Kasneci, Fabian M. Suchanek, Georgiana Ifrim, Maya Ramanath, and Gerhard Weikum. NAGA: Searching and Ranking Knowledge. In *Proceedings of the 24th International Conference on Data Engineering (ICDE)*, pages 953–962, 2008.

[LLWZ07] Yi Luo, Xuemin Lin, Wei Wang, and Xiaofang Zhou. Spark: top-k keyword query in relational databases. In *Proceedings of the 2007 ACM SIGMOD International Conference on Management of Data*, pages 115–126, 2007.

[LOF+08] Guoliang Li, Beng Chin Ooi, Jianhua Feng, Jianyong Wang, and Lizhu Zhou. EASE: an effective 3-in-1 keyword search method for unstructured, semi-structured and structured data. In *Proceedings of the 2008 ACM SIGMOD International Conference on Management of Data*, pages 903–914, 2008.

[LRO96] Alon Y. Levy, Anand Rajaraman, and Joann J. Ordille. Querying heterogeneous information sources using source descriptions. In

Proceedings of the 22nd International Conference on Very Large Data Bases (VLDB), pages 251–262, 1996.

[LT10] Günter Ladwig and Thanh Tran. Linked Data Query Processing Strategies. In *Proceedings of the 9th International Semantic Web Conference (ISWC)*, pages 453–469, 2010.

[LT11a] Günter Ladwig and Thanh Tran. Index Structures and Top-k Join Algorithms for Native Keyword Search Databases. In *Proceedings of the 20th International Conference on Information and Knowledge Management (CIKM)*, pages 1505–1514, 2011.

[LT11b] Günter Ladwig and Thanh Tran. SIHJoin: Querying Remote and Local Linked Data. In *Proceedings of the 8th Extended Semantic Web Conference (ESWC)*, pages 139–153, 2011.

[LT12a] Günter Ladwig and Thanh Tran. HybIdx: Indexes for Processing Hybrid Graph Patterns Over Text-Rich Data Graphs. Technical Report 3035, Institute AIFB, Karlsruhe Institute of Technology, November 2012.

[LT12b] Günter Ladwig and Thanh Tran. Multi-objective Linked Data Query Optimization. Technical Report 3034, Institute AIFB, Karlsruhe Institute of Technology, November 2012.

[LT12c] Günter Ladwig and Thanh Tran. Processing Flexible Hybrid Graph Patterns over Text-Rich Data Graphs. Technical Report 3036, Institute AIFB, Karlsruhe Institute of Technology, November 2012.

[LYMC06] Fang Liu, Clement T. Yu, Weiyi Meng, and Abdur Chowdhury. Effective keyword search in relational databases. In *Proceedings of the 2006 ACM SIGMOD International Conference on Management of Data*, pages 563–574, 2006.

[MF02] Samuel Madden and Michael J. Franklin. Fjording the stream: An architecture for queries over streaming sensor data. In *Proceedings of the 18th International Conference on Data Engineering (ICDE)*, pages 555–566, 2002.

[MLA04] Mohamed F. Mokbel, Ming Lu, and Walid G. Aref. Hash-merge join: A non-blocking join algorithm for producing fast and early join results. In *Proceedings of the 20th International Conference on Data Engineering (ICDE)*, pages 251–262, 2004.

[MLAN11] Mohamed Morsey, Jens Lehmann, Sören Auer, and Axel-Cyrille Ngonga Ngomo. DBpedia SPARQL Benchmark - Performance Assessment with Real Queries on Real Data. In *Proceedings of the 10th International Semantic Web Conference (ISWC)*, pages 454–469, 2011.

[MN08] Guido Moerkotte and Thomas Neumann. Dynamic programming strikes back. In *Proceedings of the 2008 ACM SIGMOD International Conference on Management of Data*, pages 539–552, 2008.

[Neu05] Thomas Neumann. *Efficient generation and execution of DAG-structured query graphs*. PhD thesis, University of Mannheim, 2005.

[NK01] Zaiqing Nie and Subbarao Kambhampati. Joint optimization of cost and coverage of query plans in data integration. In *Proceedings of the 10th International Conference on Information and Knowledge Management (CIKM)*, pages 223–230, 2001.

[NW08] Thomas Neumann and Gerhard Weikum. RDF-3X: a RISC-style engine for RDF. *Proceedings of the VLDB Endowment*, 1(1):647–659, 2008.

[NW09] Thomas Neumann and Gerhard Weikum. Scalable join processing on very large RDF graphs. In *Proceedings of the 2009 ACM SIGMOD International Conference on Management of Data*, pages 627–640, 2009.

[PH01] Rachel Pottinger and Alon Y. Halevy. Minicon: A scalable algorithm for answering queries using views. *The VLDB Journal*, 10(2-3):182–198, 2001.

[PIW10] Jeffrey Pound, Ihab F. Ilyas, and Grant E. Weddell. QUICK: Expressive and Flexible Search over Knowledge Bases and Text

Collections. *Proceedings of the VLDB Endowment*, 3(2):1573–1576, 2010.

[PY01]   Christos H. Papadimitriou and Mihalis Yannakakis. Multiobjective query optimization. In *Proceedings of the 20th ACM SIGACT-SIGMOD-SIGART Symposium on Principles of Database Systems (PODS)*, pages 52–59, 2001.

[QYC09]   Lu Qin, Jeffrey Xu Yu, and Lijun Chang. Keyword search in databases: the power of RDBMS. In *Proceedings of the 2009 ACM SIGMOD International Conference on Management of Data*, pages 681–694, 2009.

[QYC10]   Lu Qin, Jeffrey Xu Yu, and Lijun Chang. Ten thousand sqls: Parallel keyword queries computing. *Proceedings of the VLDB Endowment*, 3(1):58–69, 2010.

[RDH03]   Vijayshankar Raman, Amol Deshpande, and Joseph M. Hellerstein. Using state modules for adaptive query processing. In *Proceedings of the 19th International Conference on Data Engineering (ICDE)*, pages 353–364, 2003.

[RSSB00] Prasan Roy, S. Seshadri, S. Sudarshan, and Siddhesh Bhobe. Efficient and Extensible Algorithms for Multi Query Optimization. In *Proceedings of the 2000 ACM SIGMOD International Conference on Management of Data*, pages 249–260, 2000.

[SAC+79] Patricia G. Selinger, Morton M. Astrahan, Donald D. Chamberlin, Raymond A. Lorie, and Thomas G. Price. Access path selection in a relational database management system. In *Proceedings of the 1979 ACM SIGMOD International Conference on Management of Data*, pages 23–34, 1979.

[SAL+96] Michael Stonebraker, Paul M. Aoki, Witold Litwin, Avi Pfeffer, Adam Sah, Jeff Sidell, Carl Staelin, and Andrew Yu. Mariposa: A wide-area distributed database system. *The VLDB Journal*, 5(1):48–63, 1996.

[SGH+11] Michael Schmidt, Olaf Görlitz, Peter Haase, Günter Ladwig, Andreas Schwarte, and Thanh Tran. Fedbench: A benchmark suite for federated semantic data query processing. In *Proceedings of the 10th International Semantic Web Conference (ISWC)*, pages 585–600, 2011.

[SHH$^+$11]   Andreas Schwarte, Peter Haase, Katja Hose, Ralf Schenkel, and Michael Schmidt. Fedx: Optimization techniques for federated query processing on linked data. In *Proceedings of the 10th International Semantic Web Conference (ISWC)*, pages 601–616, 2011.

[SML10]   Michael Schmidt, Michael Meier, and Georg Lausen. Foundations of sparql query optimization. In Luc Segoufin, editor, *Proceedings of the 13th International Conference on Database Theory*, ACM International Conference Proceeding Series, pages 4–33. ACM, 2010.

[SP10]   Karl Schnaitter and Neoklis Polyzotis. Optimal algorithms for evaluating rank joins in database systems. *ACM Trans. Database Syst.*, 35(1), 2010.

[SSB$^+$08]   Markus Stocker, Andy Seaborne, Abraham Bernstein, Christoph Kiefer, and Dave Reynolds. SPARQL basic graph pattern optimization using selectivity estimation. In *Proceedings of the 17th World Wide Web Conference (WWW)*, pages 595–604, 2008.

[STW04]   Ralf Schenkel, Anja Theobald, and Gerhard Weikum. HOPI: An Efficient Connection Index for Complex XML Document Collections. In *9th International Conference on Extending Database Technology (EDBT)*, pages 237–255, 2004.

[SVHB04]   Heiner Stuckenschmidt, Richard Vdovjak, Geert-Jan Houben, and Jeen Broekstra. Index structures and algorithms for querying distributed RDF repositories. In Stuart I. Feldman, Mike Uretsky, Marc Najork, and Craig E. Wills, editors, *Proceedings of the 13th International Conference on World Wide Web (WWW)*, pages 631–639. ACM, 2004.

[TSW05]   Martin Theobald, Ralf Schenkel, and Gerhard Weikum. An Efficient and Versatile Query Engine for TopX Search. In *Proceedings of the 31st International Conference on Very Large Data Bases (VLDB)*, pages 625–636, 2005.

[TWRC09]   Thanh Tran, Haofen Wang, Sebastian Rudolph, and Philipp Cimiano. Top-k Exploration of Query Candidates for Efficient Keyword Search on Graph-Shaped (RDF) Data. In *Proceedings of the 25th International Conference on Data Engineering (ICDE)*, pages 405–416, 2009.

[TYP+05]   Yufei Tao, Man Lung Yiu, Dimitris Papadias, Marios Hadjieleftheriou, and Nikos Mamoulis. Rpj: Producing fast join results on streams through rate-based optimization. In *Proceedings of the 2005 ACM SIGMOD International Conference on Management of Data*, pages 371–382, 2005.

[UF00]   Tolga Urhan and Michael J. Franklin. Xjoin: A reactively-scheduled pipelined join operator. *IEEE Data Eng. Bull.*, 23(2):27–33, 2000.

[VM96]   Bennet Vance and David Maier. Rapid bushy join-order optimization with cartesian products. In *Proceedings of the 1996 ACM SIGMOD International Conference on Management of Data*, pages 35–46, 1996.

[VNB03]   Stratis Viglas, Jeffrey F. Naughton, and Josef Burger. Maximizing the Output Rate of Multi-Way Join Queries over Streaming Information Sources. In *Proceedings of the 29th International Conference on Very Large Data Bases (VLDB)*, pages 285–296, 2003.

[WA93]   Annita N. Wilschut and Peter M. G. Apers. Dataflow Query Execution in a Parallel Main-memory Environment. *Distributed and Parallel Databases*, 1(1):103–128, 1993.

[Wei07]   Gerhard Weikum. DB&IR: both sides now. In *Proceedings of the 2007 ACM SIGMOD International Conference on Management of Data*, pages 25–30, 2007.

[WLP+09]   Haofen Wang, Qiaoling Liu, Thomas Penin, Linyun Fu, Lei Zhang, Thanh Tran, Yong Yu, and Yue Pan. Semplore: A scalable IR approach to search the Web of Data. *J. Web Sem.*, 7(3):177–188, 2009.

[WTLF11]   Haofen Wang, Thanh Tran, Chang Liu, and Linyun Fu. Lightweight integration of IR and DB for scalable hybrid search with integrated ranking support. *J. Web Sem.*, 9(4):490–503, 2011.

[YQC10]   Jeffrey Xu Yu, Lu Qin, and Lijun Chang. Keyword search in relational databases: A survey. *IEEE Data Eng. Bull.*, 33(1):67–78, 2010.

[ZM06]   Justin Zobel and Alistair Moffat. Inverted files for text search engines. *ACM Computing Surveys*, 38(2), 2006.

Appendix A

Evaluation Queries

A.1 Keyword Queries

Name	Query	Name	Query
$DBLP_1$	miller journal	BTC_1	washington america
$DBLP_2$	proceedings 1970	BTC_2	event movie
$DBLP_3$	article journal	BTC_3	germany city
$DBLP_4$	journal 1 1980	BTC_4	soccer city person
$DBLP_5$	miller proceedings 1971	BTC_5	organization england city
$DBLP_6$	press article 1988	BTC_6	city germany person
$DBLP_7$	american university publishing 1988	BTC_7	album queen magic
$DBLP_8$	jason carolina publishing 1952	BTC_8	person harth brickley cyganiak
$DBLP_9$	journal medical article 1979	BTC_9	person conference semantic greece

A.2 Structured Queries

A.2.1 Queries used in Section 4.7.1

```
Q1: SELECT ?x ?l WHERE {
      ?x skos:subject <http://dbpedia.org/resource/Category:
         Liberal_democracies> .
      ?x rdfs:label ?l . }
Q2: SELECT * WHERE {
      ?n skos:subject <http://dbpedia.org/resource/Category:Western_Europe>
         .
      ?n owl:sameAs ?p .
      ?p factbook:area_total ?a . }
Q3: SELECT * WHERE {
```

```
       ?n skos:subject <http://dbpedia.org/resource/Category:
          Chancellors_of_Germany> .
       ?n owl:sameAs ?p .
       ?p <http://rdf.freebase.com/ns/people.person.gender> ?a .
       ?n owl:sameAs ?p2 .
       ?p2 <http://data.nytimes.com/elements/latest_use> ?u . }
Q4: SELECT * WHERE {
       ?role <http://data.semanticweb.org/ns/swc/ontology#isRoleAt> <http://
          data.semanticweb.org/conference/eswc/2010> .
       ?role <http://data.semanticweb.org/ns/swc/ontology#heldBy> ?p .
       ?paper <http://swrc.ontoware.org/ontology#author> ?p .
       ?paper <http://data.semanticweb.org/ns/swc/ontology#isPartOf> ?
          proceedings .
       ?proceedings <http://data.semanticweb.org/ns/swc/ontology#
          relatedToEvent> <http://data.semanticweb.org/conference/eswc
          /2010> . }
Q5: SELECT * WHERE {
       ?paper <http://swrc.ontoware.org/ontology#author> ?p .
       ?paper <http://data.semanticweb.org/ns/swc/ontology#isPartOf> ?
          proceedings .
       ?proceedings <http://data.semanticweb.org/ns/swc/ontology#
          relatedToEvent> <http://data.semanticweb.org/conference/eswc
          /2010> . }
Q6: SELECT * WHERE {
       ?a dbowl:artist dbpedia:Michael_Jackson .
       ?a rdf:type dbowl:Album .
       ?a foaf:name ?n . }
Q7: SELECT * WHERE {
       ?a dbowl:artist dbpedia:Michael_Jackson .
       ?a owl:sameAs ?a2 .
       ?a2 rdf:type ?x .
       ?a rdfs:label ?n . }
Q8: SELECT * WHERE {
       ?p owl:sameAs ?x .
       ?p rdfs:label ?n .
       ?paper <http://swrc.ontoware.org/ontology#author> ?p .
       ?paper <http://data.semanticweb.org/ns/swc/ontology#isPartOf> <http
          ://data.semanticweb.org/conference/iswc/2008/
          poster_demo_proceedings> . }
```

A.2.2 Queries used in Section 4.7.2

```
Q1: SELECT * WHERE {
       ?p swc:isPartOf <http://data.semanticweb.org/conference/iswc/2008/
          poster_demo_proceedings> .
       ?p swrc:author ?a .
       ?a rdfs:label ?n . }
Q2: SELECT * WHERE {
       ?proceedings swc:relatedToEvent <http://data.semanticweb.org/
          conference/eswc/2010> .
       ?paper swc:isPartOf ?proceedings .
       ?paper swrc:author ?p . }
Q3: SELECT * WHERE {
       ?paper swc:isPartOf <http://data.semanticweb.org/conference/iswc
          /2008/poster_demo_proceedings> .
       ?paper swrc:author ?p .
```

```
          ?p owl:sameAs ?x .   ?p rdfs:label ?n . }
Q4: SELECT * WHERE {
      ?role swc:isRoleAt <http://data.semanticweb.org/conference/eswc/2010>
          .
      ?role swc:heldBy ?p .
      ?paper swrc:author ?p .   ?paper swc:isPartOf ?proceedings .
      ?proceedings swc:relatedToEvent  <http://data.semanticweb.org/
          conference/eswc/2010> . }
Q5: SELECT * WHERE {
      ?a dbowl:artist dbpedia:Michael_Jackson .
      ?a rdf:type dbowl:Album .
      ?a foaf:name ?n . }
Q6: SELECT * WHERE {
      ?director dbowl:nationality dbpedia:Italy .
      ?film dbowl:director ?director.
      ?x owl:sameAs ?film .   ?x foaf:based_near ?y .
      ?y <http://www.geonames.org/ontology#officialName> ?n . }
Q7: SELECT * WHERE {
      ?x gn:parentFeature <http://sws.geonames.org/2921044/> .
      ?x gn:name ?n . }
Q8: SELECT * WHERE {
      ?drug drugbank:drugCategory <http://www4.wiwiss.fu-berlin.de/drugbank
          /resource/drugcategory/micronutrient> .
      ?drug drugbank:casRegistryNumber ?id .
      ?drug owl:sameAs ?s .
      ?s foaf:name ?o .   ?s skos:subject ?sub . }
Q9: SELECT * WHERE {
      ?n skos:subject <http://dbpedia.org/resource/Category:
          Chancellors_of_Germany> .
      ?n owl:sameAs ?p2 .
      ?p2 <http://data.nytimes.com/elements/latest_use> ?u . }
Q10: SELECT * WHERE {
      ?x dbowl:team dbpedia:Eintracht_Frankfurt .
      ?x rdfs:label ?y .
      ?x dbowl:birthDate ?d .
      ?x dbowl:birthPlace ?p .
      ?p rdfs:label ?l . }
```

A.2.3 Queries used in Section 5.6

```
Q1: SELECT * WHERE {
      ?x dcterms:subject <http://dbpedia.org/resource/Category:
          Liberal_democracies> .
      ?x rdfs:label "Germany"@en .
      ?x owl:sameAs ?p .
      ?p foaf:name ?n . }
Q2: SELECT * WHERE {
      ?p dbowl:stateOfOrigin dbpedia:Italy .
      ?p owl:sameAs ?o .
      ?o a foaf:Person . }
Q3: SELECT * WHERE {
      ?n rdf:type dbowl:PopulatedPlace .
      ?n rdfs:label "Estonia"@en .
      ?n owl:sameAs ?a .
      ?a foaf:name ?t . }
Q4: SELECT * WHERE {
```

```
            ?drug drugbank:drugCategory <http://www4.wiwiss.fu-berlin.de/drugbank
               /resource/drugcategory/micronutrient> .
            ?drug drugbank:casRegistryNumber ?id .
            ?drug owl:sameAs ?s .
            ?s <http://www4.wiwiss.fu-berlin.de/sider/resource/sider/sideEffect>
               ?eff }
Q5: SELECT * WHERE {
            ?n dcterms:subject <http://dbpedia.org/resource/Category:
               Western_Europe> .
            ?n owl:sameAs ?p .
            ?p factbook:birthrate ?a . }
Q6: SELECT * WHERE {
            ?country a dbowl:Country .
            ?country rdfs:label "Monaco"@en .
            ?country owl:sameAs ?c2 .
            ?c2 <http://www4.wiwiss.fu-berlin.de/factbook/ns#unemploymentrate> ?n
               .
            ?c2 <http://www4.wiwiss.fu-berlin.de/factbook/ns#
               literacy_totalpopulation> ?l . }
Q7: SELECT ?film ?date ?f2 ?actor ?a2 ?place WHERE {
            <http://data.linkedmdb.org/resource/director/8477> foaf:made ?film .
            ?film dcterms:date ?date .
            ?film foaf:page ?page .
            ?film owl:sameAs ?f2 . }
Q8: SELECT * WHERE {
            dailymed_orga:Mylan_Pharmaceuticals_Inc dailymed:producesDrug ?bd .
            ?bd dailymed:genericDrug ?gd .
            ?gd drugbank:possibleDiseaseTarget ?dt .
            ?dt owl:sameAs ?o .
            ?o rdfs:seeAlso ?n . }
Q9: SELECT * WHERE {
            ?a dbowl:artist dbpedia:The_Beatles .
            ?a rdfs:label "Yesterday"@de .
            ?a foaf:depiction ?img .
            ?b dbowl:previousWork ?a .
            ?b rdfs:label ?n . }
Q10: SELECT * WHERE {
             ?a dbowl:artist dbpedia:Michael_Jackson .
             ?a owl:sameAs ?a2 .
             ?a2 foaf:name ?n . }
Q11: SELECT * WHERE {
             ?country a dbowl:Country .
             ?country rdfs:label "Monaco"@en .
             ?country owl:sameAs ?c2 .
             ?c2 <http://www4.wiwiss.fu-berlin.de/factbook/ns#unemploymentrate> ?
                n .
             ?c2 <http://www4.wiwiss.fu-berlin.de/factbook/ns#
                literacy_totalpopulation> ?l . }
Q12: SELECT * WHERE {
             ?film <http://data.linkedmdb.org/resource/movie/actor> <http://data.
                linkedmdb.org/resource/actor/30064> .
             ?film <http://data.linkedmdb.org/resource/movie/
                featured_film_location> ?loc .
             ?loc rdfs:label "Hawaii (Film Location)" .
             ?film owl:sameAs ?dbp .
             ?dbp dbowl:music dbpedia:John_Williams . }
```

```
Q13: SELECT * WHERE {
        ?child geo-ont:parentFeature <http://sws.geonames.org/6269131/> .
        ?child geo-ont:officialName "Cornwall" .
        ?child geo-ont:nearby ?n .
        ?n geo-ont:name ?nn .
        ?n a ?t . }
Q14: SELECT * WHERE {
        ?x <http://dbpedia.org/property/country> <http://dbpedia.org/
            resource/Germany> .
        ?x owl:sameAs ?o .
        ?o foaf:depiction ?n }
```

A.3 Hybrid Queries

A.3.1 Queries used in Section 6.5

Name	Query
WP_1	$\langle ?x, ?y, microscope \rangle$
WP_2	$\langle ?x, ?y, sparrow \rangle$
WP_3	$\langle ?x, ?y, exploration\ of\ mars \rangle$
WP_4	$\langle ?x, ?y, bohemian\ rhapsody \rangle$
WP_5	$\langle ?x, ?y, 1755\ lisbon\ earthquake \rangle$
WP_6	$\langle ?x, ?y, nuba \rangle$
WP_7	$\langle ?x, ?y, piccadilly\ circus \rangle$
WP_8	$\langle ?x, ?y, 1840 \rangle$
WP_9	$\langle ?x, ?y, robert\ falcon\ scott \rangle$
WP_{10}	$\langle ?x, ?y, monty\ python \rangle$
WP_{11}	$\langle ?x, ?y, war \rangle$
WP_{12}	$\langle ?x, ?y, 1760 \rangle$
WP_{13}	$\langle ?x, ?y, malwa\ madhya\ predesh \rangle$
WP_{14}	$\langle ?x, ?y, international\ english \rangle$
WP_{15}	$\langle ?x, ?y, swan \rangle$
WP_{26}	$\langle ?x, ?y, separation\ of\ powers \rangle$
WP_{27}	$\langle ?x, ?y, bank\ of\ china \rangle$
WP_{28}	$\langle ?x, ?y, zelda\ series \rangle$
WP_{29}	$\langle ?x, ?y, solomons\ battle \rangle$
WP_{30}	$\langle ?x, ?y, george\ v \rangle$
WP_{31}	$\langle ?x, ?y, amda\ seyon\ i \rangle$
WP_{32}	$\langle ?x, ?y, galveston\ hurricane \rangle$
WP_{33}	$\langle ?x, ?y, dover\ cliffs \rangle$
WP_{34}	$\langle ?x, ?y, somalia\ war \rangle$

WP_{35}	$\langle ?x, ?y, william\ pitt \rangle$
WP_{36}	$\langle ?x, ?y, soviet\ casualties\ of\ world\ war\ ii \rangle$
WP_{37}	$\langle ?x, ?y, dam\ lake\ mead \rangle$
WP_{38}	$\langle ?x, ?y, irrational\ number \rangle$
WP_{39}	$\langle ?x, ?y, mona\ lisa\ artist \rangle$
WP_{40}	$\langle ?x, ?y, spanish\ flu \rangle$
WP_{41}	$\langle ?x, ?y, exxon\ valdez\ oil\ spill \rangle$
WP_{42}	$\langle ?x, ?y, einstein\ special\ relativity \rangle$
WP_{43}	$\langle ?x, ?y, pride\ and\ predjudice\ author \rangle$
WP_{44}	$\langle ?x, ?y, atomic\ numbers\ lanthanides \rangle$
WP_{45}	$\langle ?x, ?y, smallpox\ vaccination \rangle$
WP_{46}	$\langle ?z, creator ?x \rangle, \langle ?x, name, alleborgobot \rangle$
$IMDB_{1}$	$\langle ?x, ?y, denzel\ washington \rangle$
$IMDB_{2}$	$\langle ?x, ?y, clint\ eastwood \rangle$
$IMDB_{3}$	$\langle ?x, ?y, john\ wayne \rangle$
$IMDB_{4}$	$\langle ?x, ?y, will\ smith \rangle$
$IMDB_{5}$	$\langle ?x, ?y, harrison\ ford \rangle$
$IMDB_{6}$	$\langle ?x, ?y, julia\ roberts \rangle$
$IMDB_{7}$	$\langle ?x, ?y, tom\ hanks \rangle$
$IMDB_{8}$	$\langle ?x, ?y, johnny\ depp \rangle$
$IMDB_{9}$	$\langle ?x, ?y, angelina\ jolie \rangle$
$IMDB_{10}$	$\langle ?x, ?y, morgan\ freeman \rangle$
$IMDB_{11}$	$\langle ?x, ?y, gone\ with\ the\ wind. \rangle$
$IMDB_{12}$	$\langle ?x, ?y, star\ wars \rangle$
$IMDB_{13}$	$\langle ?x, ?y, casablanca \rangle$
$IMDB_{14}$	$\langle ?x, ?y, lord\ of\ the\ rings \rangle$
$IMDB_{15}$	$\langle ?x, ?y, the\ sound\ of\ music \rangle$
$IMDB_{16}$	$\langle ?x, ?y, wizard\ of\ oz \rangle$
$IMDB_{17}$	$\langle ?x, ?y, the\ notebook \rangle$
$IMDB_{18}$	$\langle ?x, ?y, forrest\ gump \rangle$
$IMDB_{19}$	$\langle ?x, ?y, the\ princess\ bride \rangle$
$IMDB_{20}$	$\langle ?x, ?y, the\ godfather \rangle$
$IMDB_{21}$	$\langle ?z, role, ?r \rangle, \langle ?r, name, indiana\ jones \rangle,$ $\langle ?x, cast\ info, ?z \rangle, \langle ?x, title, ?y \rangle$
$IMDB_{22}$	$\langle ?z, role, ?r \rangle, \langle ?r, name, atticus\ finch \rangle,$ $\langle ?x, cast\ info, ?z \rangle, \langle ?x, title, ?y \rangle$
$IMDB_{23}$	$\langle ?z, role, ?r \rangle, \langle ?r, name, james\ bond \rangle,$ $\langle ?x, cast\ info, ?z \rangle, \langle ?x, title, ?y \rangle$

$IMDB_{24}$	$\langle ?z, role, ?r \rangle, \langle ?r, name, rick\ blaine \rangle,$ $\langle ?x, cast\ info, ?z \rangle, \langle ?x, title, ?y \rangle$
$IMDB_{25}$	$\langle ?z, role, ?r \rangle, \langle ?r, name, will\ kaine \rangle,$ $\langle ?x, cast\ info, ?z \rangle, \langle ?x, title, ?y \rangle$
$IMDB_{26}$	$\langle ?z, role, ?r \rangle, \langle ?r, name, dr.\ hannibal\ lecter \rangle,$ $\langle ?x, cast\ info, ?z \rangle, \langle ?x, title, ?y \rangle$
$IMDB_{27}$	$\langle ?z, role, ?r \rangle, \langle ?r, name, norman\ bates \rangle,$ $\langle ?x, cast\ info, ?z \rangle, \langle ?x, title, ?y \rangle$
$IMDB_{28}$	$\langle ?z, role, ?r \rangle, \langle ?r, name, darth\ vader \rangle,$ $\langle ?x, cast\ info, ?z \rangle, \langle ?x, title, ?y \rangle$
$IMDB_{29}$	$\langle ?z, role, ?r \rangle,$ $\langle ?r, name, the\ wicked\ witch\ of\ the\ west \rangle,$ $\langle ?x, cast\ info, ?z \rangle, \langle ?x, title, ?y \rangle$
$IMDB_{30}$	$\langle ?z, role, ?r \rangle, \langle ?r, name, nurse\ ratched \rangle,$ $\langle ?x, cast\ info, ?z \rangle, \langle ?x, title, ?y \rangle$
$IMDB_{31}$	$\langle ?x, movie\ info, ?i \rangle,$ $\langle ?i, info, frankly\ my\ deard\ don't\ give\ damn \rangle,$ $\langle ?x, title, ?t \rangle$
$IMDB_{32}$	$\langle ?x, movie\ info, ?i \rangle,$ $\langle ?i, info, i'm\ going\ to\ make\ him\ an\ offer\ he\ can't$ $refuse \rangle, \langle ?x, title, ?t \rangle$
$IMDB_{33}$	$\langle ?x, title, ?t \rangle\ \langle ?x, movie\ info, ?i \rangle$ $\langle ?i, info, you\ don't\ understand\ coulda\ had\ class$ $could\ been\ a\ contender\ coulda\ been\ somebody$ $instead\ of\ a\ bum\ which\ is\ what\ am \rangle$
$IMDB_{34}$	$\langle ?x, movie\ info, ?i \rangle,$ $\langle ?i, info, toto\ i've\ feeling\ we're\ not\ in\ kansas\ any\ more \rangle$ $\langle ?x, title, ?t \rangle$
$IMDB_{35}$	$\langle ?x, movie\ info, ?i \rangle,$ $\langle ?i, info, here's\ looking\ at\ you\ kid \rangle, \langle ?x, title, ?t \rangle$
$IMDB_{36}$	$\langle ?c, role, ?r \rangle, \langle ?r, name, skywalker \rangle,$ $\langle ?c, person, ?p \rangle, \langle ?p, name, hamill \rangle, \langle ?x, cast, ?c \rangle$
$IMDB_{37}$	$\langle ?c, person, ?p \rangle, \langle ?p, name, tom\ hanks \rangle,$ $\langle ?x, cast, ?c \rangle, \langle ?x, year, 2004 \rangle$
$IMDB_{38}$	$\langle ?c, person, ?p \rangle, \langle ?p, name, henry\ fonda \rangle,$ $\langle ?x, cast, ?c \rangle, \langle ?x, title, yours\ mine\ ours \rangle$ $\langle ?c, role, ?r \rangle, \langle ?r, name, ?rn \rangle$

$IMDB_{39}$	$\langle ?c, person, ?p\rangle$, $\langle ?p, name, russell\ crowe\rangle$, $\langle ?x, cast, ?c\rangle$, $\langle ?x, title, gladiator\rangle$ $\langle ?c, role, ?r\rangle$, $\langle ?r, name, ?rn\rangle$
$IMDB_{40}$	$\langle ?c, person, ?p\rangle$, $\langle ?p, name, brent\ spiner\rangle$, $\langle ?x, cast, ?c\rangle$, $\langle ?x, title, star\ trek\rangle$ $\langle ?c, role, ?r\rangle$, $\langle ?r, name, ?rn\rangle$
$IMDB_{41}$	$\langle ?c, person, ?p\rangle$, $\langle ?p, name, audrey\ hepburn\rangle$, $\langle ?x, cast, ?c\rangle$, $\langle ?x, year, 1951\rangle$
$IMDB_{42}$	$\langle ?c, role, ?r\rangle$, $\langle ?r, name, jacques\ clouseau\rangle$, $\langle ?c, person, ?p\rangle$, $\langle ?p, name, ?n\rangle$, $\langle ?x, cast, ?c\rangle$
$IMDB_{43}$	$\langle ?c, role, ?r\rangle$, $\langle ?r, name, jack\ ryan\rangle$, $\langle ?x, cast, ?c\rangle$, $\langle ?c, person, ?p\rangle$, $\langle ?p, name, ?n\rangle$
$IMDB_{44}$	$\langle ?c, person, ?p\rangle$, $\langle ?p, name, stallone\rangle$, $\langle ?x, cast, ?c\rangle$, $\langle ?c, role, ?r\rangle$, $\langle ?r, name, rocky\rangle$
$IMDB_{45}$	$\langle ?c, role, ?r\rangle$, $\langle ?r, name, terminator\rangle$, $\langle ?x, cast, ?c\rangle$, $\langle ?c, person, ?p\rangle$, $\langle ?p, name, ?n\rangle$
$IMDB_{50}$	$\langle ?a, cast, ?ca\rangle$, $\langle ?a, title, lost\ ark\rangle$, $\langle ?caperson, ?p\rangle$, $\langle ?ciperson, ?p\rangle$, $\langle ?i, cast, ?ci\rangle$ $\langle ?i, title, indiana\ jones\ last\ crusade\rangle$
$YAGO-NAGA_1$	$\langle ?x, haswonprize, ?y\rangle$, $\langle ?x, hasfamilyname, curie\rangle$
$YAGO-NAGA_2$	$\langle ?x, type, ?y\rangle$, $\langle ?x, hasfamilyname, pulitzer\rangle$, $\langle ?y, subclassof, ?z\rangle$, $\langle ?z, subclassof, ?t\rangle$
$YAGO-NAGA_3$	$\langle ?y, directed, ?x\rangle$, $\langle ?x, type, james\ bond\rangle$
$YAGO-NAGA_4$	$\langle ?x, actedin, ?y\rangle$, $\langle ?x, hasgivenname, julia\rangle$
$YAGO-NAGA_5$	$\langle ?x, directed, around\ the\ world\ in\ 80\ days\rangle$
$YAGO-NAGA_6$	$\langle ?x, hasfamilyname, douglas\rangle$, $\langle ?x, actedin, ?y\rangle$
$YAGO-NAGA_7$	$\langle ?x, hasfamilyname, willis\rangle$, $\langle ?x, actedin, ?y\rangle$
$YAGO-SSEARCH_1$	$\langle ?x, hasfamilyname, rice\rangle$, $\langle ?x, type, politician\rangle$, $\langle ?x, hasgivenname, ?y\rangle$
$YAGO-SSEARCH_2$	$\langle ?x, directed, ?y\rangle$, $\langle ?x, ismarriedto, madonna\rangle$
$YAGO-SSEARCH_3$	$\langle ?x, type, mathematicians\rangle$, $\langle ?x, type, french\rangle$, $\langle ?x, bornondate, ?y\rangle$
$YAGO-SSEARCH_5$	$\langle ?x, type, composers\rangle$, $\langle ?x, type, russian\rangle$
$YAGO-SSEARCH_7$	$\langle ?x, actedin, ?z\rangle$, $\langle ?x, type, wordnet\ governor\ 110140314\rangle$
$YAGO-SSEARCH_9$	$\langle ?x, type, german\rangle$, $\langle ?x, type, physicists\rangle$, $\langle ?x, livesin, ?y\rangle$

$YAGO - SSEARCH_{10}$	$\langle ?x, bornondate, ?z \rangle, \langle ?x, type, physicists \rangle,$ $\langle ?x, haswonprize, ?y \rangle$
$YAGO - SSEARCH_{12}$	$\langle ?x, type, james \rangle, \langle ?x, type, bond \rangle,$ $\langle ?y, actedin, ?x \rangle, \langle ?y, actedin, ?z \rangle$
$YAGO - TREC05_1$	$\langle george\ foreman, bornondate, ?x \rangle$
$YAGO - TREC05_2$	$\langle kurosawa, bornondate, ?x \rangle$
$YAGO - TREC05_3$	$\langle kurosawa, type, ?x \rangle, \langle ?x, subclassof, ?y \rangle$
$YAGO - TREC05_4$	$\langle ?x, type, ?y \rangle, \langle kurosawa, ismarriedto, ?x \rangle,$ $\langle ?y, subclassof, ?z \rangle$
$YAGO - TREC05_5$	$\langle kurosawa, directed, ?x \rangle$
$YAGO - TREC05_7$	$\langle paul\ newman, actedin, ?x \rangle$
$YAGO - TREC05_8$	$\langle ?x, type, meteorite \rangle$
$YAGO - TREC05_9$	$\langle american\ legion, establishedondate, ?x \rangle$
$YAGO - TREC05_{10}$	$\langle enrico\ fermi, bornondate, ?x \rangle$
$YAGO - TREC05_{11}$	$\langle enrico\ fermi, diedondate, ?x \rangle$
$YAGO - TREC05_{12}$	$\langle rachel\ carson, type, ?x \rangle, \langle ?x, subclassof, ?y \rangle$
$YAGO - TREC05_{13}$	$\langle rachel\ carson, wrote, ?x \rangle$
$YAGO - TREC05_{14}$	$\langle rachel\ carson, diedondate, ?x \rangle$
$YAGO - TREC05_{15}$	$\langle vicente\ fox, politicianof, ?x \rangle$
$YAGO - TREC05_{16}$	$\langle vicente\ fox, bornondate, ?x \rangle$
$YAGO - TREC05_{17}$	$\langle ?x, subclassof, ?y \rangle, \langle opec, type, ?x \rangle$
$YAGO - TREC05_{18}$	$\langle ?x, subclassof, ?y \rangle, \langle nato, type, ?x \rangle$
$YAGO - TREC05_{19}$	$\langle rocky\ marciano, bornondate, ?x \rangle$
$YAGO - TREC05_{20}$	$\langle counting\ crows, created, ?x \rangle$
$YAGO - TREC05_{21}$	$\langle woody\ guthrie, bornondate, ?x \rangle$
$YAGO - TREC05_{22}$	$\langle woody\ guthrie, diedondate, ?x \rangle$
$YAGO - TREC05_{23}$	$\langle ?x, subclassof, ?y \rangle, \langle bing\ crosby, type, ?x \rangle$
$YAGO - TREC05_{24}$	$\langle bing\ crosby, actedin, ?x \rangle$
$YAGO - TREC05_{25}$	$\langle ?x, subclassof, ?y \rangle, \langle paul\ revere, type, ?x \rangle$
$YAGO - TREC05_{26}$	$\langle paul\ revere, bornondate, ?x \rangle$
$YAGO - TREC05_{27}$	$\langle paul\ revere, diedondate, ?x \rangle$
$YAGO - TREC05_{28}$	$\langle ?x, subclassof, ?y \rangle, \langle jesse\ ventura, type, ?x \rangle$
$YAGO - TREC06_1$	$\langle ?x, subclassof, ?y \rangle, \langle lpga, type, ?x \rangle$
$YAGO - TREC06_2$	$\langle warren\ moon, bornondate, ?x \rangle$
$YAGO - TREC06_4$	$\langle nascar, establishedondate, ?x \rangle$
$YAGO - TREC06_5$	$\langle mozart, bornondate, ?x \rangle$
$YAGO - TREC06_6$	$\langle ?x, subclassof, ?y \rangle, \langle imf, type, ?x \rangle$
$YAGO - TREC06_7$	$\langle judi\ dench, actedin, ?x \rangle$

$YAGO - TREC06_8$	$\langle stonehenge, locatedin, ?x \rangle$
$YAGO - TREC06_9$	$\langle hedy\ lamarr, actedin, ?x \rangle$
$YAGO - TREC06_{10}$	$\langle hedy\ lamarr, discovered, ?x \rangle$
$YAGO - TREC06_{11}$	$\langle ?x, subclassof, ?y \rangle, \langle eta, type, ?x \rangle$
$YAGO - TREC06_{12}$	$\langle johnstown, locatedin, ?x \rangle$
$YAGO - TREC06_{13}$	$\langle ?x, locatedin, ?y \rangle, \langle shakespeare, bornin, ?x \rangle$
$YAGO - TREC06_{14}$	$\langle shakespeare, bornondate, ?x \rangle$
$YAGO - TREC06_{15}$	$\langle hitchcock, bornondate, ?x \rangle$
$YAGO - TREC06_{16}$	$\langle meg\ ryan, actedin, ?x \rangle$
$YAGO - TREC06_{17}$	$\langle meg\ ryan, ismarriedto, ?x \rangle$
$YAGO - TREC06_{18}$	$\langle ?x, subclassof, ?y \rangle, \langle janet\ reno, type, ?x \rangle$
$YAGO - TREC06_{19}$	$\langle frank\ sinatra, actedin, ?x \rangle$
$YAGO - TREC06_{20}$	$\langle wal\text{-}mart, establishedondate, ?x \rangle$
$YAGO - TREC06_{21}$	$\langle john\ prine, created, ?x \rangle$
$YAGO - TREC06_{22}$	$\langle carolyn\ bessette\text{-}kennedy, ismarriedto, ?x \rangle$
$YAGO - TREC06_{23}$	$\langle patsy\ cline, created, ?x \rangle$
$YAGO - TREC06_{24}$	$\langle cole\ porter, bornin, ?x \rangle, \langle ?x, locatedin, ?y \rangle$
$YAGO - TREC06_{25}$	$\langle ?x, actedin, cheers \rangle$
$YAGO - TREC06_{26}$	$\langle heinz, establishedondate, ?x \rangle,$
	$\langle ketchup, establishedondate, ?x \rangle$
AQY_{216}	$\langle ?x, bornin, long\ island \rangle,$
	$\langle ?x, wrote, conscience\ of\ a\ liberal \rangle,$
	$\langle ?y, mentions, ?x \rangle$
AQY_{217}	$\langle ?x, created, blueprint \rangle,$
	$\langle ?x, haswonprize, grammy \rangle, \langle ?y, mentions, ?x \rangle$
AQY_{218}	$\langle ?x, bornin, melbourne \rangle, \langle ?x, bornondate, 1995 \rangle,$
	$\langle ?y, mentions, ?x \rangle$
AQY_{219}	$\langle ?y, mentions, ?x \rangle, \langle ?x, iscitizenof, iraq \rangle$
AQY_{220}	$\langle ?y, mentions, ?x \rangle,$
	$\langle ?x, produced, american\ gladiators \rangle$
AQY_{221}	$\langle ?y, mentions, ?x \rangle, \langle ?x, establishedondate, 1792 \rangle$
AQY_{223}	$\langle ?x, establishedondate, 1914 \rangle,$
	$\langle ?x, hasproduct, investment\ management \rangle,$
	$\langle ?y, mentions, ?x \rangle$
AQY_{231}	$\langle ?y, mentions, ?x \rangle, \langle ?x, label, abraham\ lincoln \rangle$
AQY_{232}	$\langle ?x, ?p1, airport\ international \rangle, \langle ?y, mentions, ?x \rangle$
AQY_{235}	$\langle ?x, bornondate, 1954 \rangle, \langle ?x, diedondate, 2006 \rangle,$
	$\langle ?y, mentions, ?x \rangle$

AQY_{237}	$\langle ?y, mentions, ?x \rangle, \langle ?x, establishedondate, 1838 \rangle$
AQY_{238}	$\langle ?x, label, damon \rangle, \langle ?x, haswonprize, ?y \rangle,$
	$\langle ?y, label, 2004 \rangle, \langle ?d, mentions, ?x \rangle$
AQY_{246}	$\langle ?x, label, michael \rangle,$
	$\langle ?x, isaffiliatedto, democratic\ party \rangle,$
	$\langle ?y, mentions, ?x \rangle$
AQY_{271}	$\langle ?x, ?p0, singers \rangle, \langle ?x, created, blaze \rangle,$
	$\langle ?y, mentions, ?x \rangle$
AQY_{272}	$\langle ?x, bornin, hawaii \rangle, \langle ?x, wrote, dreams \rangle,$
	$\langle ?y, mentions, ?x \rangle$
WDB_1	$\langle United\_States, type, ?y \rangle$
WDB_2	$\langle ?x, type, person \rangle, \langle ?x, label, david\ miller \rangle, \langle ?x, ?y,$
	$san\ diego \rangle$
WDB_3	$\langle ?x, type, work \rangle, \langle ?x, series, pong \rangle$
WDB_4	$\langle ?x, type, settlement \rangle, \langle ?x, label, sydney \rangle, \langle ?y, city, ?x \rangle,$
	$\langle ?y, type, airport \rangle$
WDB_5	$\langle ?x, type, person \rangle, \langle ?x, label, donald\ knuth \rangle,$
	$\langle ?x, nationality, ?y \rangle, \langle ?y, label, ?n \rangle$
WDB_6	$\langle ?x, type, animal \rangle, \langle ?x, label, ?y \rangle$
WDB_7	$\langle ?x, type, person \rangle, \langle ?x, homepage, ?y \rangle$
WDB_8	$\langle ?x, type, organisation \rangle, \langle ?x, foundationplace,$
	$united\ states \rangle,$
	$\langle ?y, developer, ?x \rangle, \langle ?y, type, software \rangle$
WDB_9	$\langle ?x, ?t, bestselling\ lives\ in\ los\ angeles \rangle,$
	$\langle ?x, author, ?y \rangle, \langle ?y, label, ?z \rangle$
WDB_{10}	$\langle ?x, ?y, sparrow \rangle$
WDB_{11}	$\langle ?x, ?y, exploration\ of\ mars \rangle$
WDB_{12}	$\langle ?x, ?y, bohemian\ rhapsody \rangle$
WDB_{13}	$\langle ?x, ?y, 1755\ lisbon\ earthquake \rangle$
WDB_{14}	$\langle ?x, ?y, swan \rangle$
WDB_{15}	$\langle ?x, ?y, separation\ of\ powers \rangle$
WDB_{16}	$\langle ?x, ?y, bank\ of\ china \rangle$
WDB_{17}	$\langle ?x, ?y, zelda\ series \rangle$
WDB_{18}	$\langle ?x, ?y, solomons\ battle \rangle$
WDB_{19}	$\langle ?x, type, animal \rangle, \langle ?x, ?y, swan \rangle$

A.3.2 Queries used in Section 7.5

Name	Query
WDB_1	$(type, astronaut), (moon), (birthdate)$
WDB_2	$(type, city), (europe), (population)$
WDB_3	$(type, person), (president), (america)$
WDB_4	$(type, settlement), (type, airport), (city)$
WDB_5	$(continent, europe), (capital), (type, town)$
WDB_6	$(type, person), (label, knuth), (nationality)$
WDB_7	$(league, fußball\ bundesliga), (type, soccerplayer),$ $(team)$
WDB_8	$(bestselling\ author), (british), (notablework)$
WDB_9	$(?x, ?y, bestselling), (author), (fantasy),$ $(notablework)$
WDB_{10}	$(type, settlement), (label, sydney), (city),$ $(type, airport)$
WDB_{11}	$(type, populatedplace), (country, germany),$ $(postalcode), (areacode)$
WDB_{12}	$(type, drug), (glaxosmithkline), (glucocorticoid),$ $(inhaled)$
WDB_{13}	$(smallpox\ vaccine), (knownfor), (doctoraladvisor),$ $(almamater)$
WDB_{14}	$(type, city), (population), (capital),$ $(cultural\ events)$
WDB_{15}	$(?x, ?y, metropolitan\ region),$ $(?x, type, settlement), (europe), (areametro)$
WDB_{16}	$(?x, ?y, university\ theatre),$ $(?x, type, populatedplace), (areatotal),$ $(populationtotal)$
WDB_{17}	$(?x, type, populatedplace), (asia),$ $(?x, ?y, metropolis), (postalcode), (population)$
WDB_{18}	$(?x, type, town), (?y, type, person), (dateofbirth),$ $(?y, birthplace, ?x), (occupation)$
WDB_{19}	$(?x, type, book), (?y, basedon, ?x), (language),$ $(releasedate), (country, england)$
WDB_{20}	$(?x, ?y, bestselling), (author), (fantasy),$ $(notablework, ?n), (?x, ?t, england)$
$YAGO - NAGA_1$	$(haswonprize), (hasfamilyname, curie)$

$YAGO - NAGA_3$	$(directed), (type, james\ bond)$
$YAGO - NAGA_4$	$(actedin), (hasgivenname, julia)$
$YAGO - NAGA_6$	$(hasfamilyname, douglas), (actedin)$
$YAGO - NAGA_7$	$(hasfamilyname, willis), (actedin)$
$YAGO - SSEARCH_2$	$(directed), (ismarriedto, madonna)$
$YAGO - SSEARCH_3$	$(type, mathematicians), (type, french), (bornondate)$
$YAGO - SSEARCH_5$	$(type, composers), (type, russian)$
$YAGO - SSEARCH_7$	$(actedin), (type, wordnet\ governor\ 110140314)$
$YAGO - SSEARCH_9$	$(type, german), (type, physicists), (livesin)$
$YAGO - SSEARCH_{10}$	$(bornondate), (type, physicists), (haswonprize)$
$YAGO - TREC05_1$	$(george\ foreman, bornondate)$
$YAGO - TREC05_2$	$(kurosawa, bornondate)$
$YAGO - TREC05_3$	$(kurosawa, type), (subclassof)$
$YAGO - TREC05_4$	$(?x, type, ?y), (kurosawa, ismarriedto),$
	$(?y, subclassof, ?z)$
$YAGO - TREC05_5$	$(kurosawa, directed)$
$YAGO - TREC05_7$	$(paul\ newman, actedin)$
$YAGO - TREC05_8$	$(type, meteorite)$
$YAGO - TREC05_9$	$(american\ legion, establishedondate)$
$YAGO - TREC05_{10}$	$(enrico\ fermi, bornondate)$
$YAGO - TREC05_{11}$	$(enrico\ fermi, diedondate)$
$YAGO - TREC05_{12}$	$(rachel\ carson, type), (subclassof)$
$YAGO - TREC05_{13}$	$(rachel\ carson, wrote)$
$YAGO - TREC05_{14}$	$(rachel\ carson, diedondate)$
$YAGO - TREC05_{15}$	$(vicente\ fox, politicianof)$
$YAGO - TREC05_{16}$	$(vicente\ fox, bornondate)$
$YAGO - TREC05_{17}$	$(subclassof), (opec, type)$
$YAGO - TREC05_{18}$	$(subclassof), (nato, type)$
$YAGO - TREC05_{19}$	$(rocky\ marciano, bornondate)$
$YAGO - TREC05_{20}$	$(counting\ crows, created)$
$YAGO - TREC05_{21}$	$(woody\ guthrie, bornondate)$
$YAGO - TREC05_{22}$	$(woody\ guthrie, diedondate)$
$YAGO - TREC05_{23}$	$(subclassof), (bing\ crosby, type)$
$YAGO - TREC05_{24}$	$(bing\ crosby, actedin)$
$YAGO - TREC05_{25}$	$(subclassof), (paul\ revere, type)$
$YAGO - TREC05_{26}$	$(paul\ revere, bornondate)$
$YAGO - TREC05_{27}$	$(paul\ revere, diedondate)$
$YAGO - TREC05_{28}$	$(subclassof), (jesse\ ventura, type)$

$YAGO - TREC06_1$	(subclassof), (lpga, type)
$YAGO - TREC06_2$	(warren moon, bornondate)
$YAGO - TREC06_4$	(nascar, establishedondate)
$YAGO - TREC06_5$	(mozart, bornondate)
$YAGO - TREC06_6$	(subclassof), (imf, type)
$YAGO - TREC06_7$	(judi dench, actedin)
$YAGO - TREC06_8$	(stonehenge, locatedin)
$YAGO - TREC06_9$	(hedy lamarr, actedin)
$YAGO - TREC06_{11}$	(subclassof), (eta, type)
$YAGO - TREC06_{12}$	(johnstown, locatedin)
$YAGO - TREC06_{14}$	(shakespeare, bornondate)
$YAGO - TREC06_{15}$	(hitchcock, bornondate)
$YAGO - TREC06_{16}$	(meg ryan, actedin)
$YAGO - TREC06_{17}$	(meg ryan, ismarriedto)
$YAGO - TREC06_{18}$	(subclassof), (janet reno, type)
$YAGO - TREC06_{19}$	(frank sinatra, actedin)
$YAGO - TREC06_{20}$	(wal-mart, establishedondate)
$YAGO - TREC06_{21}$	(john prine, created)
$YAGO - TREC06_{22}$	(carolyn bessette-kennedy, ismarriedto)
$YAGO - TREC06_{23}$	(patsy cline, created)
$YAGO - TREC06_{24}$	(cole porter, bornin), (locatedin)
$YAGO - TREC06_{25}$	(actedin, cheers)
$YAGO - OWN_1$	(bornondate), (type, physicists), (haswonprize)
$YAGO - OWN_2$	(directed), (type, film), (actedin)
$YAGO - OWN_3$	(actedin), (hasfamilyname, smith), (directed)
$YAGO - OWN_4$	(created, war of the worlds), (influences), (type, writer), (hasfamilyname)
$YAGO - OWN_5$	(livesin), (bornin), (locatedin, france), (hasfamilyname)
$YAGO - OWN_6$	(?x, hasgini), (haspoverty), (politicianof, ?x), (bornin)
$YAGO - OWN_7$	(?x, hasgini), (haspoverty), (politicianof, ?x), (bornin), (bornondate)
$YAGO - OWN_8$	(?x, ?y, star wars), (?z, actedin, ?x), (directed), (hasduration), (hasimdb)
$YAGO - OWN_9$	(livesin), (bornin, ?x), (?x, locatedin, germany), (influences), (created)
$IMDB_1$	(denzel washington)

$IMDB_2$	(*clint eastwood*)
$IMDB_3$	(*john wayne*)
$IMDB_4$	(*will smith*)
$IMDB_5$	(*harrison ford*)
$IMDB_6$	(*julia roberts*)
$IMDB_7$	(*tom hanks*)
$IMDB_8$	(*johnny depp*)
$IMDB_9$	(*angelina jolie*)
$IMDB_{10}$	(*morgan freeman*)
$IMDB_{11}$	(*gone with the wind*)
$IMDB_{12}$	(*star wars*)
$IMDB_{13}$	(*casablanca*)
$IMDB_{14}$	(*lord of the rings*)
$IMDB_{15}$	(*the sound of music*)
$IMDB_{16}$	(*wizard of oz*)
$IMDB_{17}$	(*the notebook*)
$IMDB_{18}$	(*forrest gump*)
$IMDB_{19}$	(*the princess bride*)
$IMDB_{20}$	(*the godfather*)
$IMDB_{21}$	($?z$, *role*, $?r$), ($?r$, *name*, *indiana jones*), (*cast info*), (*title*)
$IMDB_{22}$	($?z$, *role*, $?r$), ($?r$, *name*, *atticus finch*), (*cast info*), (*title*)
$IMDB_{23}$	($?z$, *role*, $?r$), ($?r$, *name*, *james bond*), (*cast info*), (*title*)
$IMDB_{24}$	(*role*), (*name*, *rick blaine*), ($?x$, *cast info*, $?z$), ($?x$, *title*, $?y$)
$IMDB_{25}$	($?z$, *role*, $?r$), ($?r$, *name*, *will kaine*), (*cast info*), (*title*)
$IMDB_{26}$	($?z$, *role*, $?r$), ($?r$, *name*, *dr. hannibal lecter*), ($?x$, *cast info*, $?z$), ($?x$, *title*, $?y$)
$IMDB_{27}$	($?z$, *role*, $?r$), ($?r$, *name*, *norman bates*), (*cast info*), (*title*)
$IMDB_{28}$	($?z$, *role*, $?r$), ($?r$, *name*, *darth vader*), (*cast info*), (*title*)
$IMDB_{29}$	($?z$, *role*, $?r$), (*name*, *the wicked witch of the west*), ($?x$, *cast info*, $?z$), ($?x$, *title*, $?y$)

$IMDB_{30}$	$(?z, role, ?r), (name, nurse\ ratched),$ $(?x, cast\ info, ?z), (?x, title, ?y)$
$IMDB_{31}$	$(movie\ info),$ $(info, frankly\ my\ dear\ i\ don't\ give\ a\ damn), (title)$
$IMDB_{32}$	$(movie\ info),$ $(info, i'm\ going\ to\ make\ him\ an\ offer\ he\ can't\ refuse),$ $(title)$
$IMDB_{33}$	$(movie\ info),$ $(info, you\ don't\ understand\ i\ coulda\ had\ class\ i\ coulda$ $been\ a\ contender\ i\ coulda\ been\ somebody\ instead\ of$ $a\ bum\ which\ is\ what\ i\ am), (title)$
$IMDB_{34}$	$(movie\ info),$ $(info, toto\ i've\ a\ feeling\ we're\ not\ in\ kansas\ any\ more),$ $(title)$
$IMDB_{35}$	$(movie\ info), (info, here's\ looking\ at\ you\ kid),$ $(title)$
$IMDB_{36}$	$(?c, role, ?r), (?r, name, skywalker), (person),$ $(name, hamill), (cast)$
$IMDB_{37}$	$(?c, person, ?p), (?p, name, tom\ hanks), (cast),$ $(year, 2004)$
$IMDB_{38}$	$(person), (name, henry\ fonda), (?x, cast, ?c),$ $(?x, title, yours\ mine\ ours), (?c, role, ?r),$ $(?r, name, ?n)$
$IMDB_{39}$	$(person), (name, russell\ crowe), (?x, cast, ?c),$ $(?x, title, gladiator), (?c, role, ?r), (?r, name, ?n)$
$IMDB_{40}$	$(person), (name, brent\ spiner), (?x, cast, ?c),$ $(?x, title, star\ trek), (?c, role, ?r), (?r, name, ?n)$
$IMDB_{41}$	$(person), (?p, name, audrey\ hepburn), (cast),$ $(year, 1951)$
$IMDB_{42}$	$(?c, role, ?r), (name, jacques\ clouseau),$ $(?c, person, ?p), (name), (cast)$
$IMDB_{43}$	$(role), (name, jack\ ryan), (?x, cast, ?c),$ $(?c, person, ?p), (?p, name, ?n)$
$IMDB_{44}$	$(person), (name, stallone), (?x, cast, ?c),$ $(?c, role, ?r), (?r, name, rocky)$
$IMDB_{45}$	$(?c, role, ?r), (?r, name, terminator), (?x, cast, ?c),$ $(person), (name)$

$IMDB_{50}$ $(?a, cast, ?ca), (?a, title, lost\ ark),$
$(?ca, person, ?p), (?ci, person, ?p), (?i, cast, ?ci),$
$(?i, title, indiana\ jones\ last\ crusade)$